OXFORD TEXTUAL PERSPECTIVES

World Medievalism

World Medievalism

The Middle Ages in Modern Textual Culture

LOUISE D'ARCENS

OXFORD
UNIVERSITY PRESS

OXFORD
UNIVERSITY PRESS

Great Clarendon Street, Oxford, OX2 6DP,
United Kingdom

Oxford University Press is a department of the University of Oxford.
It furthers the University's objective of excellence in research, scholarship,
and education by publishing worldwide. Oxford is a registered trade mark of
Oxford University Press in the UK and in certain other countries

First Edition published in 2021

Impression:2

Published in the United States of America by Oxford University Press
198 Madison Avenue, New York, NY 10016, United States of America

British Library Cataloguing in Publication Data

Data available

Library of Congress Control Number: 2021949391

ISBN 978-0-19-882594-4 (hbk.)
ISBN 978-0-19-882595-1 (pbk.)

DOI: 10.1093/oso/9780198825944.001.0001

Printed and bound by
CPI Group (UK) Ltd, Croydon, CR0 4YY

SERIES EDITORS' PREFACE

Oxford Textual Perspectives is a series of informative and provocative studies focused upon texts (conceived of in the broadest sense of that term) and the technologies, cultures, and communities that produce, inform, and receive them. It provides fresh interpretations of fundamental works, images, and artefacts, and of the vital and challenging issues emerging in English literary studies. By engaging with the contexts and materiality of the text, its production, transmission, and reception history, and by frequently testing and exploring the boundaries of the notions of text and meaning themselves, the volumes in the series question conventional frameworks and provide innovative interpretations of both canonical and less well-known works. These books will offer new perspectives, and challenge familiar ones, both on and through texts and textual communities. While they focus on specific authors, periods, and issues, they nonetheless scan wider horizons, addressing themes and provoking questions that have a more general application to literary studies and cultural history as a whole. Each is designed to be as accessible to the non-specialist reader as it is fresh and rewarding for the specialist, combining an informative orientation in a landscape with detailed analysis of the territory and suggestions for further travel.

Elaine Treharne and *Greg Walker*

To my mother, Paulina, with love and eternal gratitude

PREFACE AND ACKNOWLEDGEMENTS

This book has been written across a time of remarkable ongoing transformation in the related fields of medieval studies and medievalism studies. The last few years have seen an acceleration in (especially Anglophone) medievalists' self-examination about the racist, colonialist, and ethnocentric legacies we have inherited, and which we risk perpetuating through our teaching and research, and about our responsibility to pay attention to the biases and cultural assumptions that continue to shape our field.

The urgency of this transformation has been driven by world political events, in particular by the emergence, or consolidation, in many parts of the world of a political far-right with a seemingly relentless appetite for instrumentalizing, and indeed, weaponizing, the Middle Ages to its own ends. It can be easy for academic medievalists to treat such violence as an aberrant use of the Middle Ages, produced by a remote, radicalized subculture that feeds off distorting, ahistorical memes. But these recent medievalisms cannot be separated neatly from the longer tradition of institutional practices that have placed the Middle Ages in the service of nationalist, colonialist, and white supremacist ideologies. Recognizing this does not mean that academic medieval scholars need take responsibility for every rogue uptake of the period for malignant ends; but we have a collective duty to acknowledge the legacy we have inherited from our discipline's historical relationship to ideologies that have underpinned forms of social exclusion. Medievalists might not be unanimous about the role played by academic medieval studies in underpinning racist medievalism in the public sphere, but many agree on the value of academic medievalists seeking out ways to short-circuit the usefulness of academic work for racist networks. This book, by exposing and unsettling the premise that medievalism always leads us back to a familiar and comforting idea of Europe, aims to be part of this circuit breaking.

The sheer number of sharp-minded and committed scholars who have devoted themselves to addressing this issue has made medievalism studies a very fast-moving terrain, with approaches, concepts, and terminologies around decolonization and race being taken up, refined, rejected, and sometimes even revived, at a dizzying pace. Parts of this book, then, will inevitably have the discursive equivalent of archaeological cross-sections in which, to borrow a metaphor from Chapter 3, the stratigraphy of the conversation will be evident to trained eyes. In the end, books are records of the conversations in which they participate, as well as accounts of the texts and events they explore. It is my belief, however, that the issues raised here about the politics of periodization, nomenclature, space, and time are far from resolved, so to that end I hope the book will be of value for a number of ongoing discussions on how medievalism studies as a field can continue to redraw its parameters, and recognize its limitations, in pursuit of a more inclusive and interdisciplinary practice.

The writing of this book took place on the unceded lands of the Dharawal and Dharug peoples. I acknowledge them as the traditional custodians of the places where I live and work, and I pay my respects to Elders past, present, and emerging. My work on medievalism has for the last two decades been tied to a sense of my location in Australia, a country that is in the planetary south but is part of the Global North. As a European Australian attempting to understand my privilege and my status as a beneficiary of my country's practices of violent colonial dispossession, I have long been preoccupied with medievalism's presence beyond Europe as both instrument and formative discourse of settler colonialism. An earlier stage of this research eventually coalesced into my book *Old Songs in the Timeless Land: Medievalism in Australian Literature 1840–1910* (2011), which argued that the medievalism threaded through settler culture attested to colonial Australians' desire to situate themselves within deep European and British traditions. It showed that this desire was motivated not only by a desire to overcome geographical isolation but also by a wilful disavowal of the Australian Indigenous past that vastly predated the Western Middle Ages. *World Medievalism* picks up the thread of medievalism's relationship to colonialism, contextualizing it as just one impetus for medievalism's move out from Europe to the world. Parts of this book also aim to speak back to, and move beyond, the postcolonial focus of my earlier work by balancing Western narratives against the perspectives of those colonized, occupied, and/or demonized by the West. The project of decolonizing our approaches to medievalism must take its lead from the groundbreaking work of Black, Indigenous, and scholars of colour, but ultimately this must be a task shared by the many.

I owe thanks to medievalists far and wide for the inspiration they offer. International colleages who've been especially important for thinking through this book have included Candace Barrington and Jonathan Hsy, John Ganim, Seeta Chaganti, and Jeffrey Jerome Cohen. The Medievalists of Color collective has provided much-needed impetus for thinking through disciplinary decolonization and approaches to race. My thanks also to Tarren Andrews, Adam Miyashiro, Jenna Mead, and Helen Young for fruitful discussions about the intersection of medieval/ism studies and Indigenous perspectives. I'm very fortunate to be part of a vibrant antipodean community of medieval and early modern scholars. I've benefited from the scholarship and conversation of more colleagues than I can name in the Australia and New Zealand Association of Medieval and Early Modern Studies (ANZAMEMS), but will single out for special thanks Clare Monagle, Andrew Lynch, Helen Dell, Stephanie Trigg, Kim Phillips, Marina Gerzić, and Stephanie Russo. I've also benefited immeasurably over a decade from the support and concentrated brilliance of the Australian Research Council Centre of Excellence for the History of Emotions 1100–1800, which sponsored many events that enabled me to formulate the ideas in this book. The Global Middle Ages in Sydney group has been another important forum for considering the Middle Ages beyond Europe. My thanks to Hélène Sirantoine and Sahar Amer for founding and continuing this group.The Faculty of Arts at Macquarie University has provided a stimulating and supportive workplace. Of the many colleagues I could thank, I will limit myself to the Department of English, and the Global Literatures and Cultures research group: Jumana Bayeh, Alice Moody, and their reading group from which I learned so much about theories of world literature. I wish also to thank valued colleagues in Macquarie's Department of Indigenous studies, in particular Bronwyn Carlson and Lou Glover Nathan. Lou came into this project just when I most needed guidance about how to do respectful decolonizing work in Chapter 4 guided by the vital ethos 'Nothing about Us without Us', and I'm grateful for the enthusiasm and wisdom of that guidance. Any failures on this front are because my training wheels are very much still on.

Sections of this book appear in articles published in *Exemplaria, Studies in Medievalism, Parergon,* and *Digital Philology.* My thanks to the editors of those journals for permission to re-use this material. Extract from J. R. R. Tolkien, *Tree and Leaf: Including Mythopoeia* reprinted by permission of HarperCollins Publishers Ltd © 1989. My thanks also to OUP: to series editors Elaine Treharne and Greg Walker, anonymous readers, and Aimee Wright for their support and patience as I completed this manuscript through a series of challenging circumstances.

As ever, my beloved family Robert, Eva, and Mimi, have been a source of encouragement and comfort. They have urged me through crises of confidence, numerous family health crises, catastrophic bush-fires, and now global pandemic. I thank them for the purpose they bring to my life. My parents, Brian and Paulina, have offered unfailing pragmatic help throughout my career and my life. The season has come for me to return the help they've given to me. It is to them that I dedicate this book, with love and gratitude.

Louise D'Arcens

Macquarie University, Sydney, Australia

CONTENTS

LIST OF FIGURES

Introduction

Medievalism and the Missing Globe

At the bottom edge of the map of The Known World in George R. R. Martin and Jonathan Roberts's *The Lands of Ice and Fire* is the coastline of a dense green landmass. The expanse of this land is uncertain, as only its northern headland is visible, jutting into the Summer Sea; but this headland hints at a vast continent stretching far south, beyond cartographic fathoming.[1] Its continental scale is also suggested by the word written across it: SOTHORYOS—a name which, like those of the better-known continents Essos and Westeros, and the frozen reaches of The North, condenses an entire compass point and all of its meanings into a single body of land. Sothoryos is not just *in* the south; it *is* the South.

This southern land is rarely mentioned in Martin's novels, while their televisual adaptation, HBO's *Game of Thrones*, offers only a swooping glimpse in the Dragon-Cam opening credits of Season 2. The supplementary compendium *The World of Ice and Fire* provides a fuller account, but cautions that most of what is reported of Sothoryos is speculative and fantastical. Its description is a lurid medley of tropes familiar from premodern accounts of terra incognita. The continent's

---

[1] George R. R. Martin and Jonathan Roberts, *The Lands of Ice and Fire: Maps from King's Landing to Across the Narrow Sea* (New York: Random House, 2012), Map 1.

World Medievalism: The Middle Ages in Modern Textual Culture. Louise D'Arcens, Oxford University Press.
© Louise D'Arcens 2021. DOI: 10.1093/oso/9780198825944.003.0001

equatorial climate of dense jungle seems to make it uninhabitable; its deep interior, the 'green hell', is a space of monstrosity inhabited by 'brindled men' who are understood to be hominids, alongside a perverse fauna that includes vampiric bats, small vicious dragons, and what seem to be stunted dinosaurs; its abandoned interior city, Yeen, is an enormous black-stoned ruin from which even the creeping vines recoil.[2] This confused account suggests that Martin's medievalesque world entertains an 'antipodal imagination' not unlike that which Alfred Hiatt attributes to the premodern West—an imaginary which 'consider[s] the possibility of habitable land [in the terra incognita] even while arguing against the possibility of human habitation'.[3]

The account in *The World of Ice and Fire* also positions Sothoryos as what might be described as the 'Global South' of the Known World. Although the compendium purports to be compiled by a Westerosi Maester, its account refracts this fantastic-medieval world through the prism of modern geopolitics, especially in this case the long and devastating legacy of the trans-Atlantic slave trade. Martin et al. portray Sothoryos like those modern nations that function as sites of labour and resources to be exploited by the wealthy and powerful Global North under a neocolonial capitalist economy.[4] Through a logic of recognizable approximation between the Known World and our world, Sothoryos is, as Martin has confirmed elsewhere, the series' Africa equivalent, subjected to colonial looting and five thousand years of slaving raids. According to the compendium, the opulent civilizations of Slavers Bay in Essos are built on the forced labour of trafficked Sothoryosan people. Yet as part of the general occlusion of Sothoryos in the novels, there is little exploration of the origin of the slaves in the continents north of the Summer Sea, except in the case of Missandei from the island of Naath, near Sothoryos, who speaks openly of the raids on her people. The large-scale Northern theft of Southern people is alluded to in the novels, but the narrative focus remains on the slavers and the liberators rather than the enslaved themselves, whose experience is thereby rendered

---

[2] George R. R. Martin, Elio M. Garcia, and Linda Antonsson, *The World of Ice & Fire: The Untold History of Westeros and The Game of Thrones* (London: Harper Voyager, 2014), 284–6.

[3] Alfred Hiatt, *Terra Incognita: Mapping the Antipodes before 1600* (Chicago: University of Chicago Press, 2008), 59.

[4] Mignolo, Walter, 'The Global South and World Dis/order', *Journal of Anthropological Research* 67.2 (2011), 165.

insignificant. This focus reflects, and reinforces, the novels' focus on the powerful North and West rather than the disempowered South.

Sothoryos is not the only unmapped land in Martin's medievalesque fantasy world: in the bottom right corner of the map is the coastal fringe of Ulthos, a mysterious jungled terrain of unknown expanse whose name evokes the *Ultima Thule* (farthest land) of medieval geography.[5] Sothoryos is especially significant, however, for what it reflects about the series' representation of relations between the Global North and South. Martin has claimed that *The World of Ice and Fire*'s fantastical image of Sothoryos is historically accurate, in that '[e]ven though Africa was known to Europe from the earliest days of ancient Greece... we knew relatively little about sub-Saharan Africa'.[6] While it is true that North Africa was better known to Europeans, Martin's portrait of medieval ignorance is questionable given what has been established for some time about medieval Mediterranean societies' knowledge of, and contact with, Africa.[7] This is attested by such cartographic-historical evidence as the 1375 Catalan Atlas produced in Majorca by Abraham Cresques, which compiled then-current knowledge of the African societies of Ethiopia, Nigeria, and the sophisticated West African kingdom of Mali. Taking this into account, and bearing in mind Martin's wide reading in medieval history,[8] the removal of this knowledge from the Known World seems a deliberate narrowing of the compass not just of that world, but of Western (or at least Mediterranean) knowledge of Africa.

This is reinforced by the decision to locate Sothoryos below Essos, at the Southern perimeter of the wide Summer Sea. Altering the map so that there is no great Africa-like continent immediately South of the quasi-British/European Westeros shifts not just the geography but also the geopolitics of the Known World in a way that protects Westeros

---

[5] The depiction of Ulthos as jungle terrain, rather than its conventional depiction as the frozen North, might be an attempt to distance it from the German *Völkisch* (and later Nazi) appropriation of Ultima Thule as a mythical Aryan homeland.
[6] Jennifer Vineyard, 'George R. R. Martin on What Not to Believe in *Game of Thrones*', *Vulture*, 6 November 2014, https://www.vulture.com/2014/11/george-rr-martin-new-book.html.
[7] See, for instance, the discussion of the Afro-Eurasian *oikemene* in Andre Gunder Frank and Barry K. Gills, eds, *The World System: Five Hundred Years or Five Thousand?* (London and New York: Routledge, 1993).
[8] See Carolyne Larrington, *Winter Is Coming: The Medieval World of Game of Thrones* (London: I. B. Taurus, 2015); and Shiloh Carroll, *The Medievalism of Game of Thrones* (Cambridge: Boydell and Brewer, 2018).

from an expectation of knowledge about Sothoryos, and hence from a reckoning with its exploitation. It also precludes the possibility of Sothoryosan influence on or exchange with Westeros. This has particular ramifications for the Southern Westerosi kingdom of Dorne, the series' equivalent to medieval Al-Andalus. Just as the eighth-century conquest of the Iberian Peninsula linked al-Andalus to the great Islamicate world of the East, so too Dorne is tied into the culture and history of the East by the fusion of its ancient local population with an Eastern migrant people, the Rhoynar. Unlike Muslim Spain, however, which also came under the rule of the North African Almoravid and Almohad dynasties, Dorne does not enjoy any relationship to any cultures further south; below it there is only ocean. In the world of Martin's creation, moving Sothoryos East has the equivalent effect of writing the Berber influence out of the story of the Iberian Islamic empire, and hence of the Western world.

The global Middle Ages

Why have I opened a book on world medievalism by worrying at length about a sliver of land on the map of a fictional world? I take Sothoryos as my opening example not just because of what it reveals about the ideological priorities of the *Song of Ice and Fire/Game of Thrones* series, but as an example that captures the complexities of what happens when medievalism extends beyond the familiar historical imaginary based on the post-Roman European and British past. On the one hand, Martin seems to be refusing the Anglo-Euro focus of the medievalist fantasy genre into which he writes: despite having adopted the initials 'R. R.' to mark his debt to J. R. R. Tolkien, he has created a sprawling, intercontinental, and (gesturally) inter-hemispheric realm that would seem to take its contours more from the trans-oceanic domain described in Fernand Braudel's landmark study *La Méditerranée* (1949) than from Tolkien's more confined Anglo-Norse Middle Earth. Martin's Known World is one in which many diverse peoples are linked by the chaotic vectors of conquest, warfare, religion, and trade, and one that looks outward to unexplored southern and eastern hemispheres. It is, to use Alison Bashford's formulation, a 'terraqueous' realm where conflicting sovereignties play out across land, sea, and the borders where they meet.[9] On the other hand, the text's handling of Sothoryos exposes the residual ethnocentrism at the heart of the series' medievalism, which, notwithstanding its panoramic scope, ultimately confines the presence of southern actors (reinforcing what Raewyn Connell in *Southern Theory* describes as the conflation of the 'Northern' with the universal),[10] focalizes Western perspectives, and protects Western innocence concerning the exploitation of the Global South. Its cultural topography, moreover, almost perfectly replicates G. W. F. Hegel's positioning of the Mediterranean basin as the dynamic 'centre of world history' whilst relegating Africa to a static and benighted place 'beyond the day of self-conscious history'.[11] In this respect the series falls back on what Helen Young has helpfully called the fantasy genre's 'habits of whiteness', assuming the centrality of a white, Western worldview despite its expansive scale.[12] Numerous readers, many of them readers of colour, have expressed dissatisfaction with the occlusion of a broader global history not just in *Game of Thrones* but in post-Tolkien medievalist fantasy more generally. Prominent among these is the award-winning US-based Jamaican author Marlon James, whose *Dark Star* trilogy uses the familiar generic traits of fantasy, but with a new cultural and racial orientation, drawing on the great pre-1500 African civilizations for historical detail, and on African epic 'as old as *Beowulf*' for fantasy elements.[13] The first instalment of the trilogy, *Black Leopard, Red Wolf*, was published to acclaim in 2019, and its companion novels are impatiently awaited.[14]

The Game of Thrones/SOIAF series has been of keen interest to scholars of the Middle Ages because its (admittedly imperfect) attempt

[9] Bashford, Alison, 'Terraqueous Histories', *The Historical Journal* 60.2 (2017), 253–72.
[10] Raewyn Connell, *Southern Theory: The Global Dynamics of Knowledge in Social Science* (Sydney: Allen and Unwin, 2007/New York: Routledge, 2020), vii–viii.
[11] G. W. F. Hegel, 1975, *Lectures on the Philosophy of World History*, trans. H. B. Nisbet (Cambridge: Cambridge University Press, 1975), cited in Jerry H. Bentley, 'The Task of World History', in *The Oxford Handbook of World History*, ed. Jerry H. Bentley (Oxford: Oxford University Press, 2011), 4.
[12] Helen Young, *Race and Popular Fantasy Literature: Habits of Whiteness* (New York: Routledge, 2015).
[13] Natalie Zutter, 'Marlon James to Write Fantasy Trilogy Inspired by *Lord of the Rings* and African Mythology', *Tor.Com*, Tuesday 10 January 2017, https://www.tor.com/2017/01/10/marlon-james-dark-star-trilogy-fantasy-african-mythology/.
[14] Marlon James, *Black Leopard, Red Wolf* (New York: Riverhead Books, 2019).

at offering a medievalesque world characterized by transnational exchange, terraqueous expansion, and diasporic communities corresponds with an increasing scholarly interest in exploring the years between approximately 500 and 1500 CE—that is, the time that Western nomenclature calls 'the Middle Ages'—as an epoch of interconnectedness: of exchanges, migrations, and cross-race and interfaith encounters. Within this scholarly development, which Sahar Amer and Laura Doyle go so far as to declare a paradigm shift in the field of medieval studies, the Middle Ages are now increasingly coming to be understood under the auspices of a deeper historical reconceptualization of 'the global'.[15] The notion of cultural interconnectedness is a conspicuous leitmotif running throughout the recent scholarship dedicated to examining 'medieval globality'. The North American-based Global Middle Ages Project, which has been running since 2011, states on its website that it aims to 'see the world whole in a large swathe of time—as a network of spaces braided into relationship by trade and travel, mobile stories, cosmopolitan religions, global cities, cultural borrowings, traveling technologies, international languages, and even pandemics, climate and war'.[16] In the 2014 inaugural issue of the *Medieval Globe*—a development that both expresses and consolidates the status of global-orientated work in the field—the editorial statement similarly declares the journal's dedication to the interdisciplinary examination of 'varieties of connectivity, communication, and exchange' across the millennium leading up to 1500.[17] Cultural and religious exchange as symptoms of the global feature even more explicitly in a 2014 special issue of *Literature Compass* called 'the Global Middle Ages', where co-editors Geraldine Heng and Lynn Ramey evoke a millennium of 'literatures whose global themes, global subjects, global purview, and whose global imaginary were there for all

---

[15] Sahar Amer and Laura Doyle, 'Introduction: Reframing Postcolonial and Global Studies in the Longue Durée', *PMLA* 130.2 (2015), 331–5. Doyle has more recently developed the idea of the entwined or 'horizontal' nature of intercultural power relations in her book *Inter-imperiality: Vying Empires, Gendered Labor, and the Literary Arts of Alliance* (Durham and London: Duke University Press, 2020).

[16] http://globalmiddleages.org.

[17] Carol Symes, 'Introducing the Medieval Globe', *The Medieval Globe* 1.1 (2014), 2.

to consider'.[18] This premodern 'globalism', which Heng and Ramey distinguish from globalization as a symptom of late capitalism, is abundantly evident, they suggest, in medieval travel narratives tracing journeys from Iceland to India, and the East African coast.[19] Julia McClure has summarized the practice of global medieval history as 'a manifestation of the reflection on provincialization of Europe', as having the twofold objectives of inclusion and the deconstruction of 'Europe' as an autonomous entity: it aims 'to represent extra-European histories' and 'to show the ways Europe itself is the product of global interactions'.[20] This book's chapters will demonstrate how this twofold practice also reflects global medievalism as a non-scholarly, creative phenomenon.

The 2015 special issue of *PMLA* co-edited by Amer and Doyle continues this theme, celebrating and calling for more momentum toward an interdisciplinary and collaborative 'longer-durée global studies'.[21] This globalist approach, Amer and Doyle argue, not only shifts medievalists' disciplinary focus toward the 'connections of local formations to longer geopolitical histories',[22] but compels a reconsideration of the exclusive focus on modern cultures within postcolonial, transnational, and global studies. The latter theme reappears throughout the volume, especially in Heng's argument that an acknowledgement of 'the global past in deep time... productively speaks to the racial politics of the contemporary European now'.[23] More recently, in a Supplement of *Past and Present*, the co-editors Catherine Holmes and Naomi Standen attribute the marginalization of the Middle Ages to 'the still ubiquitous idea that truly global history only began with European long-distance maritime expeditions in the early modern centuries'.[24] Byzantinist Peter Frankopan, author of *The Silk Roads:*

---

[18] Geraldine Heng and Lynn Ramey, 'Early Globalities, Global Literatures: Introducing a Special Issue on the Global Middle Ages', *Literature Compass* 11.7 (2014), 389.

[19] Heng and Ramey, 'Early Globalities', 389–90.

[20] Julia McClure, 'A New Politics of the Middle Ages: A Global Middle Ages for a Global Modernity', *History Compass* 13.11 (2015), 611.

[21] Amer and Doyle, 'Reframing Postcolonial and Global Studies', 331.

[22] Amer and Doyle, 'Reframing Postcolonial and Global Studies', 332.

[23] Geraldine Heng, 'Reinventing Race, Colonization, and Globalisms across Deep Time: Lessons from the Longue Duree', *PMLA* 130.2 (2015), 365.

[24] Catherine Holmes and Naomi Standen, 'Introduction: Towards a Global Middle Ages', *Past and Present* 238, Supplement 13 (2018), 1.

A New History of the World, is somewhat blunter: 'This idea of globalisation as something Facebook taught us is rubbish—it has been happening for centuries.'[25] Directed at a general readership, Frankopan's comment does not distinguish between globalism and globalization, but in its querying of glib periodization and of modern (and particularly modern Western) self-congratulation, and in its vision of premodern cultural and economic exchange, it aligns with the key insights of the more consciously academic work discussed above.

A diverse, interculturally networked Middle Ages has also been invoked recently as a corrective to modern-centric ideas about race. Geraldine Heng's recent magnum opus, *The Invention of Race in the European Middle Ages*, queries the reduction of race to a 'presentist' concern,[26] a theme also taken up in the 'Race, Racism, and the Middle Ages' special series published on *The Public Medievalist* website throughout 2017. The purpose of this series of short online articles, also aimed at a non-expert audience, is explicitly political: to refute popular misconceptions about ubiquitous medieval European whiteness which, according to the site's founder, Paul Sturtevant, helped authorize 'the recent uptick of overt prejudice, hate crimes, and politically sanctioned racism in the US and Europe'.[27] A 2019 issue of *Literature Compass* edited by Dorothy Kim addresses itself to academic medievalists, drawing attention to how investigations into medieval race can, and should, benefit from a serious engagement with critical race theory.[28] Along with this increased momentum in academic, popular, and online publication, university courses and seminars on the Global Middle Ages are becoming increasingly frequent, as the

---

[25] Jessica Salter, 'Peter Frankopan: "This Idea of Globalisation as Something Facebook Taught Us Is Rubbish"', Interview, *The Telegraph*, 28 August 2015, https://www.telegraph.co.uk/books/authors/peter-frankopan-interview/.

[26] Geraldine Heng, *The Invention of Race in the European Middle Ages* (Cambridge: Cambridge University Press, 2018), 3–15.

[27] Paul B. Sturtevant, 'TPM Special Series: Race, Racism, and the Middle Ages', *Public Medievalist*, https://www.publicmedievalist.com/race-racism-middle-ages-toc/. See also Amy S. Kaufman and Paul B. Sturtevant, *The Devil's Historians: How Medieval Extremists Abuse the Medieval Past* (Toronto: University of Toronto Press, 2020).

[28] Dorothy Kim, 'Introduction to Literature Compass Special Cluster: Critical Race and the Middle Ages', *Literature Compass* 16.e12549 (2019), https://doi.org/10.1111/lic3.12549.

academy rebalances its histories away from an assumed Western centre of gravity.

This apparently new transnational, terraqueous, and 'distributed'/ network approach to the millennium 500–1500 CE, is of course, not new. In addition to what Alan Karras and Laura J. Mitchell call the 'recognition of multiple interpretive centers' over the past half-century in the field of world history,[29] Amer and Doyle acknowledge that within medieval studies the last few decades have witnessed the production of a growing body of work on the medieval foundations of intercultural geopolitical and economic formations hitherto deemed to be modern.[30] Scholarship on the Crusades and on medieval Byzantium, for instance, has, going back at least to the work of Steven Runciman, long focused on East-West exchange and de facto globalism *avant la lettre*,[31] querying Western triumphalism in the process. The portrayal of cultural complexity at the heart of much of this work has been reinforced by the sustained study of minority races and cultures within the medieval West, such as the Jewish presence throughout Europe and England[32] and the Western Islamic diaspora in Spain, Sicily, and North Africa.[33] It has, moreover, been thirty years since *Before European Hegemony: The World System AD 1250–1350*, Janet Abu-Lughod's medievalist intervention into World Systems Theory,[34] a domain of political historiography hitherto dominated by Immanuel Wallerstein and his followers' strong reification of an epochal divide brought about

<hr>

[29] Alan Karras and Laura J. Mitchell, 'Writing World Histories for our Times', in *Encounters Old and New in World History: Essays Inspired by Jerry H. Bentley*, ed. Alan Karras and Laura J. Mitchell (University of Hawaiʻi Press, 2017), 5.

[30] Amer and Doyle, 'Reframing Postcolonial and Global Studies', 331.

[31] Steven Runciman, *A History of the Crusades*, 3 vols (Cambridge: Cambridge University Press, 1951–4).

[32] Mark Cohen, *Under Crescent and Cross: The Jews in the Middle Ages* (Princeton, NJ: Princeton University Press, 1994); Robert Chazan, *Reassessing Jewish Life in Medieval Europe* (Cambridge: Cambridge University Press, 2010); Avraham Grossman, *Pious and Rebellious: Jewish Women in Medieval History* (Hanover, NH: Brandeis University Press, 2004).

[33] María Rosa Menocal, *The Arabic Role in Medieval Literary History: A Forgotten Heritage* (Philadelphia: University of Pennsylvania Press, 1987); Brian A. Catlos, *Muslims of Medieval Latin Christendom c.1050–1614* (Cambridge: Cambridge University Press, 2014).

[34] Janet Abu-Lughod, *Before European Hegemony: The World System AD 1250–1350* (Oxford: Oxford University Press, 1989).

by trans-Atlantic expansion. In drawing attention to predominantly Islamic trade routes that traversed Western and non-Western spaces in the twelfth and thirteenth centuries, from Persia to China, Africa, India, and the Indo-Malay region, Abu Lughod's work corresponds to research undertaken outside of medieval studies that has for some time been drawing attention to the interactions of coeval cultures in that period, including K. N. Chaudhuri's landmark *Trade and Civilization in the Indian Ocean: An Economic History from the Rise of Islam to 1750* (1985).[35]

Despite this longer developmental background, however, it is only more recently that the insights and potential of this earlier work have begun to be recognized as foundational to the current refiguring of the Middle Ages as global. This more self-conscious 'turn' toward the global is not just responding to the Western biases of medieval historical and literary studies. As Abu-Lughod's study demonstrates, they also redress the tendency within historical studies to confine the global to modernity as well as the tendency within literary studies to perceive global literature as co-extensive with the growth of a global circulation of literary commodities,[36] attempting to reclaim the global for texts and practices in deeper time.

The idea of a 'global Middle Ages' has not been unanimously embraced within medieval historical studies. Robert I. Moore's 2016 chapter 'A Global Middle Ages?', for instance, argues for the importance of not imposing Western periodization on non-European cultures, since the tripartite division of history into ancient, medieval, and modern 'makes little sense' beyond Europe—and, to a lesser extent, even within it.[37] While Moore, following world historian Jerry Bentley, does not necessarily dispute the possibility of identifying forms of cultural, material, and economic coalescence across different cultures in the period described as 'medieval', he favours describing their emergence as an 'age of intensification', since this term avoids the

---

[35] K. N. Chaudhuri, *Trade and Civilization in the Indian Ocean: An Economic History from the Rise of Islam to 1750* (Cambridge: Cambridge University Press, 1985).

[36] Peng Cheah, 'World against Globe: Toward a Normative Conception of World Literature', *New Literary History* 45.3 (2014), 303–29.

[37] Robert I. Moore, 'The Global Middle Ages', in *The Prospect of World History*, ed. James Belich, John Darwin, Margret Frenz, and Chris Wickham (Oxford: Oxford University Press, 2016), 80–92.

geographical limitation implicit within the term 'global Middle Ages'.[38] Moore's point about historical nomenclature of course reflects long-accepted practice among scholars of Asia, Africa, and other areas of non-Eurocentric focus, and it is an uncomfortable truth that medieval studies has come to this both belatedly and largely in response to the promptings of Western colleagues. For instance, Moore is corroborated, albeit from a different disciplinary perspective, by Daud Ali, whose account of South Asian historiography demonstrates that although the word 'medieval' has been taken up widely in the field, it is applied inconsistently across a sliding scale of epochs, the only commonality being that it is positioned immediately before whatever date is variously deemed to have ushered in 'the modern' in India.[39] This concern over Eurocentric naming practices is not the preserve of sceptics, either: even the most enthusiastic advocates for globalizing the medieval have conceded that the term carries with it an ineluctable Eurocentric charge. Alluding to the practice of Martin Heidegger (made more famous by Jacques Derrida) to register a term's unsatisfactory yet necessary status by placing it 'under erasure'—that is, crossed-out but still legible—Heng and Ramey suggest that the term 'the Middle Ages ... can only be embraced *under erasure*' when applied beyond Europe.[40]

The power of the phrase 'the Middle Ages' to illuminate yet also obscure is registered in the general scholarly reluctance to expand the term to encompass significant coeval non-European cultures such as, for instance, the pre-Columbian American Indian city of Cahokia, the Incan and Mayan empires, or the Tuʻi Tonga empire of Oceania. Although Cahokia can be found in the 'North American Middle Ages' project on the Global Middle Ages website (of which Heng is a founder), the written scholarship is more circumspect about the epistemological purchase of including such societies under the rubric of 'the medieval'. This is of course partly due to the fact that these cultures have not (or not yet) been found to have participated in the 'medieval

---

[38] Moore, 'The Global Middle Ages', 91.

[39] Daud Ali, 'The Idea of the Medieval in the Writing of South Asian History: Contexts, Methods and Politics', *Social History* 39.3 (2014), 382–407.

[40] Heng and Ramey, 'Early Globalities', 391. See also Candice Barrington, 'Global Medievalism and Translation', in *The Cambridge Companion to Medievalism*, ed. Louise D'Arcens (Cambridge: Cambridge University Press, 2016), 180–95.

world system' stretching from Western Europe to the Malay Straits, and so are deemed to have operated according to their own unrelated, *emic* temporalities. And yet viewed from another angle the ruling out of such societies also arguably reflects an unexamined residual Eurocentrism whereby coeval Southern cultures are only deemed to 'come into view' when they intersect with the cultures of the Northern hemisphere—in the case of the South Pacific/Oceania this is the modern era of European exploration and colonization. Despite such hesitations and occlusions, which are under constant revision as new intercultural links come to light, the increasing scholarly investment in a globalized Middle Ages is undeniable.

Globalism and medievalism

The recent turn toward the 'global Middle Ages' is inseparable from scholarly interest in medievalism; that is the myriad ways in which the medieval world has come to be interpreted, adapted, and represented in post-medieval texts, objects, and practices. It is axiomatic within the study of medievalism that post-medieval understandings of the medieval are inseparable from the creative, cultural, and ideological uses to which they are put; as such, then, the concerns of medieval studies and medievalism studies are also inseparable. As mentioned above, numerous recent portrayals of a medieval world characterized by cultural diversity and mobility have been tendered expressly as correctives to nationalist, Eurocentric, and racist instrumentalizations which feature a Middle Ages that is a site of racio-cultural purity and 'natural' segregation. While intended as urgent interventions in a pernicious political situation, these recent globalizing representations also take their place within a longer reckoning that has been underway at least since the essays collected in R. Howard Bloch and Stephen G. Nichol's *Medievalism and the Modernist Temper*.[41] Over the last two decades, and especially in the last few years, a whole host of scholars have demonstrated how closely the study of the Middle Ages has been imbricated since the nineteenth century with the nationalistic,

---

[41] R. Howard Bloch and Stephen G. Nichols, eds, *Medievalism and the Modernist Temper* (Baltimore: Johns Hopkins University Press, 1996).

linguistic nativist, and race-identitarian politics of Britain and Europe and their former colonial dependencies. There has been significant and sustained critical reflection on the legacy this has bequeathed to modern popular perceptions of the Middle Ages, which are readily co-opted into nationalist, colonialist, and, ultimately, racist causes.[42]

Recently, a welcome counterpoint to this narrative of exclusion has begun to emerge alongside this narrative of Euro-triumphalist exclusionary practice. Candace Barrington and Jonathan Hsy's Global Chaucers project is one leading example of a growing body of work that has sought to demonstrate how medieval insular and European cultural legacies have been adapted by modern cultures around the world in ways that reflect, in Barrington's words, 'dialogic transfer between a European medieval past and a non-European present' and are undertaken for the adapting cultures' own purposes.[43] Contrasting this kind of anticolonial practice to what she calls *temporal* and *spatial* global medievalisms, which have been spread via the global phenomenon of settler colonialism and have thus been vehicles to reinforce the colonizers' values, Barrington takes as a key example Ofuoma Overo-Tarimo's adaptation of The Miller's Tale, *Wahala Dey O!* (2018), which changes Chaucer's text to reflect the social, linguistic, and comic preferences of contemporary Nigerian culture. Patience Agbabi, in a recent essay on her own 2014 multicultural slam adaptation of Chaucer, *Telling Tales*, reminds readers that anticolonial politics can also be found in texts that elect, as hers does, to retain Chaucer's London setting, since the former colonial headquarters has changed profoundly to become the multicultural metropolis it is today.[44] The growing body of work examining non- or anti-colonial medievalisms

---

[42] Kathleen Davis, *Periodization and Sovereignty: How Ideas of Feudalism and Secularization Govern the Politics of Time* (Philadelphia: University of Pennsylvania Press, 2008); Kathleen Davis and Nadia Altschul, *Medievalisms in the Postcolonial World: The Idea of 'The Middle Ages' outside Europe* (Baltimore: Johns Hopkins University Press, 2009); Stephanie Trigg, ed., *Medievalism and the Gothic in Australian Culture* (Turnhout: Brepols, 2005); Michelle Warren, *Creole Medievalism: Colonial France and Joseph Bédier's Middle Ages* (Minneapolis: University of Minnesota Press, 2010); Louise D'Arcens, *Old Songs in the Timeless Land* (Cawley/Turnhout: University of Western Australia Press/Brepols, 2011).

[43] Barrington, 'Global Medievalism and Translation', 180, 190.

[44] Patience Agbabi, 'Stories in Stanza'd English: A Cross-Cultural Canterbury Tales', *Literature Compass* 15.6 (2018), n.p. (8 pages).

produced by, and relevant to, cultures beyond Europe[45] owes its impetus as much to the disciplines of world history and world literature, as well as postcolonial, transnational, and diasporic studies, as it does to medieval studies. It is true that the call within those related disciplines to 'provincialize Europe', to invoke Dipesh Chakrabarty's foundational phrase,[46] offers a particular set of challenges to those working within a discipline whose very name, medievalism studies, appears to take European geo-temporality as its starting point. But it also—and this point is central to my study—offers exciting analytical opportunities to this field of study precisely because the critical compass of medievalism expands, both temporally and geographically, far beyond its starting point.

What the above account suggests is that the dialectic at the heart of *SOIAF/Game of Thrones*, between progressive and conservative impulses, and, most importantly, between Western and global orientations, is inherent to medievalism itself, and constitutive of its attempts to engage with the Middle Ages with a view to commenting on later societies. The ideological malleability of medievalism as a historico-cultural phenomenon was remarked on as early as Charles Dellheim's study *The Face of the Past: The Preservation of the Medieval Inheritance in Victorian England* and has continued through to the present.[47] Progressive, emancipatory, and counter-cultural uses of the medieval past, from William Morris's socialism through to Pier Paolo Pasolini's sexual libertarian medievalism, have been explored alongside conservative and exclusionary forms. Methodologically speaking, this suggests that, while it is vital to keep in view medievalism's historical implication within nationalist, racist, and colonialist projects, this need not be pursued to the point of genetic fallacy,[48] in which medievalism is deemed to be so irremediably tainted by its historical and ideological

[45] For instance Robert Rouse, 'Indigenising the Medieval; or How Did Maori and Awabakal Become Inscribed in Medieval Manuscripts?', *Parergon* 32.2 (2015), 233–50; Louise D'Arcens, *Old Songs*; Nadia Altschul, Geographies of Philological Knowledge: Postcoloniality and the Transatlantic National Epic (Chicago: University of Chicago Press, 2012); Warren, *Creole Medievalism*.

[46] Dipesh Chakrabarty, *Provincializing Europe: Postcolonial Thought and Historical Difference* (Princeton, NJ: Princeton University Press, 2000).

[47] Charles Dellheim, *The Face of the Past: The Preservation of the Medieval Inheritance in Victorian England* (New York: Cambridge University Press, 1982).

[48] See Wesley Salmon, 1984, *Logic* (Englewood Cliffs, NJ: Prentice-Hall, 1984), 12.

origins that any progressive, globalist, anticolonial, and anti-racist iterations can only be regarded as unrepresentative exceptions. I wish to show in this book that acknowledging the ideological dialectic intrinsic to medievalism makes it possible to analyse the fullness of its ideological complexity. On the one hand it is possible to expose how certain forms of medievalism respond to the symptoms of globalism by retreating into (or aggressively asserting) those familiar and comforting verities of deep national, racial, and religious identity that are central to medievalism's conservative legacy. On the other hand, as Jonathan Hsy's book *Antiracist Medievalisms: From 'Yellow Peril' to Black Lives Matters* has shown, it is possible to learn from other medievalist formations that attempt to challenge and displace this legacy, adapting the medieval past in ways that reflect and serve post- or anticolonial and anti-racist priorities.[49] I aim to pursue this two-pronged approach in this book through the combination of examples I offer. Together they reflect the wide ideological span of medievalism when it reckons with a world characterized by accelerated circulations of people, capital, and knowledge, a volatile worldwide mediascape, and geopolitical connections that challenge apparently naturalized political configurations such as the nation, including the ongoing impacts of political and economic imperialism.

In historical terms, the notion of global medievalism is not, unlike 'the global Middle Ages', fraught with the same potential for oxymoron, since an enormous number of medievalist texts, objects, and practices have emerged out of the respective eras of global colonialism, transnational industrialization, global warfare, and neoliberal globalization. The medievalisms that will be examined in this book have been produced over the last twenty years or so, from the late 1990s to the first two decades of the twenty-first century, and in this respect they would seem to be located unambiguously within globalized culture. But, as I will go on now to discuss, I wish to argue that they are each also— indeed, more accurately—describable as forms of 'world medievalism' because of their trans-temporal content, scope, and practice.

---

[49] Jonathan Hsy, *Antiracist Medievalisms: From 'Yellow Peril' to Black Lives Matter* (Amsterdam: Amsterdam University Press, 2021).

Globe and world

In arguing for 'world medievalism' in this book, I wish to invoke a
capacious use of the idea of 'world' that does not preclude or disqualify
other useful overlapping terms such as 'global', 'transnational', 'transcultural', 'diasporic', or 'postcolonial', which I will continue to use
throughout the study when appropriate. But, having said that, why
single out the term 'world medievalism'? How is the idea of 'world'
being used here? And why not 'global'? Anyone familiar with the
adjacent field of world literature studies will be aware that its ongoing
debates around competing nomenclature, in which all of the terms
mentioned above are submitted to fine-grained analysis of their relative
virtues and limitations, can seem daunting and even intractable. Such
debates are symptomatic of the quest for terms that do not reproduce
textual hierarchies that are non-inclusive or reaffirm Euro-Anglo dominance. To that end, electing to use 'world' as a descriptor for medievalism here requires careful framing.

Scholars have repeatedly signalled the importance of operating with
care in relation to the cosmopolitan formulation inherited from Goethe
in his 1827 coining of 'Weltliteratur', a literature he envisaged as
reaching beyond the stultifying strictures of (implicitly European)
national traditions, out into the world beyond. Emily Apter, for
instance, points to the necessity of recognizing the capacity of world
literature, under the auspices of Goethe's 'Eurocentric universalist
humanism',[50] to flatten out important differences between local literatures. She argues, furthermore, in accord with others such as Barbara
Herrnstein Smith, that this universalism can potentially reinforce
centre-periphery hierarchies and overlook the power differentials
between literary cultures bequeathed by both colonial histories
and the global capitalist literary market, which leads it to emphasize
similarity and assume translatability between cultures. Indeed,
she argues that the word 'world' itself needs to be more 'worldly',[51]

[50] Emily Apter, 'Afterword: The "World" in World Literature', in *Transnational French Studies: Postcolonialism and Littérature-monde*, ed Alec G. Hargreaves, Charles Fosdick, and David Murphy (Liverpool: Liverpool University Press, 2012), 288.
[51] Apter, 'The "World" in World Literature', 294–5.

accommodating its different nuances and conceptualizations in different languages and places.

Pheng Cheah, on the other hand, argues that the universalism inherited from Goethe has been too readily dismissed as 'effete, idealist, and humanist'.[52] Cheah claims that a careful re-examination of this cosmopolitan impulse reveals that it need not be Euro-triumphalist but can endow world literature with the capacity to 'reveal...universal humanity *across particular differences, even as such differences are valued*', as its fictions 'open and make worlds' as a way of contesting capitalist globalization.[53] Cheah calls for a renewed acknowledgement of world literature's normative ethical project as 'a modality of cosmopolitanism that is responsible and responsive to the need to remake the world as a hospitable place, that is, a place that is *open* to the emergence of peoples that globalization deprives of world'.[54] He contrasts this with what he sees as a more limiting view of world literature as merely a reactive expression and reification of hegemonic global capitalist market exchange, 'a symbolic expression of social relations [and] merely a relay of social forces, a medium for refracting them'.[55]

Cheah's argument for world literature as an ethical creative project that actively 'makes worlds' is significant for my account of medievalism as a transhistorical phenomenon because it is buttressed by his call for a renewed attention to the 'temporal-historical dimension' inherent within the idea of 'world'.[56] He queries the scholarly tendency to perpetuate spatialized conceptualizations that 'conflate the world with the globe'[57] and hence reify an idea of world literature's scope as intelligible mostly 'in terms of spatial circulation, the paradigmatic case of which is global capitalist market exchange'.[58] A temporalized conception of 'world', conversely, perceives it as 'an ongoing dynamic process of becoming, something that is continually being made and remade because it possesses a historical-temporal dimension'.[59] This perspective makes possible a conceptualization of a world literature that, even when participating in modern globalized exchange, can also

---

[52] Cheah, 'World against Globe', 306.
[53] Cheah, 'World against Globe', 318–19, emphasis mine.
[54] Cheah, 'World against Globe', 326.   [55] Cheah, 'World against Globe', 315.
[56] Cheah, 'World against Globe', 318.   [57] Cheah, 'World against Globe', 309.
[58] Cheah, 'World against Globe', 303.   [59] Cheah, 'World against Globe', 319.

transcend it ethically and imaginatively through envisaging historical change—past, present, and future. Cheah is not alone in arguing that world literature earns its name through its engagement with deep temporality. Debjani Ganguly has also queried what she calls the 'assumptions concerning the synchronous temporality of world literature with global capital and its imperial geopolitics'.[60] Ganguly argues that it is precisely world literature's 'unpredictable routes of circulation and horizons of reception across crisscrossing temporal arcs' that interrupt contemporary 'flows of political economy'. It is far from incidental that Ganguly cites as her example of this 'refractory, elastic, even anarchic temporality' Osip Mandelstam's essay *Conversations about Dante*, in which the anti-Stalinist Russian Jewish poet celebrates the medieval laureate's 'transmutable and convertible' theme.[61] Suzanne Conklin Akbari uses this cross-temporal model to argue that the culturally diverse extant body of medieval literature can be properly perceived as a world literature.[62] For my purposes, Cheah's and Ganguly's temporalizing accounts not only emphasize the transformative (rather than static universalizing) potential of world literature but, I wish to suggest, reveal a key reason why 'world' is a more amenable concept for a cultural phenomenon such as medievalism: it exceeds the global in its temporal depth and horizon, accommodating an idea of transcultural ecumene that reaches back beyond the period when 'globe' became synonymous with global capitalism.

So, while this study embraces the general 'globalist' impulse to destabilize those medievalisms that make nationalist territorial, political, and racial claims on the Middle Ages, it nevertheless argues for medievalism as a transtemporal 'world' phenomenon. In so doing, it also addresses some other reservations raised by medievalists about the potentially troubling implications of modern portrayals of the Middle Ages as 'global'. Kathleen Davis, for instance, despite recognizing the capacity of such portrayals to 'undo the foundational narratives of European nations, [give] space to hitherto slighted histories, and...

---

[60] Debjani Ganguly, 'Literary Globalism in the New Millenium', *Postcolonial Studies* 11.1 (2008), 126.

[61] Ganguly, 'Literary Globalism', 126. See also Wai Chee Dimock, 'Literature for the Planet', *PMLA* 116.1 (2001), 173–88.

[62] Suzanne Conklin Akbari, 'Modeling Medieval World Literature', *Middle Eastern Studies* 20.1 (2017), 2–17.

disrupt some of the premises of medieval/modern periodization',[63] has raised concerns about whether creating a *longue durée* account of the 'global' offers a long historical justification for neoliberal globalization:

> Unpicking the attachments of a foundational Middle Ages to the national histories of northwestern Europe, and reconfiguring them as global, stretched across trade routes, enmeshed economies, and intercultural experience, is precisely what is necessary for globalization—particularly its economic forms—to have a legitimizing past.[64]

This concern is reiterated by Holmes and Standen, who caution against a 'global' Middle Ages being understood teleologically as a stage in the 'relentless development' toward modernity's 'global order'.[65] These scholars' fear has in part been realized, as John Ganim (2011) and Bruce Holsinger (2016) have shown, in the concept of 'new medievalism' developed in the field of international relations (IR) theory, especially as a legacy of Hedley Bull's watershed contribution, *The Anarchical Society: A Study of Order in World Politics* (1977).[66] In the 'neomedievalist' IR narrative, supranational medieval European entities such as the Catholic Church function genealogically as precursors to today's multinational conglomerates. Holsinger points out that since IR theorists are not themselves medievalists, they are 'less interested in the accuracy or verifiability of its claims about the medieval past than in the power of its historical analogies to shape the future'.[67] Although this is not the Eastern-weighted Middle Ages of 'enmeshed' trade and cultural exchange envisaged by Abu-Lughod and her successors, it is nevertheless an attempt, to borrow a term from Saskia Sassen, to link medieval and modern supranational 'assemblages'.[68] Although

---

[63] Kathleen Davis in Kathleen Davis and Michael Puett, 'Periodization and "The Medieval Globe": A Conversation', *The Medieval Globe* 2.1 (2015), 3.

[64] Davis in 'Periodization and "The Medieval Globe"', 3.

[65] Holmes and Standen, 'Towards a Global Middle Ages', 2.

[66] John Ganim, 'Cosmopolitanism, Sovereignty and Medievalism', *Australian Literary Studies* 26.3–4 (2011), 6–20; Bruce Holsinger, 'Neomedievalism and International Relations', *The Cambridge Companion to Medievalism*, ed. Louise D'Arcens (Cambridge: Cambridge University Press, 2016), 165–79; Hedley Bull, *The Anarchical Society: A Study of Order in World Politics* (New York: Columbia University Press, 1977).

[67] Holsinger, 'Neomedievalism and International Relations', 166.

[68] Saskia Sassen, *Territory, Authority, Rights: From Medieval to Global Assemblages* (Princeton, NJ: Princeton University Press, 2006).

Holsinger's account does not offer an explicit warning about the post hoc reifying effect of constructing a 'global' Middle Ages, his investigation into IR nevertheless leads him to conclude that neomedievalist modellings of the past:

> have, for better or worse, been thoroughly absorbed into the language and logic of globalisation... and will continue to have an important bearing on how we comprehend our geopolitical relation to the medieval past and how we understand the emergent and residual forces shaping our future in the global age.[69]

I wish to suggest that the multi-temporal conceptualization of 'world' as (re)formulated by Cheah offers greater flexibility for creative post-medieval reimaginings of a 'connected' and decentred medieval world, as it does not inadvertently provide portrayals of the period that naturalize global capitalism.

I am also persuaded by the efficacy of the concept of 'world' for the current study because of its relationship to the conceptual approach of phenomenology, which introduces an important experiential dimension into my discussion of medievalism rather than only seeing it as a historical and geopolitical phenomenon or a field of cultural and textual practices. The advantage of using a phenomenologically derived frame to describe a medievalist epistemology is that it brings into focus, and offers a language for discussing, the obvious yet unarticulated knowledges and experiences informing medievalist understandings of the Middle Ages. Its chief strength lies in its querying of empiricism, since empirical knowledge is often not at the heart of medievalist creative practice, which relies at least as much on hermeneutic and 'felt' understandings of 'the medieval world' as it does on historical knowledge. Hubert Dreyfus and Mark Wrathall argue that phenomenological understanding is not the knowledge of the analytical subject contemplating or mastering a world of objects, but rather emerges 'intimately and inextricably' out of our experiential or engaged 'interdependence... with the world and the entities around us'.[70] By

---

[69] Holsinger, 'Neomedievalism and International Relations', 178.

[70] Hubert L. Dreyfus and Mark A. Wrathall, 'Martin Heidegger: An Introduction to his Thought, Work, and Life', in *A Companion to Heidegger*, ed. Hubert L. Dreyfus and Mark A. Wrathall (Malden, MA: Blackwell, 2005), 4–5.

arguing that knowledge emerges out of the contact between the medieval remnant and the medievalist, a phenomenological-hermeneutic account of medievalism appeals as a 'practical' approach for describing the modes of transhistorical perception that post-medieval people experience when they come into contact with articulations of the medieval (texts, artefacts, buildings, and so on).[71]

Of particular value for my study of creative medievalisms is the replacement within phenomenology of disinterested *comprehension* with interested *apprehension*, a term that aptly describes medievalist knowing because it implies receptivity and a grasp that it not fully conceptual. This thick apprehension (in Clifford Geertz's sense) comprises not just intellectual responses, as well as social intuitions and beliefs but also cognitive, somatic, and emotionally inflected understanding. This form of understanding, which Martin Heidegger calls 'involvement' (*Bewandtnis*), is part of the phenomenological experience of being engaged with and dwelling in a 'world', where 'world' is understood to be a background context of meaning, action, and communication.[72] But how can 'the medieval world'—whatever temporal and geopolitical parameters are ascribed to it—be experienced phenomenologically as a 'world' by those who, by dint of time, cannot physically dwell in it? I wish to suggest that it is best understood as the kind of world described by Heidegger that is not a neutral world of objects but rather an apprehended constellation of beliefs, practices, values, and events—what he calls a 'referential context of significance'.[73] Cristina Lafont argues that Heidegger's idea of world can be applied to 'entities such as cultures' including past cultures; notably for this study, she points out that 'we...refer to cultures as "worlds" in expressions such as "the world of the Renaissance man" or "the medieval world"'.[74] Within a Heideggerian schema, Lafont argues, humans can dwell in such culture-worlds 'in a non-spatial sense of the term'—that is in a phenomenologically rich or engaged sense—understanding or

---

[71] Michael Heyns, 'An Epistemology of Engagement', *Koers* 71.1 (2006), 75.

[72] Martin Heidegger, *Being and Time*, trans. J. Macquarrie and E. Robinson (Oxford: Blackwell, 1962), 117.

[73] Heidegger, *Being and Time*, 167.

[74] Cristina Lafont, 'Hermeneutics', in *A Companion to Heidegger*, ed. Hubert L. Dreyfus and Mark A. Wrathall (Malden, MA: Blackwell, 2005), 71.

interpreting these worlds without having direct physical perception of them.[75]

Taking this into account, medievalism can be thought of as a transhistorical experiential state which, to use Heidegger's term, enables acts of 'world-disclosure'[76] in relation to 'the medieval world', making the possibilities of meaning within this world available to post-medieval people. The affective and encompassing state that facilitates, and is achieved through, these kinds of medievalist world-disclosures is what Heidegger calls *Stimmung*, a musicologically inflected term that is expressive of engaged *attunement*. Such states of affective attunement open and make accessible meaningful dimensions of a world, rather than responding to specific objects, although objects within that world can elicit affective responses that in turn reveal a broader sense of their context. To take just one example, which I have discussed elsewhere, heritage tourism sites do not recreate 'the Middle Ages' for visitors empirically and factually through displaying objects in glass cases with explanatory placards, but through using space evocatively as well as relying on the transitive senses of hearing and smell to create a powerful sonic and olfactory sense of connection to the medieval past, filling visitors with the presence of the past.[77] As I will go on to argue in the first two chapters, creative texts such as novels rely on imaginative rather than reconstructed sensory encounters to disclose medieval worlds or to depict characters' encounters with these disclosed worlds. To do this, they both draw on and add to their readers' attunement to the Middle Ages.

A consideration of medievalist *Stimmung* does not preclude an acknowledgement of more determinate 'intellectual' or conceptual interactions such as, for instance, reading and analysing medieval texts, or dating artefacts, nor does it deny the very specific joys and/ or frustrations these might elicit. Importantly, it also does not conjure away the ideological underpinnings of postmedieval attitudes toward the medieval. Rather it claims that these are all always suffused with, and sometimes even exceeded (or even obfuscated) by, an experience of

---

[75] Lafont, 'Hermeneutics', 271.

[76] Heidegger, *Being and Time*, 120–1; Hubert L. Dreyfus, *Commentary on Being and Time* (Cambridge: MIT Press, 1999), 89.

[77] See Louise D'Arcens, 'Smelling the Past: Medieval Heritage Tourism and the Phenomenology of Ironic Nostalgia', in *Comic Medievalism: Laughing at the Middle Ages* (Cambridge: Boydell and Brewer, 2014), 161–84.

transhistorical attunement. As my opening example of *Game of Thrones* demonstrates, and the book's chapters will elaborate, creative evocations of medieval pasts are acts of world disclosure—or, to use another Heideggerian term, 'worlding'—that either invite audiences into immersive experiences of those pasts, or at the very least explore the capacity of 'the medieval world' to offer such transhistorical experiences. But as my discussion of the limitations of Martin's world also reveals, the experience need not prevent us from calibrating the cultural and ideological implications of the medieval worlds that are disclosed, especially when those worlds are expanded culturally and geopolitically beyond Europe. Indeed the later chapters of this book, both of which explore Southern hemisphere engagements with the medieval, evaluate the ways in which ideas of 'the medieval', when applied to phenomena emerging in cultures before the Middle Ages and beyond the Eurasian continent, can have the effect of recentring imaginary European heritage at the expense of local material history and cultural practices.

Sensitively used, a phenomenological approach to medievalism accords with, but deepens, David Damrosch's argument that the workings of transcultural phenomena such as world literature are better understood by a phenomenology than an ontology.[78] Damrosch argues that a phenomenological approach registers the transformations brought about by texts' traversal of geographical and cultural boundaries, and the new meanings generated by transcultural reception and translation. A theory of phenomenological medievalism can similarly recognize the proliferation of 'medieval worlds' in reception, but adds to this a powerful recognition of the affective experience involved in, and even motivating, the 'worlding' of the Middle Ages.

World Medievalism: the arrangement of this book

With a growing awareness of the necessity to expose and displace the unmarked Eurocentrism of historical disciplines, a number of scholars

---

[78] David Damrosch, *What Is World Literature?* (Princeton, NJ: Princeton University Press, 2003), 6.

have broached the question of how to handle cultural and geographical coverage when it comes to producing world-spanning accounts. Earlier in the scholarly life of this question, when it was being raised under the auspices of world systems theory, Andre Gunder Frank and Barry K. Gills argued that a Eurocentric approach to world history 'need not be replaced by "equal time" for the history of all cultures' or by shifts in gravity that lead to 'Islamo-, Nippo-, Sino-, or whatever other centric' accounts to counter Eurocentrism.[79] Although Carol Symes's more recent editorial statement in the *Medieval Globe* does not subscribe to Frank and Gunder's world systems model, she nevertheless acknowledges that 'a global approach to medieval studies need not encompass the globe in any territorial sense':[80] tracing worldwide trajectories of medieval culture cannot at all times be a project of equal geographical representation, but proceeds rather by an uneven accrual of multiple accounts of localities beyond the Eurosphere as well as within it. Areas (for example the Pacific) that are less proximate culturally, linguistically, or geographically to the centres of scholarship—and indeed to medieval Europe—or whose archives are less available to the epicentres of medieval studies have received less attention than more familiar areas such as the Middle East—a trend that can be overcome by a concerted effort to learn and collaborate beyond the field with scholars working on coeval societies. The cumulative and fragmentary picture that will emerge from this is, however, likely to be resistant to being organized into an overarching 'global' narrative. Bentley's compatible claim that 'global periodization' can only 'chart historical development in approximate rather than finely calibrated fashion'[81] leads him to argue that any attempt to account for large-scale historical formations must be prepared to accommodate how local and regional histories intersect with or depart from those formations. The medieval 'globe' will not have an even or seamless surface.

In accordance with these perspectives, the four case studies of world medievalism explored in this book are far from geographically or

[79] Frank and Gills, eds, *The World System*, 12.
[80] Symes, 'Introducing the Medieval Globe', 2.
[81] Jerry Bentley, 'Cross-Cultural Interaction and Periodization in World History', *American Historical Review* 101.3 (1996), 751.

culturally exhaustive of this worldwide phenomenon, although two cover distant points of the Northern hemisphere and two are from the Global South. I have, rather, as I discuss below, aimed to feature examples that are, in the words of Vilashini Cooppan, 'locally inflected and translocally mobile'[82]—that is, reflective of four very specific sets of historico-cultural and geopolitical conditions but also reflective of larger trends in how concepts of 'the medieval' have been taken up across the world. Taken together they reveal how imperial and global legacies have ensured that the medieval period continues to be per- ceived as a commonly held past that can be retrieved, reclaimed, or revived in response to the accelerated changes and uncertainties of global modernity. In accordance, furthermore, with Karras and Mitch- ell's methodological point that with world histories 'the available ter- rain is too vast to tackle if you do not have a clear organising principle in mind',[83] the organizational principle shaping this book is chiefly heuristic: its four cases are intended to exemplify possible approaches to thinking through medievalism as a 'world' phenomenon, with each chapter reflecting a *disposition* toward 'worldliness' and a specific medievalist world disclosure that is closely reflective of its geo-cultural location but not reducible to it. The book's case study-based approach also enables what Shu-Mei Shih has called 'effective scaling',[84] a key technique when dealing with a phenomenon of this scope, which enables flexible movement between a macro-analysis of a global phe- nomenon against close analysis that engages with the micro-dynamics of texts in their contexts of production and reception.

As a study of medievalism this book is primarily concerned with texts, including, but not limited to, literary, cinematic, televisual, jour- nalistic, scientific, scholarly, legal, and musical texts. But it also exam- ines spatial and material artefacts that have proven highly amenable to textual interpretation, including buildings, photographs, paintings, caves, fossils, rock art, and statues. These readings do not discount the materiality of these objects and spaces, but are principally interested

---

[82] Vilashini Cooppan, 'World Literature and Global Theory: Comparative Literature for the New Millennium', *Symplokē* 9.1 (2001), 15–43.

[83] Karras and Mitchell, 'Writing World Histories for our Times', 7.

[84] Shu-Mei Shih, 'World Studies and Relational Comparison', *PMLA* 130.2 (2015), 432.

in the cultural meanings attributed to them through the lens of world medievalism. Insofar as it continues to deal with core questions such as 'what Middle Ages is being presented in these texts?' and 'whose interests are served by such representations of the past?', this book adopts a cultural-historicist approach that engages with a number of the ongoing concerns being explored under the disciplinary auspices of world history. But the book's concerns are predominantly aligned with those of world literature studies, aiming to investigate how we might understand the circulation of medieval and medievalist texts as world phenomena, not just traversing different times but also different spaces, often caught within the circuits of global capitalism but also sometimes short-circuiting them. It does not use the methodology of comparative literature insofar as it is not my primary aim to represent the medievalism of a range of language groups from a position of linguistic expertise. I am conscious that, being shaped in part by my primary language competencies, it is vulnerable to a criticism levelled at both world literature studies and medievalism studies, which is that both of these fields gravitate toward Anglophone and Francophone literatures (even if, in the case of world literature, this is extended to the post-colonial sphere of Anglo- and Francophonie). But I have also aimed to counter this potential limitation by creating an account that is implicitly, and sometimes explicitly, comparative in offering a cross-cultural map across its four chapters. This is a map that will need to be filled in and re-drawn by many hands other than mine; a prospect which, as Christine Chism has recently argued, reflects medieval histories and medieval afterlives that are increasingly 'open in both period and geography, subject to strange collusions, politicized, heterogeneous, and necessarily collaborative'.[85]

The book traces medievalism's fanning out across a number of geographical and cultural networks, from the land- and sea-paths cut by the rapacious vectors of European colonialism and neocolonialism to the homogenizing web of fantasy spun by Hollywood across the world. Because of the asymmetrical economic and political arrangements that uphold these networks, part of the story I tell is that of medievalism as a symptom of, or a justification for, conquest, exclusion,

---

[85] Christine Chism, 'Tawaddud/Teodor and the Stripping of Medieval Mastery', *Digital Philology* 8.1 (2019), 136.

and domestication. But the other part of the story is different, and reveals how, as they travel from the centre, these networks become rhizomes, taking unpredictable paths and making surprising conjunctions. It shows how, in environments beyond Europe, medievalist world-disclosure heralds resistance and appeals for justice and inclusion, and how its premodern strangeness makes it an unexpected portal into the deep time of peoples who predate even the thought of Europe. This mixture of hegemonic and resistant medievalisms reflects Arlene B. Tickner and Ole Waever's argument that moves toward 'worlding' a discipline must acknowledge that 'colonizing, resisting and reshaping' all require attention as intersecting practices involved in 'imagining and creating worlds'.[86]

The first half of the book comprises two chapters examining medievalisms which, while both nominally produced in the Northern hemisphere, make radically different use of the Middle Ages to reflect opposing ideological approaches to the question of Western nationhood and (neo)colonialism in the context of global politics and economy.

Chapter 1, 'Medievalism Disoriented: The French Novel and Neo-reactionary Politics', will examine the specific valency of the Middle Ages as a period in the recent French political imaginary and in recent vocabularies of nationhood, tracing how the European nationalist medievalisms of recent decades can be read as a symptomatic response to the perceived threats and uncertainties of globalization. Although a number of French political commentators in the twentieth and twenty-first centuries have viewed the later Middle Ages as the truest expression of French greatness, for others the Middle Ages is the period that sowed the seeds for a cultural and political decline that continues today. The most prominent, and controversial, recent instance of this view has emerged in the writings of the French 'nouveaux réactionnaires', including Éric Zemmour in his *Mélancolie française* (2010) and *Le Suicide français* (2014). The chapter will examine how Zemmour's idea of post-Roman 'French melancholy' sparked a heated debate among commentators and historians alike, as a result of his ideological use of the Middle Ages to account for what he regards as the rise of

---

[86] Arlene B. Tickner and Ole Waever, eds, *International Relations Scholarship around the World* (New York: Routledge, 2009), 9.

French cultural malaise and its loss of identity in the era of multiculturalism and the globalized economy. It will also analyse some vital debates that emerged in the French public sphere before and after Zemmour, including those clustering around the French neoreactionary polemics of the 'Great Replacement', the anti-Islamic tracts such as Bat Ye'or's *Eurabia* and *Dhimmitude*, and the militant uptake of the early Middle Ages by France's Front National.

The chapter will also analyse how these debates play out in three recent high-profile French novels that can be regarded as vehicles for three very different medievalist explorations of contemporary French identity. First, Jérôme Ferrari's novel *Le sermon de la chute de Rome/ Sermon on the Fall of Rome* (2012) offers a searching exploration of the perception of France's past as a post-Roman vacuum, as a way of reckoning with the geopolitical and emotional fallout from France's loss of its modern colonial empire. I will trace how the novel draws a parallel between the present and the early medieval period via an invocation of the sermons delivered by Saint Augustine in the wake of Rome's fall, which converge with the novel's meditation on the ultimate futility of empire-building as a human endeavour. The chapter will then explore the notorious creative uptake of 'decline' and 'Great Replacement' theses in Michel Houellebecq's 2015 novel *Soumission/ Submission*. It will argue that Houellebecq's satiric portrait of France's transformation into a post-secular 'Eurabian' polity is presented not as a violent upheaval but as the menacingly benign harnessing of France's medieval religious and sexist impulses, which have been only superficially suppressed by the Enlightenment, feminism, and secular republicanism. Finally, the chapter will examine how Mathias Enard's 2015 novel *Boussole* ('Compass') makes complex use of medieval literary and historical legacies to expose the complexities of the West's rapprochement with the East in the twenty-first century. It will show that the novel grapples with two opposing impulses: on the one hand the cosmopolitan desire to emphasize cross-cultural empathy in order to combat Islamophobia; and on the other the need to recognize the unequal power dynamic underpinning orientalism and to acknowledge Europe's implication in the legacies of colonialism. Examining these texts together enables a nuanced account of how France in the age of globalization has used the Middle Ages to understand its own long, contradictory love affair with ideas of nation, empire, and world.

Chapter 2, 'Medievalism Re-orientated: Tariq Ali's Islam Quintet and the "Arab" Historical Novel', examines the staging of interfaith encounter and conflict in the Islam Quintet, a suite of historical novels written between 1992 and 2010 by British-Pakistani author and commentator Tariq Ali. Ali is better known for his political activism, his commentary on Israel and Palestine, and his account of the Middle East and U.S. neocolonialism in the 2002 polemic *The Clash of Fundamentalisms*, his post-9/11 response to Samuel Huntington's thesis of inter-civilizational conflict in his 1996 book *The Clash of Civilizations*. This chapter will explore Ali's fictionalized medievalist engagement with Huntington's thesis and with neocolonial politics, particularly in the three novels within the Quintet that are set in medieval Islamicate contexts shaped by interfaith and intercultural encounters: *Shadows of the Pomegranate Tree* set in fifteenth-century Al-Andalus, *A Sultan in Palermo* set in twelfth-century Sicily, and *The Book of Saladin*, set in Crusade-era Egypt, Syria, and Palestine. Written with the intention of offering a corrective to Eurocentric occlusions of the Arab contribution to global knowledge and a riposte to misperceptions of Islam as a static culture of fanaticism, the novels offer Ali a creative way of meditating on contemporary East-West geopolitics, in particular the occupation of Palestine. I will argue that through their imaginative narration of a longer history of cross-cultural encounter and conflict in the medieval Islamicate diaspora, the novels develop a central, unstable tension between *convivencia*, an ideal polity built on interfaith cohabitation achieved under Arab governance, and *occupation*, a hostile monocultural regime imposed under Christian rule. My account of these novels will place them in the longer context of the Arabic historical novel over the past century or so, considering the vital role of this genre in forging a fictional-historicist response to the Western presence in the Middle East, and its promotion of nationalist and pan-Arabist perspectives. As a precedent to Ali, the chapter singles out Jurjī Zaidan (1861–1914), the prolific Cairo-based Lebanese-Egyptian public intellectual and historical novelist whose fictional titles include *The Battle of Poitiers*, *Saladin and the Assassins*, and *The Conquest of Andalusia*. The chapter will examine Zaidan in the context of the lively Middle Eastern cultural scene of the Arab *nahḍa* (awakening), in which early Arabic texts and language were recovered as part of a complex attempt to define modern Arab cultural identity and nationhood.

The chapter does not seek to recuperate the Islamicate world into Western chronologies; rather, it will complicate current Western understandings of 'the medieval' by exploring how these texts highlight the linked destinies of Western and Islamic societies. Its account demonstrates that the Islamicate world, like the West, has felt an attraction/repulsion to the premodern past since the late nineteenth century, reclaiming this period as a cultural Golden Age but also as a time of East-West encounters and of critical reflections (*ijtihad*) and multiple truths.

The two final chapters move not just to the Southern hemisphere, but to the Global South shaped by colonialism and its unequal configurations of wealth and power. As a scholar located in a place that is part of the economic Global North yet also self-consciously part of the Asia-Pacific region, I am taking up this region as an under-discussed arena in the study of medievalism. Anticipating by several years Alison Bashford's 'post-terrestrial area studies',[87] in *Premodern Places* David Wallace's analysis of the 'humanist Atlantic' of the fourteenth and fifteenth centuries troubled epochal premodern/modern divisions.[88] In these chapters I examine the Asia-Pacific as a 'premodern place', out of which surprising and singular medievalisms have emerged. One chapter is a story of medievalism's capacity to open up deep human history beyond Europe but also of the costs and limitations of this. The last chapter is a story of a 'Middle Ages' that is taxonomically entirely detached from Western periodization, instead using Indigenous time, but responds to the medievalism bound up with colonialism in the Pacific. These two chapters also query the tendency of world history as a discipline to focus, in the words of Karras and Mitchell, on 'important civilisations, typified at the height of their political power',[89] by focusing instead on two so-called 'remote' places whose claims to world attention are not due to political power but rather due to their significance in humanity's deep historical story. Sothoryos has come into view, and it's far from the terra nullius of Westerosi imagining.

---

[87] Bashford, 'Terraqueous Histories', 258.

[88] David Wallace, *Premodern Places: Calais to Surinam, Chaucer to Aphra Behn* (Malden, MA; Oxford; Carlton: Blackwell, 2004).

[89] Karras and Mitchell, 'Writing World Histories for our Times', 6.

Chapter 3, 'The Name of the Hobbit: Halflings, Hominins, and Deep Time', moves the study from the Northern to the Southern hemisphere, arriving at a cultural, religious, linguistic, and scientific crossroads. It takes as its focus the collapsing of fantastic medievalism and palaeontology in the scientific, media, and creative narratives surrounding the discovery of *homo floresiensis*, the petite, large-footed hominid species which has gone informally by the name of 'the hobbit' since an Australian-Indonesian archaeological team uncovered its remains in a cave on the island of Flores in 2003. The chapter will explore the convergence of two aspects of global medievalism by analysing how the discovery of the Asian hominin came to be seen through the prism of the globally exported medievalist fantasy of J. R. R. Tolkien's Middle Earth novels and their film adaptations. The chapter will argue that although the medievalizing of this hominin might be seen simply as a convenient analogy, or an accident of history (it was discovered just before the third instalment of Peter Jackson's *Lord of the Rings* trilogy), in fact the relationship is closer: for, just as Tolkien's multi-species Middle Earth explores the moral contours of humanity, so too the scientific debates waged over *homo floresiensis* trace the biological, anthropological, and historical parameters of the human species across its global migrations. A rich range of textual forms will be covered in this examination, including Tolkien's novels, archaeologists' memoirs, scientific and media reporting, films (both the Jackson Middle Earth films and Asian Tolkienesque films based on the Flores discovery), electronic memes, South-East Asian folklore, and the fossil finds from the Flores excavations themselves.

While the previous two chapters examined Middle Eastern and European recoveries and re-examinations of the historical past, this chapter takes us to the outer edges of creative medievalism as a discursive and material phenomenon, showing the unexpected byways down which medievalism as a global phenomenon can stray. But this is why it is of interest. However incidentally it might have begun, the extensive medievalizing of the Flores hominid is culturally revealing because it exposes the potency of the medieval for the popular understanding of the deep historical past. This chapter will argue that the discursive field that grew up around *homo floresiensis* discloses how medievalism, with its often mythic or legendary vision of the medieval past, functions as the hinge into a non-specific 'premodernity', a space that has the urgency of history but also the scale of prehistory. It will examine what the remarkable scientific saga of the Flores hobbit can tell us about the capacity for 'the medieval' to stand in not just for global human history writ large but for the ways we figure 'deep time' and the primeval past. The chapter will also examine the difficult racial politics underlying this episode, arguing that the framing of *homo floresiensis* within Tolkien-influenced medievalism ultimately constructs a limiting image of a globally conceived humanity. Since it overwrites the Flores hominid's femaleness, Austronesian identity, and paleolithic age, at the same time confirming genre fantasy fiction's staple image of the medieval past as white, male, and European, it serves as a reminder that global medievalism has the potential to reinforce rather than unsettle the Eurocentric legacy of the Middle Ages in the modern world.

Chapter 4, '*Ten Canoes* and 1066: Aboriginal Time and the Limits of Medievalism', continues and deepens the book's Southern-hemisphere focus by examining an Australian Aboriginal interpretation of a period that is apparently coeval with the European Middle Ages as it unfolded in the north of the Australian continent. Over the past decade, a growing body of research has explored colonial perceptions, and indeed creations, of 'the medieval' as an imaginative category, with an emphasis on how these have been implicated within the European imperialist projects that have been such a significant vehicle for the spread of medievalism across the globe. Focusing so far almost exclusively on white settler perceptions and reconstructions of the Middle Ages, this research has widened the geopolitical scope of medievalism but has not fundamentally challenged its Eurocentric paradigm. This chapter will take a different approach, examining what might constitute a postcolonial Australian medievalism by looking at the 2006 Cannes award-winning Australian film *Ten Canoes*, a joint Aboriginal/non-Aboriginal production by Rolf de Heer, Peter Djigirr, and the Yolŋu people, which sets its story in the Yolŋu territories of Arnhem land 'a thousand years ago'.

This film's communication of deep Yolŋu history to a general audience is, the chapter will argue, part of a broader historical project. For just as recent work on the global Middle Ages emphasizes international networks of cultural, economic, linguistic, and material exchange as an alternative to narratives of Western dominance, so too research into Aboriginal Australian history prior to colonization is giving increased attention to its long social, trade, and even religious networks with other non-European societies. In order to convey fully the ideological significance of the film's 'medievalization' of Yolŋu culture, the chapter will give a contextual account of how white settler culture has long relegated Australian Aboriginal culture to a 'timeless' place outside of history, as opposed to Euro-British culture, which is understood to be properly historical in its inheritance of long traditions reaching back to the Middle Ages. This film's creation of a non-European 'medieval' past for the Yolŋu is, it will be argued, a highly sophisticated instance of a non-European Aboriginal culture recreating a deep past—an impulse with which scholars of Eurocentric medievalism are very familiar. Exploring how the film presents its ancestral memory of the Yolŋu world 'a thousand years ago', I will argue that a properly global approach to medievalism needs to take into account how the period known in the West as 'the Middle Ages' has figured for cultures whose contact with colonialism has left them negotiating, but also displacing, European and non-European ideas of time and the distant past. This chapter also argues that a discussion of this film demands that the concept of 'world' be replaced with the Australian Aboriginal concept of 'Country', which expresses a deeply intertwined phenomenological relationship between human and the more-than-human existence. While Chapter 3 showed how global medievalism can suppress difference when introduced into non-European environments, this final chapter demonstrates the extent to which the very idea of the 'medieval world' can be queried and even displaced from outside Europe.

These last two chapters, with their persistent return to the specific materiality of place, remind us that 'world', phenomenologically conceived, is also finally a concept that has a deeper materiality to it than 'global'. To adapt Alfred Korzybski's famous distinction between 'the map' and 'the territory',[90] 'world' is grounded in territory, in place, while 'globe' is conceived as a diagrammatic arrangement and representation of space. As such, 'world' in this book touches on the

---

[90] Alfred Korzybski, 'A Non-Aristotelian System and its Necessity for Rigour in Mathematics and Physics', a paper presented before the American Mathematical Society at the New Orleans, Louisiana, meeting of the American Association for the Advancement of Science, 28 December 1931.

planetary not just because both latitudinal hemispheres are discussed but also because its Southern medievalisms raise questions about how ideas of the medieval relate to the planet—how they interpret and occlude the environment, and how they provide ways of understanding and misunderstanding time, the deep temporality of human habitation, and the strata of the earth itself.

| 1 |

Medievalism Disoriented

The French Novel and Neo-reactionary Politics

Nation and 'globophobia'

How is a nation a world? Is it a part of the larger world, or a rejection of and retreat from that world? The question of what constitutes a world is intensively pursued in Jérôme Ferrari's 2012 Prix Goncourt-winning novel *The Sermon on the Fall of Rome*, whose narrator muses:

> The truth is that we do not know what worlds are. But we can watch out for the signs of their coming to an end. The release of a shutter in summer daylight, a tired young woman's delicate hand resting on that of her grandfather, or the square sail of a ship sailing into the harbor at Hippo, bringing with it, from Italy, the inconceivable news that Rome has fallen.[1]

In this multi-temporal novel, which loops from twenty-first century France back to fifth-century North Africa, the fall of Rome figures as the world-historical cataclysm that sets the paradigm for all Western

---

[1] Jerome Ferrari, *Sermon sur la chute de Rome* (Paris: Éditions Actes Sud, 2012); *Sermon on the Fall of Rome*, trans. Geoffrey Strachan (London: Maclehose Press, 2016). All future references are to these editions.

World Medievalism: The Middle Ages in Modern Textual Culture. Louise D'Arcens, Oxford University Press.

imperial destinies, and shapes the regional, national, and trans-oceanic destinies that emerge in the wake of empire's collapse. The worlds that are created in the vacuum of empire are not necessarily large in scale: they range, as the quotation above shows, from family units through to whole cities and even nations. Worlds are defined, rather, by the collective will of their members, whether these be friends, lovers, governors, or soldiers—a will which, to draw on the phenomenological approach formulated in my Introduction, apprehends worlds as constellations of shared beliefs, practices, values, and events that are grounded in a recognized past. The awareness of the historical past among the world-builders in Ferrari's novel corresponds to Cheah's formulation of world as 'an ongoing dynamic process of becoming, something that is continually being made and remade because it possesses a historical-temporal dimension'.[2] By this construction, a modern nation that understands itself as a post-Roman entity is engaging in a form of nationalist medievalism that is also an act of world creation, and as such warrants a place in this study of world medievalism.

And yet in a more directly geopolitical sense it would seem counterintuitive to take recent French uses of early medieval France as my opening case study of world medievalism. This is especially so since these reclamations of the medieval past, as I will show, are often expressly in the service of nationalist ideologies and as such would seem to be the opposite of 'worldly' in their orientation. I argue, however, that European nationalist medievalisms of recent decades differ from the nationalist medievalisms of the nineteenth century in that they function as a symptomatic and in many cases explicit response to the perceived threats and uncertainties of globalization, with its supranational flows of capital and of people. This seems especially to be the case with France in the past two decades. Sarah Waters is among those who have identified the increasingly insistent recourse to notions of French cultural identity as a symptom of a widespread 'globophobia' that has arisen in response to the rise of globalization and its attendant by-products of economic disparity and displacement of people. Waters argues that French opponents of

---

[2] Cheah, 'World against Globe', 319.

globalization have framed its impost not just as economic but rather in civilizational and even ethnic terms, as an 'Anglo-Saxon' (that is, American) menace to France's distinctive social forms and traditions, and have characterized the tension as a 'war of worlds', due to the perceived opposition between French and 'Anglo-Saxon' *Weltan-shauungen*.[3] The slippage evident here between 'world' as way of life or perspective and 'globe' as a geopolitical-economic entity is charac-teristic of the semantic elasticity of the word *mondialisation* in French discourse, which is used interchangeably with globalization, although some, such as Jean-Luc Nancy, have disarticulated them in order to emphasize globalization as what he calls the 'un-world' (*l'im-monde*), a force of inequity and disintegration which does the opposite of world-making.[4] Much of this critique, as Waters has demonstrated, issues from France's prominent intellectual Left. In this chapter I will focus more closely on the Right-wing response, exploring how anxieties about the movement of people into France, especially from the Islami-cate world, as an effect of globalization has given rise to more virulently expressed forms of French nationalist identification, forged under the star of an idiosyncratic medievalism.

This chapter's examination of some of the flashpoints of 'early medievalism' in recent French politics and culture evaluates both the significant overlaps and the important differences between nativist and recent neoreactionary approaches to the Middle Ages. Nativism here refers to the far-Right nationalist ideology that advocates a preservation of France's unified 'native' complexion as a white Christian society, an identity whose origins are located in premodern, pre-Revolutionary French history.[5] France's neoreactionaries share the nativists' rejection of immigration and supranational entities such as the European union which are deemed to impinge on France's national sovereignty, but defend modern France's secular Republican and post-Enlightenment values, with public figures such as Alain Finkielkraut appealing to national secularism to condemn the wearing of religious garb by

[3] Sarah Waters, 'French Intellectuals and Globalisation: A War of Worlds', *French Cultural Studies*, 22.4 (2011), 303–20.
[4] Jean-Luc Nancy, *The Creation of the World or Globalization*, trans. and intro. François Raffoul and David Pettigrew (Albany, NY: SUNY Press, 2007).
[5] Hans-Georg Betz, 'Nativism across Time and Space', *Swiss Political Science Review* 23.4 (2017), 337.

Muslim immigrants.[6] This difference shapes their different accounts of
how the early Middle Ages figure in the long story of France's national
destiny. This chapter also considers some recent responses that critique
or refuse such nationalistic-imperialist French medievalisms, exploring
how these critical responses present early medievalism as fraught with
forms of post-imperial trauma.

Populism and the loss of 'deep France'

Anyone following French politics over the past two decades or more
can hardly fail to have noticed the conspicuous recourse made to
France's medieval past by the populist and nationalist Front National
(FN) led by Jean-Marie Le Pen from 1972 and by his daughter Marine
since 2011. The blatant populism of the party's positions and of its use
of public spectacle means it can be easy to overlook the depth and
seriousness of the FN's account of history, which, as José Pedro
Zúquete has shown, is based on the philosophies of historical continuity argued in the nineteenth century by Ernest Renan and Hippolyte
Taine.[7] The FN's philosophy of nation, as stated in the Front National's
2001 party platform, is that it is a primordial spiritual and ethnic
community held together by shared language and heritage, and gov-
erned by what Jean-Marie Le Pen has called a 'profound law of immo-
bility' that underlies superficial change.[8] For Le Pen the dominant
historical narratives that privilege the French Revolution and the
French Republic as a secular state fail to acknowledge the true, premodern origins of the French nation.

The medieval figure most persistently and conspicuously adopted by
the FN is, as many images recorded from mass rallies attest, the iconic
fifteenth-century warrior and martyr Joan of Arc, whose image continues to be reworked across three generations of Le Pens, and has
gained new significance now that two of them, Marine and Marion

[6] See, for instance, Alain Finkielkraut, *L'Identité malheureuse* (*The Unhappy Identity*)
(Paris: Stock, 2013), which argues that Muslim immigration is a threat to French
Enlightenment secularism.
[7] José Pedro Zúquete, *Missionary Politics in Contemporary Europe* (Syracuse: Syracuse
University Press, 2007), 34–5.
[8] Zúquete, *Missionary Politics*, 35.

Maréchal-Le Pen, are female. Despite the predictability of the FN's invocation of Joan as a martyr of national defence, their rhetoric of historical parallelism has proven flexible across the decades: her original 'English' foes have been refigured as a series of supranational entities that have been deemed as diminishing France's national sovereignty. These have ranged from the Soviet States in the 1980s to the European Union and Schengen Area from the 1990s on, and, more amorphously, the global capitalist system, especially, as mentioned earlier, the Anglo-Saxon neoliberal economy—and, most recently, Islam.

Despite her iconographic potency, Joan is, in fact, only the latest medieval figure in the FN's historical catalogue. Decades earlier, Le Pen senior was invoking the early medieval roots of the French nation, the *Ur*-moment of which was, for him, the fifth- to sixth-century king Clovis's uniting of the Frankish tribes. An indispensable part of Clovis's enduring legacy for the FN was his conversion to Catholicism. His baptism, according to a speech given by Le Pen in 1995, 'achieved the sacred union of Christianity and Roman civilization and the youthful vigor of the Frank people that would become, through fifteen centuries, the French people'.[9] This historical vision, in which the Christian faith was an indispensable part of the French national identity, is an overt rejection of *laïcité*, the secularism at the heart of French society in the wake of the 1905 Combes laws that separated Church and state.

The year 1996 revealed, however, that Clovis's baptism was far from being the sole property of the minority clustered on the extreme Right. In that year, then-President Jacques Chirac invited Pope Jean-Paul II to preside over celebrations in Reims Cathedral to commemorate 1,500 years since Clovis's baptism, which was dated, using Gregory of Tours's *Historia Francorum*, as being Christmas Day 496.[10] The announcement and planning of this event generated a storm of controversy across several months which involved, in the amusing summary of *The New Yorker*'s French correspondent Adam Gopnik:

[9] Quoted in Zúquete, *Missionary Politics*, 36.

[10] Martin Heinzelmann, 'Heresy in Books I and II of Gregory of Tours' *Historiae*', in *After Rome's Fall: Sources of Early Medieval History. Essays Presented to Walter Goffart*, ed. Alexander Callander Murray (Toronto, Buffalo, and London: University of Toronto Press, 1998), 67–8.

pamphlets, a bomb, protest marches, an excited op-ed piece in *Le Monde* debating the proper conjugation of two 5th-century Greek verbs, and a fierce polemic written by the head of Yves Saint Laurent. Like all French public controversies, it was a mixture of the absurd, the profound, the inscrutable, the enviable, and, always, the metaphoric.[11]

Though there were a myriad of stances for and against the event, Henri Tincq, the religious commentator for the newspaper *Le Monde*, characterized the controversy as a 'war of the two Frances',[12] and indeed reactions did generally tend to polarize along Left and Right lines. On the Left, those with Republican and secularist sympathies objected not only to the Royalist fetishism of the event but to the idea of tax-payers' money being used not just for a religious event in a secular state—but for a religious event that celebrated the intertwining of religious and national baptism. For them, a state-sponsored event celebrating France as 'the oldest daughter of the Church' rather than a post-Enlightenment republic was not only culturally retrograde but illegal. This was made worse by the scheduling of the event on 21 September, the date commemorating the National Convention's proclamation in 1792 of the abolition of the French monarchy, rather than on either of the other two traditionally accepted dates of 13 April or Christmas Day. While conservative accounts emphasized the genuineness of the king's Catholic conversion, Leftist accounts countered this by presenting it as an act of secular *Realpolitik* that allowed Clovis to extend his territories and consolidate his alliance with the Church as a power base.[13] Those on the Right, especially those with Catholic Royalist sympathies, tended to share Le Pen's historical account of France's premodern spiritual and ethnic roots, although, as I will go on discuss, some attempted to soften the FN's hijacking of the Clovis commemoration to buttress an anti-immigration stance.

The competing commentaries of politicians, media pundits, historians, and novelists offered divided assessments of the meaning of the legacy of the so-called 'first Frenchman' for France in the age of

[11] Adam Gopnik, 'The First Frenchman', *The New Yorker*, 7 October 1996, 44.
[12] Susan J. Terrio, 'Crucible of the Millennium? The Clovis Affair in Contemporary France', *Society for the Comparative Study of Society and History* 41.3 (1999), 439.
[13] Terrio, 'Crucible of the Millennium?', 445–6.

globalization and in particular the age of increased immigration. When members of the FN gathered on 13 April to commemorate the baptism, Le Pen seized on the event to point to the contrast between France's heroic Christian age and its current age of immigration (especially North African Muslim immigration), criminality, and unemployment. As Susan J. Terrio has recounted in her thorough account of the controversy, Leftist historians such as the eminent Suzanne Citron claimed that it was ludicrous to speak of the barbarian Clovis as the embodiment of primordial Frenchness when his kingdom encompassed parts of what would become Germany and the low countries. Emphasizing this plurality enabled Citron to call for 'a historiography which is no longer that of a nation ... but that of a plural, intercultural France which encompasses religious, ethnic, philosophical, and regional diversity, open to others'.[14] Rightist historians, while holding themselves aloft from Le Pen's crude ethnic essentialism, nevertheless reinforced his assimilationist agenda around immigration by casting Clovis as a 'good immigrant' king whose exemplary adoption of his people's religion led to further religious unification across his realm. This orientation toward unity was under threat, they argued, from external supranational forces such as the European Union, Anglo-liberalism, and the internal forces of secularism and multiculturalism.

While the 1996 Clovis storm eventually blew over, the larger debates around contemporary France's relationship to its longer historical past have continued vigorously in the politico-cultural debates of twenty-first-century France. Within these debates, one of the dominant narratives that has emerged is that which has come to be called *déclinisme*. As its name implies, this position argues that France is in decline relative to its former glories. Anyone familiar with the histories of Gibbon, the German strain of *Verfallsgeschichte*, or indeed the Book of Jeremiah knows that this trope is not particular to contemporary France but has long been used to mark boundaries between earlier societies and their degenerate aftermaths. Clifford Ando and Andrew Gillett have both pointed out that the decline narratives are, to quote Ando, 'seductive' because they can attribute the collapse of a civilization either to its intrinsic problems or to external assaults, or to a

---

[14] Suzanne Citron, 'A propos de Clovis', *Le Monde*, 28 February 1996; cited in Terrio, 'Crucible of the Millennium?', 447.

combination of both.[15] This flexibility, as I will go on to demonstrate, makes the trope especially serviceable to those wishing to draw parallels between the fall of earlier great societies and perceived or predicted decline in the present. The recent French iteration of declinology, which Sarah Waters shows had already gained traction among nativists in the 1990s,[16] is notable in the twenty-first century for refracting the trope of decline through the prism of French identity in the face of globalization.

As a discourse *déclinisme* is bipartisan: the Left focuses on impacts of neoliberalism while the Right dwells on immigration, multiculturalism, and moral and linguistic decline. While the extreme Right of French politics, especially the Front National, is notorious beyond France for its prosecution of this view, the less-known Right-wing commentariat is a volatile domain that ranges from Republican secularists to religious conservatives. Despite its volatility, a thesis expounded across the Right argues that France has fallen into a malaise characterized by a nihilistic lack of cultural identity, and this malaise has made it ripe for cultural overthrow by unintegrated Muslim residents. This discourse is characterized by two notable impulses. The first is *valedictory*: at least since Jean-Marie Rouart's book *Adieu à la France qui s'en va*,[17] numerous commentators have been bidding farewell to their idea of France as the beacon of Europe. This is accompanied by the second impulse, which is *valetudinarian*, that is preoccupied with diagnosing France's social pathologies and with the idea of France as decadent and suicidally enfeebled, a state evoked in neoreactionary media pundit Éric Zemmour's polemic *Le suicide français*.[18] These pathologies are frequently characterized in emotional terms: as dejection, discontent, and, to cite the title of Zemmour's best-selling book *Mélancolie française*,[19] as

---

[15] Clifford Ando, 'Decline, Fall, and Transformation', *Journal of Late Antiquity* 1.1 (2008), 31–60; Andrew Gillett, 'The Fall of Rome and the Retreat of European Multiculturalism: A Historical Trope as a Discourse of Authority in Public Debate', *Cogent Arts & Humanities* 4.1, 1390915, https://doi.org/10.1080/23311983.2017.1390915.

[16] Sarah Waters, 'The 2008 Economic Crisis and the French Narrative of Decline: Une causalité diabolique', *Modern and Contemporary France* 21.3 (2013), 335–54.

[17] Jean-Marie Rouart, *Adieu à la France qui s'en va* (Paris: Éditions Grasset, 2003).

[18] Éric Zemmour, *Le Suicide français* (Paris: Éditions Albin Michel, 2014).

[19] Éric Zemmour, *Mélancolie française: L'histoire de France racontée par Éric Zemmour* (Paris: Librairie Anthème Fayard et Éditions Denoël, 2010). All future references will be to this edition.

melancholy, an arrested mourning that can neither retrieve what is lost nor reconcile itself to that loss. France is melancholic for a deep French past that bequeathed to modernity a contradictory inheritance of noble striving and tragic missed opportunity. It is this view of the early medieval past's melancholic legacy that distinguishes Zemmour's neoreactionary narrative of decline from the nativists' nostalgic view of the Frankish past as a unified and unifying white Christian heritage that has been betrayed.

Amid the books of French declinology, *Mélancolie française* is particularly relevant because it presents France's current maladies against the backdrop of its deep historical past. Although the trope of social decline is implicitly historical, Zemmour's book stands out for being the most expressly historicist in the prosecution of its diagnosis of France's ills: its subtitle is 'The History of France, Told by Éric Zemmour'. Among Zemmour's numerous Jeremiads, this one nests its neoreactionary purpose within a populist 'long national history' format. His book is of interest for the way the Middle Ages, and especially the early Middle Ages, feature in its account of French history. Because his concern lies primarily in post-revolutionary history, Zemmour gives only a few pages to whole swathes of medieval history, from the fifth-century beginnings of the Merovingian kingdom through to the end of the Capetian dynasty in the fourteenth century (9–27). The period is significant, however, in its illumination of the modern.

The Middle Ages are deemed by Zemmour to haunt the modern in that they set the agenda for France's *temperamental history* and its historical self-image. According to Zemmour the birth of the French Middle Ages after the destruction of the Gallo-Roman empire ushered in a cultural melancholy that was, with only brief periods of respite, to drive the course of French history. He attributes this melancholy to France's abiding sense of itself as an empire *manqué,* expressed in its serial attempts across fifteen centuries, from the Frankish kingdoms on, to institute forms of centralized governance, sovereignty, and cultural assimilation in the image of the lost Roman empire. While other conservatives have dated France's identity crisis to the sexual revolution, the rise of feminism, the loss of religion, and especially to increased immigration, for Zemmour these merely exacerbate this primordial medieval melancholy. In portraying his country as perennially striving for imperial status he unknowingly invokes the medieval political concept of *translatio imperii*. Within Zemmour's elastic polemicization of French history, even when this *translatio* is temporarily achieved, whether by Charlemagne, Napoleon, or Charles de Gaulle, melancholy persists because of empire's fragility, especially at moments such as the present which are characterized by decadence and impending collapse. This is most evident in his final chapter 'La Chute de Rome', 'the Fall of Rome', in which he openly parallels Rome's collapse with modern France's imminent demise as a result of Muslim immigration. In order to draw this parallel, he relies on Alessandro Barbero's account of the battle of Adrianopolis in *The Day of the Barbarians: The Battle That Led to the Fall of the Roman Empire*, claiming that Rome's collapse began as a result of its failure to assimilate Eastern Goths to whom it had granted asylum.[20] Although Barbero's book does not emphasize Roman decadence, Zemmour's depiction of France as suicidally succumbing to globalization, multiculturalism, and neoliberalism demands that he retain the familiar account of Rome as weakened from within and oblivious that the barbarians are not only through the gates but are there by invitation.

Zemmour, it is true, is not scrupulous in his use of the term 'melancholy'. Although the book's title is reprised in a single declaration that France is afflicted by '[u]ne souffrance, une tristesse, une mélancholie française' (124), elsewhere he refers to its 'nostalgie d'empire', (13) and claims his nation has 'une inexpugnable nostalgie pour l'unité originelle survécut à toutes les allégeances postérieures pourtant si glorieuses' ('an insurmountable nostalgia for originary unity that survives all subsequent allegiances, however glorious', 15). It is nevertheless possible to identify throughout Zemmour's account an abiding emotional condition that corresponds closely to the seminal description of melancholy in Freud's 1917 essay 'Mourning and Melancholia'. For Freud, melancholia is a pathological state in which 'loss of a loved one' or of 'some abstraction ... such as one's country, liberty, an ideal' does not result in the subject's gradual acceptance of the loss. Instead, rather than withdrawing the libido from the lost love object and 'displac[ing] it on to a new one', as a healthy mourner would do, the melancholic

[20] Alessandro Barbero, *The Day of the Barbarians: The Battle That Led to the Fall of the Roman Empire*, trans. John Cullen (New York: Walker & Company, 2007).

subject identifies its ego with the lost object.[21] Because object-loss is transformed into ego-loss in melancholia, Freud argues, the painful mood and feelings of dejection are exacerbated by an 'extraordinary diminution in...self-regard' which leads the melancholic subject to 'extend...his self-criticism back over the past' in order to confirm an enduring unworthiness and continuing decline.[22] All of these characteristics are present in Zemmour's pessimistic narrative, which portrays modern France in the grip of an affective-ideological condition predicated on the irresolvable tension between its protracted failure to secure a dreamed-of imperial destiny and its unwillingness to relinquish its originary imperial ambitions. The phrase 'inexpugnable nostalgie' is the operative term distinguishing this melancholic state from the self-serious nostalgia of extreme Right groups such as the Front National, whose reclaiming of premodernity in events such as their notorious 1996 re-enactments of Clovis's baptism are founded on a belief that the past can be re-experienced. Within the historico-emotional economy of melancholy, restoration of the lost object or ideal, even temporarily, is impossible. This is especially so, Zemmour claims, in demographically altered modern France, for which 'L'Europe continental sous domination Français est une chimère qui s'éloigne' ('continental Europe under French domination is a receding illusion', 124).

Zemmour's idea of a collective post-imperial melancholy rests on an exclusionary idea of France as a unanimous community made up of those whose identities are grounded in its deep in situ past. This racist melancholy has been challenged by alternative examinations of the migrant melancholy experienced by groups ranging from Asian-Americans to Misrahi Jews. Merav Alush-Levron, David L. Eng, and Shinhee Han all argue that migrant melancholy is directed not only toward the homeland that cannot be regained, but also toward the alienating ideal of the model 'happy' migrant who 'passes' by conforming

---

[21] Sigmund Freud, 'Mourning and Melancholia', in *The Standard Edition of the Complete Psychological Works of Sigmund Freud*, trans. and ed. James Strachey, in collaboration with Anna Freud, Volume XIV (London: Hogarth Press, 1917/57), 243–6.
[22] Freud, 'Mourning and Melancholia', 247.

to the dominant culture.[23] Although, as Sara Ahmed points out, the unintegrated 'melancholic migrant' is a folk devil of host culture scripts, mobilizing its disruptive power can challenge the imperative that migrants be compliantly grateful to the host culture in the face of systemic racism.[24] Acknowledging migrant melancholy disrupts Zemmour's fantasy that this affective state is restricted to those who, as 'real' French people, are mourning their wasted imperial mandate, and exposes the sense of perpetual loss experienced by those who are expected to participate gratefully in it despite being perceived as interlopers.

Jérôme Ferrari's *Sermon on the Fall of Rome*: colonial trauma

Despite its historical account being vigorously contested by French historians, *Mélancolie française* sold surprisingly well, and its impact is evident not only in numerous heated public discussions on immigration and national identity in France[25] but in the fact that, in addition to the public debates surrounding it, a number of significant novelistic efforts extrapolated creatively (though not uncritically) on its historical thesis. An important instance of this is Jérôme Ferrari's novel *Le sermon de la chute de Rome/Sermon on the Fall of Rome*, cited at the beginning of this chapter, which offers a searching exploration of the perception of France's past as a post-Roman vacuum. In this Prix Goncourt-winning novel, Ferrari traces the fortunes of a family living in the French territory of Corsica to reckon with the geopolitical and emotional fallout from France's loss of its modern colonial empire in Indochina and Africa—with a particular emphasis on Algeria—and the

---

[23] David L. Eng and Shinhee Han, 'A Dialogue on Racial Melancholia', in *Loss: The Politics of Mourning*, ed. David L. Eng and David Kazanjian (Berkeley: University of California Press, 2013), 343–71; Merav Alush-Levron, 'The Politics of Ethnic Melancholy in Israeli Cinema', *Social Identities* 21.2 (2015), 169–83.

[24] Sara Ahmed, *The Promise of Happiness* (Durham: Duke University Press, 2010), 121–59.

[25] Pauline Bock, 'How Right-Wing Thinker Eric Zemmour Is Fuelling France's Identity Wars', *New Statesman*, 30 October 2019, https://www.newstatesman.com/world/europe/2019/10/how-right-wing-thinker-eric-zemmour-fuelling-france-s-identity-wars.

concomitant fall of the Fourth Republic. What Ferrari's novel shares with Zemmour's manifesto is its portrait of ex-imperial France as sunk in a malaise from which it seems no new life or vigour can emerge. Furthermore, it also draws an historical analogy between the present and the cusp of the classical and early medieval periods, via a contemporary invocation of the sermons delivered by Saint Augustine in December 410 to his congregation at Hippo in the wake of Rome's fall. A crucial difference between Zemmour's and Ferrari's accounts, however, is that for Ferrari it is not failed imperial ambitions that have led to a melancholic French yearning dating back to the Middle Ages, but rather the experience of *having had an empire* that has left a deadening traumatic legacy that still plays itself out after empire has fallen. Augustine's sermons, like the *City of God* treatise which emerged out of them, converge with the novel's meditation on the ultimate futility of empire-building as a human endeavour.

The Augustinian leitmotif that runs through the novel—its sections all have epigrams taken from the saint's sermons—emerges because one of the central characters, Libero, has written an undergraduate thesis on Augustine's response to the fall of Rome. Having become thoroughly disenchanted with Augustine, who he sees as taking 'vengeful and perverse relish' in the replacement of 'an ancient world of gods and poets' by 'Christianity and its repellent cohort of ascetics and martyrs' (52), Libero returns to his native Corsica with his childhood friend and fellow philosophy student Matthieu, so they can take over the management of a failing local bar. It becomes apparent through the novel's lightly philosophical narrative that the friends' respective studies influence their attitudes to running the bar, which they regard as an act of world creation. For Matthieu, a student of Gottfried Wilhelm Leibniz, the bar is the 'best of all possible worlds' (90), and reflects Leibniz's famous doctrine in *La Monadologie* of pre-established harmony (§56):[26]

> A diverse and cheerful clientele was to be found there, a mixture of regulars, young people from the neighbouring villages and tourists of all nationalities, amazingly brought together in a festive and bibulous

[26] G. W. Leibniz, *La Monadologie*, ed. E. Boutroux (Paris: Librairie Générale Française, 1892/1991).

> communion which, against all expectations, was not troubled by any
> discord. It was as if this were a place chosen by God for an experi-
> ment in the reign of love upon earth. (79)

Matthieu enjoys his benevolent reign over the bar and its increasing
orbit of influence, and at first Libero shares Matthieu's optimistic view;
but as he becomes disenchanted with the bar's creeping state of dis-
harmony, the Augustinian neoplatonism he had abandoned reasserts
itself. He begins to see himself and Matthieu not as world creators but
as demiurges who have unconsciously fabricated a debased 'man-made
world' which will, and should, be destroyed (91)—a task he himself
hastens with increasing unrestraint, escalating tensions until a final
sequence of violent acts brings it all to a cataclysmic end.

   Libero's view of the bar as a corrupt and ephemeral domain corresponds directly to the representation of the fallen Roman empire in the
Augustinian sermons ventriloquized in the novel's final section. Here
Augustine admonishes mourners in his congregation, including its
numerous Roman refugees, saying 'Was not Rome built by men like
yourself? Since when do you believe men have the power to build things
that are eternal? Man builds upon sand' (184). This meditation on the
transience of empire is further reinforced by the novel being principally
set in Corsica, an island with a long history of serial occupation by
empires that did not last.[27] According to this Augustinian framework,
empire and its end, as acts of human world-building and destruction,
barely cause disturbance: the saint proclaims 'Rome has fallen... but
the earth and the heavens have not been shaken' (185). This sentiment
is closely echoed in one character's experience of the end of the French
colonial empire in 1962: 'six months later... the empire had ceased to
exist. Is this how empires die, without even a tremor being heard?'
(132). But the diminution of human trauma implicit in the Augustinian
view of empire is ultimately contested in the novel: just as Libero and
Matthieu's ownership of the bar ends in carnage and disintegration, so
too in the era of French decolonization 'men come heavily down to

---

[27] Marcel A. Farinelli, 'Island Societies and Mainland Nation-Building in the
Mediterranean: Sardinia and Corsica in Italian, French, and Catalan Nationalism',
Island Studies Journal 12.1 (2017), 21–34.

earth in the new gravitational field of their fallen country' (132), experiencing trauma and loss.

It is true that *Sermon* focuses on the trauma of former French colonial agents—the men who have 'come heavily down to earth' at the end of empire—rather than that of the colonized; but this is effective in that the novel replaces the *mélancolie française* diagnosed by Zemmour with what can be described as a *traumatisme français*. Cathy Caruth's renowned formulation of trauma identifies it as a trans-temporal experience that 'is not locatable in the simple violent or original event in an individual's past, but rather in the way that its very unassimilated nature ... returns to haunt the survivor later on'.[28] While Caruth's broader theory has been contested by other trauma theorists, including Ruth Leys,[29] I invoke her description above because it is useful for recognizing trauma's structural parallels with melan-choly, in that both are based on compulsive affective-memorial repeti-tion due to the failure to assimilate suffering across time. Unlike melancholy's foundation in unresolved loss of a beloved object or idea, however, the novel's depiction of *traumatisme* in the wake of empire combines a loss of power with an unassimilated recognition of the suffering one has inflicted on others in the wielding of that power. As such Ferrari's novel focuses less on the victim trauma with which Caruth, Leys, and others are concerned, and more on what Raya Morag has called 'perpetrator trauma'.[30] Exploring such trauma has, Morag says, been 'perceived as unseemly or even unimaginable' because it risks shifting the focus away from victims; but she argues that it is in fact vital to understanding the full spectrum of the brutalizing impacts of state-sponsored violence, and need not diminish victims' specific experi-ences. In particular she points to South Africa's Truth and Reconcili-ation Commission in the 1990s as being responsible for major theoretical developments in the understanding of trauma due to its finely calibrated system for identifying post-traumatic states based on

[28] Cathy Caruth, *Unclaimed Experience: Trauma, Narrative and History* (Baltimore: Johns Hopkins University Press, 1996), 4.

[29] Ruth Leys and Marlene Goldman, 'Navigating the Genealogies of Trauma, Guilt, and Affect: An Interview with Ruth Leys', *University of Toronto Quarterly* 79.2 (2010), 658–9.

[30] Raya Morag, 'Perpetrator Trauma and Contemporary Israeli Documentary Cinema', *Camera Obscura* 80 (2012), 93–133.

type and level of involvement—a system which included, importantly, an acknowledgement that post-traumatic symptoms can also be experienced by those who have participated or been complicit in atrocities. Morag's own focus is on Israeli cinema's recent portrayal of perpetrator trauma among Jewish soldiers who have permitted or participated in violence against Palestinian people in occupied territories or refugee camps, and whose experience of PTSD combines intergenerational Holocaust trauma with perpetrator trauma resulting from their 'active complicity with the government war machine'.[31] Although Ferrari's novel differs in its focus, the traumatic fusion of victim and perpetrator identity described by Morag is suggestive for understanding a number of Ferrari's Corsican characters, who despite being subject to colonization have themselves been part of the machinery of French colonial rule in North and West Africa, and find themselves fallen when that empire falls.

The symptoms of perpetrator trauma Morag describes, in particular emotional numbness and unresolved guilt, certainly apply to these characters. Matthieu's grandfather Marcel Antonetti is an almost catatonic figure not simply because his tenure as a colonial administrator in West Africa ended, but because he experienced the post itself as hollow and dehumanizing, culminating in his chillingly matter-of-fact rape of his African maid. An even shadowier figure is Lieutenant-colonel André Degorce, a 'reclusive and mute' (132) former torturer in the Algerian War. Degorce had been a central character in Ferrari's harrowing novel *Où j'ai laissé mon âme/Where I Left My Soul* (2010),[32] and his reappearance here ties the two novels together. But whereas the earlier novel minutely anatomizes the atrocities committed by Degorce in Algeria, *Sermon* is concerned with their traumatic after-effect in Corsica, when, in the wake of his dehumanization of both himself and others, 'he returns to his wife's arms seeking the redemption he will never be granted' (132). The fact that both characters are Corsican rather than denizens of the French hexagon further complicates their traumatic participation in the oppression of others only marginally more colonized than themselves. Their later withdrawal from the world registers a deep visceral apprehension on their part that they

[31] Morag, 'Perpetrator Trauma', 96–7, 99.
[32] Jérôme Ferrari, *Où j'ai laissé mon âme* (Paris: Éditions Actes Sud, 2010).

have been complicit functionaries of a brutal colonial regime that does not recognize them as fully legitimate members.

The clear historical echoes in the novel between Roman and French imperialism do appear to situate ex-imperial France as a kind of modern medieval equivalent, 'bearing witness...to the end and at the same time to the beginning' (187). But unlike the long melancholic epoch that in Zemmour's account spans from the Middle Ages to today, Ferrari's novel hints at the transition from the ex-imperial into the postcolonial. In the novel's triangulated twenty-first-century setting, Paris features but has been provincialized, in Dipesh Chakrabarty's sense that despite still being the French metropolis, its vitality now largely derives from its exchanges of people with the novel's other two Mediterranean centres, Corsica and the Algerian port city of Annaba.[33] Annaba, now decolonized but formerly the Roman-African city of Hippo Regius and later the French colonial city of Bône, becomes a compass point of the novel when Matthieu's sister Aurélie joins an archaeological team digging there for the remains of Augustine's cathedral. Aurélie's time in Annaba has transformed her so that she feels increasingly at home in North Africa and disconnected from the metropolis, where the rituals of life seem 'incomprehensible' and 'pointless' (104). Her love affair with an Algerian colleague puts an end to her disintegrating relationship in Paris. But Ferrari is careful not to paint a glibly optimistic portrait of decolonization. Instead, the lovers are driven quietly but inexorably apart by the asymmetries of the former colonial arrangement that persist all around them: Aurélie, for instance, can travel freely and afford restaurant meals, both luxuries unavailable to Algerians even of the professional classes, and the discrepancy humiliates her lover. His name, Massinissa, which he shares with the ancient king of Numidia who fought the Romans but then collaborated with them, evokes the long recursive history of North Africa's colonial subjection and occupation. In the novel's final scene, Augustine lies dying as Genseric's forces lay siege to Hippo, and he wonders whether those in his congregation who were unpersuaded by his diminution of Rome's fall in fact saw that they were on the brink of a new human era (187). This new medieval world, though it is not given

---

[33] Dipesh Chakrabarty, *Provincializing Europe: Postcolonial Thought and Historical Difference* (Princeton, NJ: Princeton University Press, 2000), 16.

this name by Ferrari, will, like contemporary France, develop in the traumatic vacuum left behind by empire, though neither Augustine nor Ferrari's narrator knows what form it will take.

Michel Houellebecq's *Submission*: melancholic medievalism

France's long post-imperial legacy is nested in a larger exploration of the French Middle Ages in controversial author Michel Houellebecq's *Submission/Soumission*.[34] This novel plumbs the significance of the premodern for a near-future France characterized by the return of religious impulses that have been only superficially suppressed by the Enlightenment and secular republicanism. Here, contact with 'la France profonde' is a contradictory emotional relationship played out via religious tourism, patriotic poetry, and neoreactionary politics, though which France revisits its Catholic and patriarchal traditions. Trafficking with the ideas of neoreactionary pundits like Zemmour, Houellebecq adopts but also satirizes the Right's argument that France's relationship to the premodern past is essentially melancholic.

Narrated through the perspective of the anomic academic François, *Submission* presents a satire of a near-future France (2022) which is moving toward transformation into a post-secular polity ruled by a Muslim president. This transformation is presented not as a violent upheaval, but as the menacingly benign harnessing of French men's yearning for patriarchal and religious impulses reaching back to *la France profonde*—traditions which have been only superficially and, it seems, temporarily suppressed by the French Enlightenment, secular republicanism, and progressive movements like feminism. Although François (whose name positions him as a white French Everyman) is initially disorientated by this change, which leads to the dismissal of all women and non-Muslim men from the now-Islamic Sorbonne, by the novel's end he has adapted to the new regime, and looks ahead to his

---

[34] Michel Houellebecq, *Soumission* (Paris: Groupe Flammarion, 2015)/*Submission*, trans. Lorin Stein (London: William Heinemann, 2015). All future references are to these editions.

imminent conversion to Islam, the restoration of his career, and the three wives with which he will be gifted by the university's new administration. Houellebecq has regularly been compared to pundits like Zemmour, and not without reason given his derogatory comments about Islam and the fact that *Submission* features characters who entertain *décliniste* views about Europe's inevitable demise. But reading *Submission* alongside polemics such as *Mélancolie française*, astute commentators have argued that the novel's sometimes infuriatingly ambiguous satire makes it more elusive in its allegiances and in its vision of France's pre-secular past and post-secular future. In this novel Houellebecq satirically narrativizes one possible outcome of the trajectory traced by Zemmour: Islamic rule in France, and soon. Like Zemmour's book, moreover, the novel identifies a medieval inheritance in France that enables the rise of such a post-secular Islamic polity; but in this case it is not post-Roman melancholy but rather the legacy of the Catholic Middle Ages. *Submission* portrays a France that is detached from, yet surrounded by the remnants of, its long Christian history.

The novel explores this conflicted legacy through François's response to medieval material environments and commemorative rituals. When the Sorbonne temporarily closes after the Muslim president is elected, François stays for several weeks in southwestern France in the medieval towns Martel and Rocamadour. Here he encounters not only the feudal grandeur of Martel's Hotel de la Raymondie, but also other monuments that bear witness to a history of interfaith conflict. The very name Martel and the town's three-hammered coat of arms allude to its founding by Charles Martel, 'the hammer', whose defeat of the Muslim forces in 732 at the Battle of Poitiers marks, according to one character, 'the real beginning of the Christian Middle Ages' (121). This character, a former government intelligence expert, links the medieval past to the present by remarking that this region proves 'that Christianity and Islam have been at war for a very long time' (121).

Houellebecq's handling of the Martel episode is typically ambiguous and confounding. As a writer clearly acquainted with the preoccupations of the far Right, he could hardly be unaware of Charles Martel's iconic status among racist and anti-Muslim groups in France and beyond; and François's description of Martel's Church of St Maur as an 'ecclesiastical fortress...built to resist the many attacks of the infidels who used to populate the region' (109), dutifully repeats the received account of Islamic incursion (though with dubious accuracy, since the church was built long after any Muslim presence in region). Yet just when the novel appears to be trading in populist anti-Islamic medievalism, Martel's legacy for racist, nationalist, or Christian triumphalism is pointedly negated: the intelligence expert, whose voice carries authority within the novel, announces to François, '...with Islam, the time has come for an accommodation; for an alliance' (122). After a brief sojourn in the town, François's attention shifts to a more compelling material remnant from the Middle Ages, the nearby shrine containing the famous statue of the Black Virgin of Rocamadour. This statue and the enduring rituals of worship surrounding it mark the ascendancy of high medieval Christianity with its cult of Marian worship.

When François is advised to visit the shrine, it is recommended as evidence of 'what a great civilization medieval Christendom was' (131). But François responds to this rich artefactual environment with mixed feelings. As a twenty-first-century secular Frenchman his relationship with the past is heavily mediated via heritage industries. He admits he had previously only experienced medieval France via lifestyle television, and that Rocamadour originally attracts him because its history as a medieval pilgrimage site has made it a tourist destination. François's mediated experience is significant given that area of academic expertise is Karl Joris Huysmans, who wrote a series of novels in which the main character, Durtal, seeks to immerse himself in the medieval past. As Elizabeth Emery has demonstrated, the most successful of these novels, *La Cathédrale*, with its extensive descriptions of Chartres cathedral, was important for the development of cathedral tourism in late nineteenth-century France.[35] François's day-tripper mentality, then, continues a legacy bestowed by his master, though not in the way Huysmans might have wished.

In spite of this, François still finds himself drawn to the vestiges of medieval French Christianity. Every day of his month-long stay in Rocamadour he visits the shrine of the Black Virgin, 'the same one who for a thousand years inspired so many pilgrimages, before whom so many saints and kings had knelt' (135). Repeating his daily ritual of

[35] Elizabeth Emery, 'J. K. Huysmans, Medievalist', *Modern Language Studies* 30.2 (2000), 119–31.

contemplating the serenity of the statue, absorbed by its 'extraterrestrial' remoteness and 'intangible energy', he is drawn into the Middle Ages it embodies. For François this statue represents a Romanesque world in which 'moral judgement, individual judgement, individuality itself' are dissolved into a 'communal' identity. For the young pilgrims who visit the shrine to attend a reading of the patriotic Catholic poems of Charles Péguy, 'community' equals nation; for François, conversely, this is a spirituality beyond 'attachment to a homeland'. Although this Romanesque Middle Ages is represented as a more 'indigenous' and hence more enduring form of religiosity, the novel refuses the facile nationalist instrumentalizations of premodern France carried out by the Zemmours and Le Pens.

Just when it seems that medieval Catholicism has survived the convulsions of religious war, statutory secularism, and the rational scepticism of the Enlightenment, on his last visit François's melancholy returns, as he is deserted by the spirit of communion with the past: 'little by little I felt myself losing touch, I felt her moving away from me in space and across the centuries while I sat there in my pew, shrivelled and puny' (139). Given that novel equates François' state with that of France, this image evokes the enfeebled body politic of the secular modern nation, which in turn contrasts starkly with the serene, incorruptible body of the medieval Virgin. His self-description as a diminished modern man separated from his religious heritage echoes Freud's description of the melancholic subject whose loss of ego is attached to the loss of the irrecoverable object. Later, when François stays at the Benedictine abbey of Ligugé in which Huysmans lived as an oblate, he again finds it impossible to enter into its spiritual life. The abbey, once caught up in the Christian-Muslim conflicts of the eighth century, now offers meditation 'staycations' which attract celebrities as well as heritage tourists and well-being devotees. François, however, can only experience melancholic alienation because he is unable to participate either in traditional Catholic spirituality or in the abbey's commercialized replacement of it with 'self-care' practices.

The novel's extended portrait of religious melancholy presents it as a cultural condition that lays the ground for France to become a quasi-Muslim nation. Through François, Houellebecq proffers the affective profile of a melancholic France in which a deep but weakened atavistic leaning toward religion coexists paradoxically with the agnostic cultural relativism of modernity (209). This cultural confusion makes it ripe for conversion, to submission to a new politico-religious order whose attraction lies precisely in allowing those wearied by the strain of relativism to repose in the reassurances of benign absolutism.

This depiction of a disorientated France softened up for takeover by Islam in some key ways corresponds to the infamous 'Grand Remplacement' anti-immigration thesis peddled by Renaud Camus in his 2011 book of that name,[36] as well as to Zemmour's 'French melancholy' thesis, which again explains why some have aligned Houellebecq with the French far Right. Houellebecq's use of ambiguous satire and humour, however, distinguishes him from the thunderous warnings about cultural dissolution issued by Zemmour, Camus, and others, and complicates his relationship to the broad neoreactionary position. The main satiric technique here is making his narrator and protagonist François a satiric literalization of the clichés used by the far Right, in a way that exposes the paranoid absurdity of these clichés while not actually disconfirming them. For instance, in a satiric nod to the vulgar far-Right fulminations against the 'halalization' of France, François comes to discover his love for Lebanese mezze plates. The fact that this culinary conversion slightly precedes his ideological and religious conversion simultaneously plays out *and* ridicules the 'slippery slope' paranoia of the neoreactionaries.

This precarious satiric strategy is especially visible in Houellebecq's treatment of François's masculinity. At one level François is the quintessential melancholic French male of neoreactionary paranoid fantasy: nihilistic, partnerless, childless, and tepidly resigned to the deracinating secular pluralism of his times, he offers no resistance to the traditionalist certainties of the new Islamic order, even to the point of accepting without protest when he is pensioned off from his academic job. But it is not this apathy that ultimately leads him to the conversion that is imminent at the end of the novel. Rather the trigger is his sexism, which is explored with confronting candour. Despite his rapport with female colleagues, François privately questions whether the enfranchisement of women has caused France's social and demographic decline. Later

---

[36] Renaud Camus, *Le Grand Remplacement*, 1st edn (Paris: David Reinharc, 2011).

on, the same thesis is proffered by the new president of the Sorbonne, a former far-Right nativist turned suave Muslim convert, who persuades François that societies which have maintained patriarchal reproductive structures are destined to overwhelm the decadent non-reproductive societies of the West. Here we see Houellebecq mobilizing the anti-feminist clichés of the neoreactionaries in a way that turns their narrative back on them: for whereas the extreme Right argues that French men's submission to Islam will result from their effeminate melancholy, Houellebecq's narrative suggests that the cause will be their bitterness about being deprived of their patriarchal inheritance. When François is courted back to his post at the Muslim Sorbonne, any last scruples have given way to his excitement at receiving the wives the university president has arranged for him on his submission to Islam—wives he could never have hoped to snare in the neoliberal sexual marketplace.

Houellebecq is regularly condemned for the misogyny of his works; and there is no doubt that his novels frequently feature sexist protagonists. But the way he represents sexism, including François's in this novel, does not necessarily solicit the reader's approval. The sexist thoughts François confesses to the reader might be deliberately *outré*, but they are also tendered as symptomatic of his social and sexual dysfunction. At times he even shows direct awareness of this: when he contemplates Nietzsche's rejection of democracy, he says 'as I got older, I found myself agreeing more with Nietzsche, as is no doubt inevitable when your plumbing starts to fail' (228). So, when he finally decides to convert, relishing above all the prospect that 'Muslim women were devoted and submissive' (247), the novel is not endorsing the traditionalist gender regimes either of the neoreactionaries or of conservative Islam. Rather, what Houellebecq takes great satirical relish in elaborating is that most of the key views of the Islamophobic Right, such as gender conservatism, traditionalism, and the rejection of progressive secular ideologies, in fact converge with those of the fantasized Islam it reviles. This is, indeed, the view urged by the Sorbonne president, who despite being 'the first to admit the greatness of medieval Christianity' has converted to Islam because, he claims, unlike Christianity it has not had to compromise with rationalism or progressivism and hence is better equipped to bring about the 'moral and familial rearmament of Europe' (230–1). He has left behind the melancholy of the washed-up

Frenchman and willingly replaced the medieval Christian past with its new Islamic semblance.

Scholars have repeatedly noted the widespread tendency in Western public discourse to view the tensions between the West and Islam as an epochal struggle between rational modernity and medieval backward-ness.[37] Houellebecq differs from those polemicists who simplistically align France with secular modernity, by presenting melancholic France as still vestigially religious. Moreover, the novel's depiction of France's newly elected Islamic leadership short-circuits racist characterizations of Islam as 'medieval' by presenting Mohammed Ben Abbes's govern-ment as a moderate, Socialist-Muslim Brotherhood coalition formed to prevent Marine le Pen's Front National from taking power. As a moderate, Ben Abbes does not force conversions, prevent other faiths from worshipping, or introduce Sharia law into France. Nevertheless, under him France is a polity in which a renewed emphasis on the religions of the book brings with it soft-power social engineering. Significant cuts to the secular education budget drive people into the well-funded Islamic schools, while the workforce becomes more male due to a government subsidy offered to women who return to domestic duties. Dress and behavioural codes are not imposed, but the change in public mood nevertheless leads women, in a kind of tacit acquiescence, to adopt modest clothes. Additionally, despite there being no obvious signs that France's Jews are in danger of the restricted citizenship or *dhimmitude* feared by conspiracy theorists such as Bat Ye'or,[38] they nevertheless start voluntarily to emigrate to Israel, including François's ex-girlfriend Myriam.

Rather than being one of the autocratic 'medieval' Muslims of Right-wing fable, Abbes in fact aspires to establish a Roman-style empire across an expanded Europe that includes surrounding Islamic nations; in short, his ambition is to create a 'Eurabian' empire that corresponds closely to that envisaged by Ye'or in her 2005 book *Eurabia*[39] which is explicitly referenced by the Intelligence expert in Houellebecq's novel.

---

[37] Bruce Holsinger, *Neomedievalism, Neoconservatism, and the War on Terror* (Chicago: Prickly Paradigm Press, 2007).

[38] Bat Ye'or, *The Dhimmi: Jews and Christians under Islam*, trans. David Maisel, Paul Fenton, and David Littman (Rutherford, NJ: Fairleigh Dickinson University Press, 1985).

[39] Bat Ye'or, *Eurabia: The Euro-Arab Axis* (Cranbury, NJ: Fairleigh-Dickinson University Press, 2005).

Here again we see Houellebecq's futuristic projections directly, and satirically, addressing both Ye'or's widely discredited thesis and Zemmour's notion that France still mourns its lost chance to be Rome. But the novel's iconoclastic solution, voiced particularly through the mouthpiece of the Islamic Sorbonne president, is that a Eurabian empire led by a French Muslim might offer France the chance that not even the greatness of its Romanesque, Carolingian past could provide.

Although Ben Abbes might not aspire to reproduce France's medieval Christian models, his policies owe much to the medievalist thought of the early twentieth century. He is especially and explicitly influenced by the social-economic theory of Distributism developed by English Catholics G. K. Chesterton and Hilaire Belloc. Chesterton and Belloc's vision of an ideal society was modelled on the late medieval craft guilds which were, they argued, organically emerging 'democratic' entities in which labour, production, and capital are linked, and collectivism and individualism are balanced. As developed by Chesterton in particular, Distributism was intended as a third way between socialism and capitalism, with the moral health of the society as the ultimate goal. It challenged capitalism's logic of infinite growth, arguing instead for the values of tradition and for a sustainable decentralized economy consisting of widespread small-scale property ownership rather than monopolies.[40] The fundamental unit of this economy is the small family business, a structure whose scale, Chesterton argued in *The Outline of Sanity* (1926), places limits on the amassing of individual wealth and thereby curbs the pernicious cycle in which humans are 'chained eternally to enlargement without liberty and progress without hope'.[41] Ben Abbes implements this system to the great pleasure not just of craftsmen and farmers but also of Brussels, thereby pulling off a medievalist economic coup. As an economic model that reflects a social and moral theory with the family at its centre, however, Distributism also enables him to dismantle the French welfare state and devolve care for the vulnerable back to the traditional locus of the family.

What develops in the novel, then, is a neo-medievalist state interpreted via moderate Islam, at the heart of an aspiring neo-Roman

---

[40] Richard Gill, 'Oikos and Logos: Chesterton's Vision of Distributism', *Logos: A Journal of Catholic Thought and Culture* 10.3 (2007), 64–90.

[41] G. K. Chesterton, *The Outline of Sanity* (London: Methuen, 1926), 19.

Eurabian empire. This multi-temporal polity is perfectly encapsulated in the home of the Sorbonne president, a turreted 'fantastical neo-Gothic' mansion which overlooks the remains of the Roman arena (203–4). In an audacious, ironical amendment to Zemmour's thesis, Houellebecq prompts readers to consider that this modern Islamic medieval-Roman space embodies not French melancholy but its antidote, French optimism. Melancholic France, with its logic of irreplaceable loss, can give way to a dynamic Islamic 'remplacement' which is traditionalist but points resolutely forward. Contemplating the benefits of his imminent conversion, François's last words are far from melancholic, recalling instead Freud's healed subject: 'I would have nothing to mourn' (250). In customary Houellebecquian fashion, the dense ambiguity of this statement allows it to be read as tragic acquiescence, resigned submission, rational concession, or sanguine adaptation, and it is out of this ambiguity that key debates over the text's ideological sympathies have arisen. But, however it is read, its replacement of François's French melancholy is indisputable.

Mathias Enard's *Compass*: medievalism and dis-orientalism

In the ongoing dialectical movement of France's reflection on nation and globe, another medievally inflected riposte to French Islamophobia is visible in the awarding of the 2015 Prix Goncourt to *Boussole/Compass*, Mathias Enard's prodigious novelistic reflection on the place of music in the history of European orientalism[42]—a novel which has repeatedly been described as an 'éloge amoureux des rapports entre l'Orient et l'Occident'.[43] It is surely not incidental that *Boussole* was awarded France's most prestigious literary prize in a year bookended by devastating domestic jihadist attacks—the massacre

---

[42] Mathias Enard, *La Boussole* (Arles: Actes Sud, 2015)/*Compass*, trans. Charlotte Mandel (New York: New Directions, 2017). All future references are to these editions.

[43] Stéphanie Vidal, 'Interview de Mathias Enard—Fragments d'un discourse amoureux entre l'Orient et l'Occident', *ONORIENT*, 28 September 2015, http://onorient.com/interview-de-mathias-enard-fragments-dun-discours-amoureux-entre-lorient-locident-9056-20150928.

of the staff of *Charlie Hebdo* in February, and the Bataclan nightclub attack just ten days after the award was announced. The fact that the 2015 finalists were announced in Tunis's Bardo National Museum, the site only months earlier of an Al Qaeda-planned massacre, underlines the Académie Goncourt's determination to underline its commitment to Western-Islamicate solidarity in the face of terror; and *Boussole*, which Enard dedicates to the people of Syria, was the perfect novel to express that commitment.

Narrated in the historical moment of its writing, *Boussole* is striking for moving between immersion in the centuries-long, convoluted history of orientalism and an almost pained awareness of the ideologically tangled climate into which it speaks. This temporal oscillation and ideological entanglement is captured perfectly in the city where the novel's narrator is situated: Vienna, whose renown as the place at which invading Ottoman forces were turned back in 1683 has led to its contradictory status as *porta orientis et propugnaculum occidentis*: both gateway to the East and bulwark of the West.[44] While for the political far Right Vienna is the historical bastion of Western resistance (epitomized by the Islamophobic 'Gates of Vienna' website, whose masthead declares 'At the siege of Vienna in 1683 Islam seemed poised to overrun Christian Europe. We are in a new phase of a very old war'), the novel's characters conversely parse the dubious but appealing fantasy of the city as 'pointing East' and the status of the Danube as 'the river that links Catholicism, Orthodoxy, and Islam' (18). This hyperawareness of contemporary ideological tension shapes the fugue-like recollections of the novel's narrator, a terminally ill middle-aged Austrian musicologist named Franz Ritter. Narrated across the course of an insomnia-tossed night, Franz's ruminations shuttle uncertainly between countering Eurocentric fears of Islam, denouncing Muslim extremism, rebutting postcolonial suspicions about orientalism, and acknowledging its reputation for cultural appropriation and even violation. It is true that Enard's narrator, dwelling on the emotional

[44] Johannes Feichtinger, 'Komplexer k.u.k. Orientalismus: Akteure, Institutionen, Diskurse im 19. und 20. Jahrhundert in Österreich', in *Orientalismen in Ostmitteleuropa: Diskurse, Akteure und Disziplinen vom 19. Jahrhundert bis zum Zweiten Weltkrieg*, ed. Robert Born and Sarah Lemmen (Bielefeld: Transcript Verlag, 2014), 38.

force of the West's deep fascination with the Middle East (all of this underpinned by his infatuation with another orientalist, the elusive French-Jewish Sarah) is repeatedly drawn to highlight the possible rather than the typical in historical East-West relations. The novel itself, however, does not offer a naïvely apologistic genealogy of orientalism. Rather, through the figure of Franz *Boussole* exposes the deadlock of the West's rapprochement with the East in the twenty-first century: its cosmopolitan desire on the one hand to combat Islamophobic dehumanization by emphasizing cross-cultural empathy, admiration, and fascination, and its need on the other hand to acknowledge its implication in the legacies of colonialism and to calibrate with honesty the uneven distribution of power underpinning orientalism.

Franz weaves his own learned appreciation of Middle Eastern music into a wider and denser web of the West's passionate yet agonistic encounters with the East. But in celebrating the influence of Eastern aesthetics on Western art forms, an influence he repeatedly describes as an 'irrigation', he seems anxious to pre-empt any imputations that Western music is made up of superficial and exoticizing appropriations. He insists:

> it was not a matter of 'exotic procedures', as was thought before...it made external elements, alterity, enter...over all of Europe the wind of alterity blows, all these great men use what comes to them from the Other to modify the Self...to use the external procedures to undermine the dictatorship of church chant and harmony. (140)

In subscribing to this idea that orientalism permits the discovery of the 'Other within the Self', he is in fact ventriloquizing the words of his *inamorata* Sarah, who is prominent among those cosmopolitan critics who have sought to modify the legacy of Edward Said's watershed analysis of orientalism. In what has become a legendary definition, Said has described orientalism, whereby Eastern and Islamic cultures are 'known' through the prism of Western values, as 'a *distribution* of geopolitical awareness into aesthetic, scholarly, economic, sociological, historical and philological texts' but also a political project, underpinned by the objective of 'dominating, restructuring, and having authority over the Orient'.[45] Sarah's principal objection is more to the

---

[45] Edward Said, *Orientalism* (New York: Vintage Books, 1979), 12, 3.

uptake of Said, and in particular to what she sees as his readers' habit of sedimenting asymmetric power between East and West at the exclusion of acknowledging cultural exchange throughout history (323–4). Franz claims to be agnostic about Sarah's argument that the West needs 'to admit not only the terrifying violence of colonialism, but also all that Europe owed to the Orient—the impossibility of separating them from one another' (324); yet his earlier defence of Western music's orientalist 'alterity' would appear to accord with her cosmopolitan outlook. The same can be said of a remark he makes about Said's creation, along with the legendary pianist-conductor Daniel Barenboim, of the West-Eastern Divan Orchestra, which he says is managed by 'a foundation in Andalusia, where the beauty of sharing and diversity is stressed' (171). Named after Goethe's famous anthology and made up of musicians from Spain, Israel, and the Islamicate Middle East, the orchestra counts in its discography works by a number of the West's best-known adopters of Eastern aesthetics. By raising this, Franz emphasizes Said's belief in the potential for music to be a vehicle for what in *Culture and Imperialism* he calls 'unhierarchical influence' between cultures.[46]

Franz's invocation of Andalusia as a paradise of diversity is not incidental. Rather, this trope, alluding to the region's much-lauded reputation as an interfaith *convivencia* before the Catholic Reconquista, is part of a medievalist line that runs quietly but persistently through Enard's novel. Franz's preoccupation with the knotted histories of orientalism is not restricted to the era of global European colonialism, but returns persistently to the era known in the West as the Middle Ages. Just as the Orient is presented as the cultural 'other within the self' of the West, so too the medieval becomes the temporal 'other within the self' of the modern, its long afterlife still shaping the culture and politics of the Eurasian continent. Despite the brevity of Franz's allusion to Andalusia, its history as a Western Islamicate kingdom—an 'other within the self'—crystallizes his portrayal of the medieval period as an era of seemingly unforced cultural porosity in which the West was profoundly transformed, at least culturally and aesthetically, by its contact with the East.

---

[46] Edward Said, *Culture and Imperialism* (New York: Knopf, 1994), 331.

This convergence of the medieval and the oriental is by no means unique or even unusual within the broader perception of the Middle Ages in the modern imaginary. From a temporal perspective, the medieval period is regarded as the crucible of the modern West, while also being the superseded Other of democratic, secular, and scientific modernity. This contradiction is further intensified by a cultural-geographical perspective wherein the medieval West is imagined contradictorily to be both the cradle of Western nationhood and a site of Eastern influence (a point which will be taken up at greater length in Chapter 2). In *Boussole*, the significance of the orientalized Middle Ages is somewhat difficult to pin down to any single cultural or historical thesis: sometimes medieval events or cultural phenomena are identified as origins or at least precedents to a modern opera, symphony, story, or ideology, while at other times medieval legends are read by Franz as parallels with modern stories, disclosing a universal storytelling and musical impulse across human societies. As with the ideological tensions in the text, these historical inconsistencies are not resolved. Rather, within the fuguelike structure of Franz's ruminations, this premodern time-place is best thought of as *contrapuntal* to Western modernity, a line running beneath and breaking across the main line in a kind of echoic structure.

This contrapuntal relationship is witnessed in Franz's identification of what he regards as narrative patterns across centuries of Eastern verse romance and Western music. A prime instance of this is his provocative assertion that in the work of the most notoriously nationalistic of Western composers, Wagner, one can find traces of medieval Eastern literature. He links the protagonists of the iconic Wagnerian opera *Tristan and Isolde* not just to those of its twelfth-century German source but, more deeply, to the tragic lovers in Persian tales: 'Vis and Ramin are in Tristan and Iseult. There is the passion of Majnun the Mad for Layla, the passion of Khosrow for Shirin' (276).

Despite arguing for this transcultural irrigation, Franz refuses to account for its operation. He is less interested in explanation than in rendering legends rhizomatic, their root systems horizontal and entangled. By his account Sarah takes the search for transcultural analogues even further, drawing parallels between a lay in Thomas of Britain's *Roman de Tristan*, in which a woman is forced to eat the heart of her lover, and practices of symbolic cannibalism in Sarawak, at the furthest southeastern fringes of the Islamicate world (439). Franz and Sarah's preference for discovering analogues rather than origins reflects their general thesis of culture not as pure and autochthonous but as co-created via exchange and bastardization. This idea is also extended to the canso tradition of the troubadours, which is both invoked and disavowed as an origin for a modern French love song Franz contemplates at dawn: 'you have to...love this song that is all songs, ever since the *Songs of Dawn* by the troubadours, by Schumann and all the ghazals of creation' (444). Here Franz appears to assert a dual East-West medieval lineage in which the Occitan alba and the Arabo-Persian ghazal have equal claim to inspiring a vibrant and diffuse afterlife of song.

The significance to *Boussole* of the medieval courtly tradition is imprinted in the narrator's very name: Franz Ritter, French knight. This allusion, which Enard himself has gone so far as to call 'une clé de lecture du livre aussi exposée que cachée' (a key for reading the book, as exposed as it is hidden),[47] is borne out in the novel's love story, a decades-long *amor de lonh* that leaves Franz tortuously unfulfilled. Just as the troubadour cansos sing incessantly of the male lover's longing for an inaccessible woman, revelling in an economy of virtuous suffering, so too the lovelorn Franz circles back repeatedly to his frustrated but undiminished passion for the brilliant, mercurial Sarah. In a deliberate—and deliberately medievalist—complement to Franz's chivalric surname, Sarah's is never revealed: in an interview Enard says of her 'elle reste fantasmée de la même façon que l'étaient les héroïnes médiévales dont on ne connaît que le prénom' (she remains fantasized, in the same way that medieval heroines were, of whom we know only their first name).[48] Sarah's namelessness also marks the fact that, as a French Jew, she embodies a diasporic 'other within the self' of Europe, something Franz believes he detects in 'something indefinably Oriental in her face, in her complexion and in the shape of her eyes' (35). Franz's futile desire for Sarah, comprised equally of a will to possess her and a recognition of her elusiveness, threatens at times to devolve into a hackneyed allegory of his relationship with an Orient he can study obsessively but never truly know. But lest he, or indeed Enard, seem like reactionaries unthinkingly reproducing orientalist and medieval

---

[47] Vidal, 'Interview de Mathias Enard', n.p. Translation mine.
[48] Vidal, 'Interview de Mathias Enard', n.p. Translation mine.

courtly paradigms in the twenty-first century, it is worth underlining that Sarah elicits not just desire but professional admiration and even envy in Franz. He repeatedly cites her books and articles, and it is often difficult to tell where his ideas end and hers begin.

The evocation of French knighthood in Franz Ritter's name has another, less romantic implication which is vital for shining a light on the darker history of the West's interactions with the Islamicate East. The other prominent image of medieval knighthood in the book is the crusaders, who were referred to as 'the Franks' (*Franj*) by the people whose lands they occupied. Franz's view of the crusaders and their conduct is typically ambivalent, poised uncomfortably between condemnation and sympathy. His first mention of them would appear to bear the influence of famous studies such as Amin Maalouf's *Les Croisades vues par les Arabes*[49] or eminent Byzantine historian Steven Runciman's study *A History of the Crusades* (1951–4),[50] which view the crusaders as barbarians who invaded the lands of a more advanced people. Contemplating his own recently diagnosed illness, Franz says:

> God knows what rot of the soul I could have caught in those distant lands. The way the crusaders, the first Orientalists, returned to their somber villages in the West loaded with gold, bacilli, and sorrow, aware of having, in the name of Christ, destroyed the greatest wonders they had seen, pillaging the Churches of Constantinople, burning Antioch and Jerusalem. (189)

This passage is striking on several counts. First, its suggestion that modern orientalists are the heirs of the crusaders is the novel's most overt alignment of apparently innocuous cultural practices with a long history of dispossession and destruction. Its arresting triangulation of 'gold, bacilli, and sorrow' furthermore creates an intimate link between the material enrichment of the West at the East's expense and the introduction of disease and corrosive guilt into the Western soul. Here orientalism is not based on the 'sharing and continuity' he invokes when discussing music, but rather on theft and rupture. Trying to make sense of his terminal diagnosis, Franz seems genuinely to entertain the

[49] Amin Maalouf, *Les Croisades vues par les Arabes* (Paris: J. T. Lattès, 1983).

[50] Steven Runciman, *A History of the Crusades*, 3 vols (Cambridge: Cambridge University Press, 1951–4).

idea that his physical illness is in some way a legacy of the violent lineage to which he belongs extending back to the twelfth century. He goes on to imagine how the crusaders' cultured Levantine adversaries faced the 'violent sobriety' and barbarism of these foreign occupiers. Immediately, after this, however, he retreats from his reckoning with violence and theft, saying instead 'the Franks ended up learning Arabic, tasting apricots and jasmine, and nourishing a certain respect for the lands they had just delivered from the infidels' (191). This backpedalling into a portrayal of benign aestheticism, focalized through the crusaders' own view of themselves as 'deliverers' of the land, is both conspicuous and unconvincing, revealing the rapid reflex of Franz's denial when contemplating the uglier medieval past that inflects his own cultural endeavours.

Franz's retreat here to a benign conception of medieval orientalism is part of his larger discomfort with limiting the period's legacy to the Western theft of Eastern culture and material goods—an approach he believes does not capture the richness of the 'medieval' Middle East's relationship with its own traditions. Having called the crusaders 'the first orientalists', he later goes on to re-bestow the title on the twelfth-century Persian philosopher Suhrawardi, whose construction of a distinctive Iranian wisdom fusing Islamic and Zoroastrian ideas made him 'the first Orientalist in the strict sense of the word' (301). This cross-cultural expansion of orientalism's origins reflects Sarah's and Franz's 'common construction' thesis of orientalism. The consummate example of this for Franz is the Azerbaijani composer Uzeyir Hajibeyov, whose 1908 opera *Layla and Majnun* he calls 'the first Oriental Orientalist opera' (192), both because it is based on medieval Persian legend and because it uses Eastern modes within a Western genre. Hajibeyov is but one example within a novel that bristles with examples of painters, poets, politicians, and composers from across the Islamicate world whose expressions of their cultures bear witness to, and engage actively with, the influence of orientalist discourse and aesthetics.

It is unsurprising that the instability characterizing Franz's account of medieval orientalism and medieval conflict is also evident in his scattered and overwhelmed discussions of contemporary warfare in the Middle East, especially the ongoing conflict in Syria. At times he is unsparing in his indictment of Western involvement in Eastern geopolitics, repeatedly singling out the British and the French for their neocolonial interference. On other occasions, however, he is equally scathing of political pathologies that are apparently endogenous to the Middle East. For the most part, however, he attributes Middle Eastern conflicts to an entangled East-West agency, a position that is most apparent in his views on Jihadism. While he reserves special contempt for the actions of Jihadists, he does not regard Jihadist extremism as an endogenous product of Islam, but claims, rather:

> It's such a European story, in the end. European victims, killers with London accents. A new and violent radical Islam, born in Europe and the United States, from Western bombs, and the only victims that count when it comes down to it are Europeans. (263)

Whether the last remark is a response to the Western 'Je Suis Charlie' movement that emerged in the wake of the attack on the staff of *Charlie Hebdo* in January 2015, or a more general comment on the West's indifference to Jihadist slaughter in the Middle East, Franz ultimately complicates the picture by attributing Middle Eastern conflicts not simply to the West or the East, but to an intractable dynamic between the two, a deep and complicated intertwining of these apparently opposed cultures reaching back to the Crusades.

The contradictions, blind spots, and discomforts of this narrative are not faults, but are the novel's point. Enard, a scholar of Arabic and Persian, uses the novelistic form not to mount an argument about foreign or domestic policy, but instead to capture a mood of contemporary paralysis, in which desire, denial, fascination, guilt, and the weight of history all move in counterpoint. The affair it conveys between East and West is a vibrant but fractious one in which the lovers have, like Franz and Sarah, a long, unequal history punctuated by misunderstandings and missed opportunities. But the novel ends with Franz thinking at dawn of the Danube, flowing between the two compass points, and realizing, finally, that it's 'not shameful to give in ... to the warm sunlight of hope' (445). At a time of rising nationalist sentiment, it is an ingenious image with which to conclude: flowing through ten countries, this river that inspires hope is the opposite of a national boundary, a fertile source of 'irrigation' that opposes the aridity of solipsistic nationalism. In short, it points beyond the nation to the world. Written at a time when the far Right is fomenting hostility toward the Muslim 'other within the self', *Boussole*'s solution of giving in to hope is not practical but emotional. This might not seem enough; but in a contemporary narrative of melancholy and trauma, and in a year that began in despair and hardened into defiance, hope seems like a start.

Most recently, the supranational impulse underlying Enard's novel has made its way into popular historiography, in the form of medievalist Patrick Boucheron's almost eight-hundred-page blockbuster edited volume *Histoire mondiale de la France/France in the World: A New Global History*.[51] Although, major reviews of the volume point out, it does not allude to the specifics of contemporary politics, the anti-nationalist, anti-racist nature of its agenda is stated explicitly:

> Cette ambition est politique, dans la mesure où elle entend mobiliser une conception pluraliste de l'histoire contre l'étrécissement identitaire qui domine aujourd'hui le débat public. (The result is political inasmuch as it seeks to mobilize a pluralist concept of history against the general shrinkage of national identity that is such a central component of the public debate in France today.)[52]

This volume, made up of short chapters that take a significant year or event as their starting point, exploits the full semantic range of *mondiale* in its approach to telling the story of France in the world. As might be expected, its later chapters nominate important dates or events in France's travels through the age of globalization, with an emphasis on issues of immigration and national identity: to take just two examples, '1974: Reflux migratoires' ('Curbing Migration') argues that from this date 'l'immigration s'inscrit durablement au centre du débat politique national' ('immigration [was turned into] a central topic of political debate in France, which it has remained ever since'),[53] while '2015: Le retour du drapeau' ('The Return of the Flag') examines the domestic and international response to the terrorist attacks in Paris, which are themselves placed within a global context

---

[51] Patrick Boucheron et al., *Histoire mondiale de la France* (Paris: Éditions de Seuil, 2017)/*France in the World*, ed. Stéphane Gerson (New York: Other, 2019).

[52] Boucheron, *Histoire mondiale de la France*, 7/translation, xxxii.

[53] Alexis Spire, '1974: Reflux migratoires', in *Histoire mondiale de la France*, 712/translation, 838.

of terrorism reaching from Africa to Australia.[54] But the *mondiale* of the title also refers to France's long and deep embeddedness in world history, that is events and movements reaching far beyond France yet connected with it. Numerous chapters on the Middle Ages seek to challenge the triumphalist narratives of medieval history that have fuelled nationalist and racist ideas of French purity. One especially pointed instance of this for the purposes of this chapter is '719: L'Afrique frappe à la porte du pays des Francs' ('Africa knocks on the Franks' door'), which, using an engaging second-person address, reconstructs the coming of 'la menace Islamique' to the Roussillon— already the site of other previous occupations—and the decades of Muslim rule that followed. In focusing on Ruscino in 719 the chapter diminishes the significance of the Franco-Islamic encounter at Poitiers/ Tours in 732, that flashpoint of 'European victory' so beloved of the far Right. This narrative decision is addressed explicitly:

> Bien sûr, il aurait été possible de choisir d'autres dates ou d'autres lieux... pour parler de cette rencontre. On aurait peut-être dû parler de l'autre incursion, celle que la mémoire collective a conservée comme une relique précieuse, parce-que c'est une victoire. (Of course, we could have chosen other dates or other places... to evoke this encounter. Perhaps we should have looked at another incursion, the one that collective French memory has preserved like a precious relic, because it ended in French victory.)[55]

It caps off its deflationary account of Martel's apparently epochal victory by describing it as one 'escarmouche' (skirmish) among dozens fought around the time, and a minor event in the epic history of Islam's expansion. The very earliest chapters take French-based events as a starting point but pursue their examinations in such a way as to decentre France within the much larger story of human history. Again to take just one example, the opening chapter '34,000 avant J.-C: Inventer le monde dans les entrailles de la Terre' ('Creating the World Deep inside the Earth'), the title of which links 'world' to the deep materiality of its synonym 'earth', locates France's famous

---

[54] Emmanuel Laurentin, '2015: Le retour du drapeau', in *Histoire mondiale de la France*, 763–6/translation, 902–7.

[55] François-Xavier Fauvelle, '719: L'Afrique frappe à la porte du pays des Francs', in *Histoire mondiale de la France*, 93/translation, 90.

Chauvet cave complex not within a story of chthonic local habitation but instead within the ancient story of human migration which fans out from Africa across the planet.[56]

To return to the questions posed at the beginning of my chapter, in this volume's act of world creation a nation is not a world but is of the world, and of the globe, and of the earth. France is, as the title of the larger opening section states, 'un bout du monde'[57]—not 'un bout' in the temporal sense of an end, but in the spatial sense of a tip of the Eurasian continent (the English translators render this as 'a corner')—a mere scrap of world. This image of incompletion corresponds to the novelistic accounts discussed above, which query, seriously and satirically, the pursuit of deep historical purity. Together these texts expose the yearning for national completion and the contradictory role of the Middle Ages as both the origin and the fulfilment of this yearning.

[56] François Bon, '34,000 avant J.-C: Inventer le monde dans les entrailles de la Terre', in *Histoire mondiale de la France*, 19–23/translation, 7–12.

[57] Boucheron, *Histoire mondiale de la France*, 15.

| 2 |

Medievalism Re-oriented

Tariq Ali's Islam Quintet and the 'Arab'
Historical Novel

The Islam Quintet as diasporic fiction

The story has become lore among his followers: one day in early 1991, as Tariq Ali was taking in the television coverage of the First Gulf War, he heard a commentator offer the following pronouncement on the conflict: 'the Arabs are a people without political culture.'[1] The statement incensed Ali on two fronts: first of all, he rejected its reduction of the diversity of Middle Eastern cultures into the flattening descriptor 'the Arabs'. Secondly, Ali—a Pakistani Brit whose post-partition childhood was shaped by his family's deep commitment to Marxism—also rejected the statement's fundamental assertion of Islamicate cultures as religious rather than 'properly' political. As a Leftist and anti-colonial activist of some decades' standing, he had closely

---

[1] Talat Ahmed, 'Interview: Tariq Ali', *Socialist Review* 311, November 2006, 6–9, http://socialistreview.org.uk/311/interview-tariq-ali.

World Medievalism: The Middle Ages in Modern Textual Culture. Louise D'Arcens, Oxford University Press.

followed the politics of the Middle East[2] and the wider Islamicate world, writing journalism, nonfiction tracts, and creative works on a range of issues, including, at that stage, a book on the political fortunes of his native Pakistan (*Can Pakistan Survive? The Death of a State*, 1983). Among his recent works had been *Iranian Nights* (1989), a co-authored play for the Royal Court Theatre on the Salman Rushdie Affair, which criticized both the Islamic fundamentalism that had emerged in Iran over the past decade and the problem of anti-Muslim racism in Britain and the West.[3] Most significant for this chapter, though, is that Ali's chief objection to the throwaway remark on television in 1991 was to what he saw as its heedless ahistoricism—its dismissal at one stroke of centuries of conquest, governance, and struggle throughout the Islamicate world. Initially planning to research and write an essay to rebut these claims, he instead found himself travelling to Southern Europe and throughout the Mediterranean to make an episode of the Channel 4 programme *Rear Window*, 'Islam in Spain: The Final Solution', where he experienced the spectacular palaces, fortresses, and mosques of the great Islamic kingdoms of al-Andalus and Sicily in order to understand the history of Islam's political and cultural influence on European society.[4]

What Ali reports of this travel experience in an interview in *Socialist Review* is strongly reflective of the kind of transhistorical apprehension that is characterized in the Introduction of this book as

[2] Just as the term 'Middle Ages' reflects a Western epochal mentality, numerous postcolonial scholars have pointed out that the term 'Middle East' is a reflection of Anglo-European and North American geopolitical coordinates; a pioneering voice is Hassan Hanafi, 'The Middle East, in Whose World?', in *The Middle East in a Globalized World: Papers from the Fourth Nordic Conference on Middle Eastern Studies, Oslo, 1998*, ed. Bjørn Olav Utvik and Knut S. Vikør (Bergen, London: Nordic Society for Middle Eastern Studies, 2000), 1–9. Where possible I will avoid this phrase (which also fails to accommodate southern hemisphere perspectives) by using the phrase 'the Islamicate world' or variations thereof, as derived from Marshall G. S. Hodgson, 'The Role of Islam in World History', *International Journal of Middle East Studies* 1.2 (1970), 106. Since the latter term comprises cultures as distinct and as geographically distant as Turkey and Indonesia, occasionally I will use 'the Middle East' as a shorthand to refer to the lands of the Eastern Mediterranean/Levant region, the Arabian Peninsula, and parts of Western Asia.

[3] Tariq Ali, *Can Pakistan Survive: The Death of a State* (London: Penguin Books, 1983); Tariq Ali and Howard Brenton, *Iranian Nights* (London: Nick Hern Books, 1989).

[4] Claire Chambers, 'Tariq Ali', in *British Muslim Fictions: Interviews with Contemporary Writers* (Basingstoke: Palgrave Macmillan, 2011), 33–55.

phenomenological 'world disclosure'. Far from simply beholding architectural remains—or indeed architectural absences in the case of the now-vanished 'hundred mosques' of medieval Muslim Palermo—he describes the experience as an encounter with a 'lost world'.[5] While visiting these places, Ali experienced what Heidegger and romantic hermeneuticists have described as transhistorical *Stimmung*—a rich attunement with what he sensed of the beliefs, practices, values, communities, and events that had shaped different parts of the medieval Islamicate world. And this attunement would in turn lead to further transhistorical world-disclosures through his writing of texts designed to invite audiences into immersive experiences of those pasts: in Ali's words, he found himself wanting to 'bring back the people who had lived around there'—'there' being the Muslim Mediterranean and Levant—for his modern followers.[6] The method he determined would best achieve this world disclosure was fiction; and so out of this process the 1992 novel *Shadows of the Pomegranate Tree* was born.[7] Set in and around Granada in 1499–1501, it was the first of what was to be Ali's Islam Quintet, written across a decade and a half. No fewer than three novels in the Quintet are set in the period widely known as the Middle Ages. In addition to *Shadows of the Pomegranate Tree*, *The Book of Saladin* (1998)[8] follows the rise of its eponymous warrior sultan as he unifies Egypt, Syria, and Palestine in the period before and during the third Crusade, while *A Sultan in Palermo* (2005)[9] is set in Sicily in the final year of the Norman king Roger II's life and rule. As I shall explore in this chapter, Ali's novels show that despite having existed hundreds of years ago, the medieval Islamicate world, especially in its exchanges and conflicts with the Christian West, continues to attract the modern imagination to a past that can be 'scaled up' to offer commentary on volatile modern geopolitical events while also 'scaling down' to offer intimate portraits of cross-cultural and interfaith

---

[5] Ahmed, 'Interview: Tariq Ali', 7.   [6] Ahmed, 'Interview: Tariq Ali', 7.

[7] Tariq Ali, *Shadows of the Pomegranate Tree* (London: Verso, 1992). All future references will be to this edition.

[8] Tariq Ali, *The Book of Saladin* (London: Verso, 1998). All future references will be to this edition.

[9] Tariq Ali, *A Sultan in Palermo* (London: Verso, 2005). All future references will be to this edition.

friendship. Sharon Kinoshita has remarked that 'historical fiction set in the Middle Ages has become a place to explore the complexities of Muslim-Jewish-"European" relations';[10] this is certainly true of the Islam Quintet. Written with the intention of offering a corrective to Eurocentric occlusions of the Arab contribution to global knowledge and a riposte to misperceptions of Islam as a static culture of fanaticism, the novels offer Ali a creative way of meditating on contemporary East-West geopolitics.

The Islam Quintet arguably qualifies as 'world medievalism' not just in the sense that it emerged out of the author's experiences of phenomenological world disclosure but also because these popular and much-translated novels have attracted a widespread audience throughout the West and the Islamicate world who have read them in over a dozen languages. In the ideological and historical sense, however, the novels' status as 'world' literature and as medievalism requires more careful qualification. Although their corrective portrait of Arab political history reflects Cheah's argument that world literature can express a 'modality of cosmopolitanism that is ... responsive to the need to remake the world as a hospitable place',[11] describing these Anglophone novels as 'world literature' is potentially problematic. First, it risks reinforcing what Emily Apter refers to as the fantasy of 'oneworldedness'[12] in which the idea of uniform 'world culture' continues to privilege Anglo-European literatures and authors with access to networks of distribution and as such is, as Jumana Bayeh has argued, 'still infected by pre-existing relations of power within the international system'.[13] As an influential public figure who has lived in a Western metropolis for several decades, Ali is in demand as a voice on world politics, but should not be taken to represent a 'world' perspective. The homogenizing potential of the 'oneworlded' version of world literature risks, moreover, neutralizing

[10] Sharon Kinoshita, 'Deprovincializing the Middle Ages', in *The Worlding Project: Doing Cultural Studies in the Era of Globalization*, ed. Rob Wilson and Christopher Leigh Connoly (Santa Cruz: New Pacific Press, 2007), 75.

[11] Cheah, 'World against Globe', 326.

[12] Emily Apter, *Against World Literature: On the Politics of Untranslatability* (New York: Verso, 2013), 83.

[13] Jumana Bayeh, 'Anglophone Arab or Diasporic? The Arab Novel in Australia, Britain, Canada, the United States of America', *Commonwealth Essays and Studies* 39.2 (2017), 16.

the historico-cultural specificity of the various worlds disclosed in Ali's novels and the transnational Islamicate perspective in which they are anchored.

I wish to suggest, alternatively, that these novels' authorship and content both suggest that they are more usefully understood under the rubric of diasporic Arab-Islamicate fiction. Ali's familial background in Pakistan implicates him in the diasporic spread of Islam, and exposed him in his youth both to Quranic Arabic and to the Islamic history which is so central to his novels. This diasporic sensibility continues into the novels' portrayals of medieval Islam, which anticipate by some years calls by scholars of the Middle East for twentieth-century national and territorial paradigms to be replaced with a 'diasporic cartography' that discloses the Islamicate world to be 'a set of networks holding together . . . people and things, places and practices'.[14] As this chapter will go on to show, Shadows of the Pomegranate Tree, The Book of Saladin, and A Sultan in Palermo present a dynamic, culturally sophisticated, and intellectually open-minded supranational ummah (Muslim community) shaped by physical mobility and intercultural encounters within and between the Mediterranean, Levantine, and Arabian regions.

Lest this seem like too sanguine a portrayal, it is worth clarifying that the dominant condition for contact in these novels is occupation. As this intercultural dynamism spirals into volatility and, eventually, conflict with the forces of the Christian West, Ali's Arab-Islamic diaspora becomes conspicuously analogous to the colonized and riven Islamicate sphere of the late twentieth and early twenty-first century. Ali is better known for his political activism, his journalistic commentary on Israel and Palestine, and his account of the Middle East and U.S. neocolonialism in his 2002 manifesto The Clash of Fundamentalisms: Crusades, Jihads and Modernity, a post-9/11 response to Samuel Huntington's Clash of Civilisations (1996) in which Ali replaces Huntington's grandiose thesis of inter-civilizational conflict with a detailed account of intertwined global politics. The novels offer a clear fictionalized and historicist complement to his political commentary

---

[14] Andrew Arsan, John Karam, and Akram Khater, 'On Forgotten Shores: Migration in Middle East Studies and the Middle East in Migration Studies', Mahjar & Mashriq: Journal of Middle East Migration Studies 1.1 (2013), 5–6.

in that book and elsewhere. Indeed, Ali's comment in *Clash of Fundamentalisms* that 'the world of Islam has not been monolithic for over a thousand years'[15] clearly points to the parallel thinking going on in his fictional and nonfictional writing, as do the allusions he makes to events from Islam's first centuries, many of which form the basis of the novel's narratives. The historical novel has long operated as a mode of soft political intervention, something which has been apparent since Walter Scott allegorized British union in his 1820 novel *Ivanhoe*, set in England during the Norman occupation.[16] It seems especially apparent, however, in novels whose author regards the novels, as Ali does, as a part of their larger political practice.

Given their determinedly Islamicate perspective, describing the novels as 'medievalist' also requires some justification. The Introductory chapter to this book has already discussed critics' reservations about the colonizing gesture implicit in extending the term 'medieval', with its stubbornly Eurocentric resonance, to encompass societies whose histories owe little to the temporal coordinates of Western empires or Christianity. Ali's novels, however, notwithstanding their focalization through Muslim characters, anchor their narratives in periods and events that are flashpoints in Islam's (frequently conflictual) encounters and intersections with Christianity and with Jewish diasporic cultures, and as such are able to be described more readily as medievalist texts. He is careful not to treat Islamic-Christian contact as a phenomenon that simply 'adds colour' to Western history, but frames the novels' episodes within the story of Islam's fluctuating fortunes. The refusal to anchor the events in the Western timeline means that on the whole the novels are sparing in their allusions to actual dates, and when dates are explicitly mentioned it is not uncommon for them to be located simultaneously within Muslim and Christian calendars. This parallel dating system is established on the very first page of *Shadows of the Pomegranate Tree*, where a character's birthday is narrated as taking place in '905 AH [*Anno Hegirae*, "in the year of the Hijra"] which was 1500, in the Christian calendar' (1, text in square brackets mine).

---

[15] Tariq Ali, *The Clash of Fundamentalisms: Crusades, Jihads and Modernity* (London: Verso, 2002), 274.

[16] Sir Walter Scott, *Ivanhoe* (Harmondsworth: Penguin, 1820/2000).

The effortless interculturalism of Ali's portrayal works as an effective riposte to the orientalist anxieties directed at the medieval in the contradiction-riven modern Western imaginary. As John M. Ganim has argued, although the medieval period is deemed to be 'the point of origin of [Western] national identities' it is also, conversely, 'the result of foreign incursion, of alien influence'.[17] This perception of foreignness, Ganim argues, is attributable to a pervasive 'twinned association' of the medieval with the Oriental, in which 'geography [is] transmuted into history'.[18] The Western imaginary has long attributed both barbarity and primitive vitality to the Middle Ages and the Middle East alike, with the result that the medieval is frequently Orientalized while the Oriental is deemed to be 'medieval'. The geopolitical tensions of the past decades, and in particular the period since the attacks of 11 September 2001, have led to an increasing, and increasingly negative, collocation of Islamic culture with the 'Middle Ages' understood as a period of violence, authoritarian religion, and social stasis.[19] Ali's riposte does not so much dismiss the notion of an 'oriental' Middle Ages as reinterpret it more literally by actually locating this period within Islamic history, thereby shifting the cultural centre of gravity in such a way as to take for granted the powerful—and, his novels suggest, wholly beneficial—impact of Islamicate culture on Western Christendom. By viewing the Middle Ages through a transnational and transcultural lens, Ali's novels participate in the growing scholarly and creative tendency to challenge the formerly prevalent Eurocentric and nationalistic views of the Middle Ages, offering instead, to again cite Amer and Doyle, a Middle Ages that is 'global' *avant la lettre*.[20] This 'reorientating' of an orientalized Middle Ages helps expand and nuance the language already in place to understand how the period that the

---

[17] John M. Ganim, *Medievalism and Orientalism: Three Essays on Literature, Architecture and Cultural Identity* (Basingstoke and New York: Palgrave Macmillan, 2005), 3.

[18] Ganim, *Medievalism and Orientalism*, 7.

[19] See Holsinger, *Neomedievalism, Neoconservatism, and the War on Terror*; Nickolas Haydock, 'Introduction: "The Unseen Cross upon the Breast": Medievalism, Orientalism, and Discontent', in *Hollywood in the Holy Land: Essays on Film Depictions of the Crusades and Christian-Muslim Clashes*, ed. Nickolas Haydock and E. L. Risden (Jefferson, NC and London: McFarland & Company, Inc., 2009), 1–30.

[20] Amer and Doyle, 'Reframing Postolonial and Global Studies'.

West calls 'the Middle Ages' has been understood and mobilized within the political cultures that interact with the West but are also distinct from it.

Predecessors: pan-Arabism and the historical novel

As an author of Islamic-orientated historical fiction, Ali has some worthy predecessors, including Abdul Rahman Munif, of whose *Cities of Salt* (*Mudun al-milh*) quintet Ali has spoken admiringly.[21] Indeed, some of the earliest novel-like narrative texts to emerge out of the Islamicate diaspora based their material on Islamic history. The best-known author of these is Jurji Zaidan (1861–1914), the Lebanese-born Egyptian writer, journalist, and architect of pan-Arabism and modern Arabic literatures. As a Christian Arab living in an Islamic nation in the later years of Ottoman rule, Zaidan was a hugely influential figure in the pan-Arabist movement and the *nahḍa* (the Arab cultural Renaissance, which gained momentum in the late nineteenth and early twentieth centuries), as well as being vital to the modernization and standardization of the Arabic language, and a promoter of Arab literature. A vital part of the cultural renewal sought by Zaidan and other proponents of the *nahḍa* was tied up with the recovery of a premodern Arabic heritage, in pursuit of earlier linguistic and cultural models that could unify modern people across the Arab world and correct the diminution of Arab culture after several centuries under the Ottomans. Jonathan Phillips has recently offered a helpful account outlining how the rich cultural scene of the late nineteenth and early twentieth century was a 'particularly fertile time' in Egypt and the Levant for recovering the medieval past, especially the Crusade era, to understand contemporary politics and culture.[22] Zaidan's literary contribution to this effort was no fewer than twenty-two prose historical fictions, set in

---

[21] Ali, *Clash*, 81–5.

[22] Jonathan Phillips, '"Unity! Unity between All the Inhabitants of our Lands!" The Memory and Legacy of the Crusades and Saladin in the Near East, *c.*1880 to *c.*1925', in *Perceptions of the Crusades from the Nineteenth to the Twenty-First Century*, ed. Mike Horswell and Jonathan Phillips (New York: Routledge, 2018), 80.

the early centuries of Islam's emergence, spread, and consolidation. Many of these have nothing to do with the West, geographically or culturally: they are set on the Arabian Peninsula or in the Levant, and focus on Islamic dynasties and Caliphates. The two exceptions to this are *The Conquest of Andalusia* (1903) and *The Battle of Poitiers: Charles Martel and 'Abd al-Rahman* (1904), which are based respectively, as their titles suggest, on the Muslim taking of the Iberian Peninsula from the Visigoths and the defeat of Muslim forces at the 732 battle of Poitiers.[23] Here Zaidan sets a precedent for the Eastern novelization of the complex tensions between Christianity and Islam.

Kamran Rastegar has argued that the Arabic term *riwayat* is preferable to 'novel' for Zaidan's historical fictions, since Zaidan himself referred to them as *silsilat riwayat tarikh al-Islam* (a series of narratives of the history of Islam), and because the term has implications of literary innovation that are specific to their linguistic and cultural milieu and only partly overlap with the innovation associated with the novel as a form.[24] It is also true, however, that Zaidan cited Walter Scott's historical novels as one of his key influences,[25] and that the structure of his narratives, which move between historical events and fictional romantic subplots, bear the imprint of the Western genre, which was consumed avidly in loose translation at the time.[26] In this respect Ali can certainly be seen to be, however inadvertently, one of Zaidan's heirs.

Zaidan's *riwayat* have long been translated into the languages of the Islamicate world, including Persian, Azeri, Turkish, Javanese, Uighur, and Urdu—Ali might have encountered him in the latter, although this

[23] Zaidan's three novels featuring medieval East-West engagement are: *The Conquest of Andalusia*, trans. with an Afterword and Study Guide by Roger Allen (Bethesda, MD: The Zaidan Foundation, 2010); *The Battle of Poitiers: Charles Martel and 'Abd al-Rahman*, trans., with a Study Guide, by William Granara (Bethesda, MD: The Zaidan Foundation, 2011); and *Saladin and the Assassins*, trans. Paul Starkey (Bethesda, MD: The Zaidan Foundation, 2011).

[24] Kamran Rastegar, 'Literary Modernity between Arabic and Person Prose: Jurji Zaydan's *Riwayat* in Persian Translation', *Comparative Critical Studies* 4.3 (2007), 362.

[25] Rastegar, 'Literary Modenity', 375, n. 9.

[26] M. Peled, 'Creative Translation: Towards the Study of Arabic Translations of Western Literature Since the 19th Century', *Journal of Arabic Literature* 10 (1979), 129–50; Rebecca C. Johnson, 'Importing the Novel: The Arabic Novel in and as Translation', *Novel: A Forum on Fiction* 48.2 (2015), 250.

is difficult to prove—as well as being more sporadically translated into some European languages. They have only reached Anglophone audiences in the twenty-first century, however, as the result of a concerted (though currently incomplete) translation scheme inaugurated by the Zaidan Foundation, established in 2009 and based in Maryland in the U.S.A. The foundation's stated purpose, strongly reminiscent of Zaidan's own, is to offer his career as an example of a sophisticated cosmopolitan vision of the Arabic past and the Arabic future, and to translate his novels in the name of 'international dissemination of the secular and progressive view of the Arab and Islamic heritage'. The Foundation's intended audience for the translations encompasses 'the broader English-speaking world: the United States, England, and Canada . . . but also English-speaking Muslim populations with little or no knowledge of Arabic, such as Bangladesh, India, and Pakistan'.[27] Where they differ is that, rather than engaging as Zaidan did in using history for broadly conceived 'national' consciousness raising, the Foundation instead revives his cosmopolitan vision in an attempt, in the name of 'enhance[ing] understanding between cultures'[28] to educate a wider public suspicious of or hostile to Islam. Academic scholars such as Roger Allen and William Granara are involved in the Foundation's translation project, but the apparatus they include in the novels is pedagogic in a public, rather than scholarly, way: all of the editions offer a brief sketch of the key events and historical figures featured in the novels, with study notes and questions to prompt historical, cultural, and even ethical reflection from readers. While critics of Ali's Islam Quintet have faulted the novels on their didacticism, Zaidan's *riwayat* in both their original and translated forms also have an explicitly consciousness-raising function that affords a forerunner to the approach Ali takes.

Shadows of the Pomegranate Tree

As telecasts throughout 1991 showed black plumes billowing from hundreds of burning Kuwaiti oil wells in the wake of the First Gulf

[27] Zaidan, *Conquest of Andalusia*, xii.   [28] Zaidan, *Conquest of Andalusia*, xii.

War, Ali chose to open his novel *Shadows of the Pomegranate Tree* with another conflagration: the infamous burning in Granada in December 1499 of five thousand Arabic manuscripts on the orders of the recently arrived Archbishop of Toledo, Ximénes de Cisneros. Within the novel's portrayal of the history of Muslim al-Andalus, the blaze is both a rupture and a continuation. For Ali's Muslim characters, it is a shocking violation of the religious protections offered them under the 1491 Treaty of Granada (or 'Gharnata', as they call it), and a pitiless reversal of the more moderate 'hearts-and-minds' approach to Christian conversion taken by Cisneros's predecessor, the Hieronymite Hernando de Talavera, who had been Archbishop of Granada since 1492. Yet on a longer timeline Granada's despairing Muslims see it as the brutal culmination of the centuries-long Christian-Castilian war on Islamic Spain known by many today (including Ali) as the Reconquista, escalated to a new level of inevitability by the looming arrival of the Inquisition. In a further gesture toward Spain's—and by extension the Christian West's—future of global conquest and colonization, Ali presents the destruction of Andalusian Muslim culture as a precursor to even larger-scale violations in the New World.

In choosing to write about Islam in Spain after the Fall of Granada, Ali is hardly unique among modern novelists of the Islamicate Middle East and diaspora. In addition to the established Western tradition of novelization, dramatization, and visual portrayal of this tragic moment in history, Arabist William Granara has demonstrated that al-Andalus between the eighth and fifteenth century has been the favoured chronotope ('time-place') for depictions of the cosmopolitan past in modern novelizations from across the Islamicate diaspora.[29] In his account of the potency of this chronotope in the development of the Arabic novel across the twentieth century, Granara argues that medieval al-Andalus has both historical and literary significance: it 'creates a recognizable and credible fictional space where Arabic literature can be read on equal footing with the hegemonic western canon: and it allows for an allegorization of contemporary political problems that, mapped onto the literary, enables fantasies of a better life'.[30] In the 1990s alone,

[29] William Granara, 'Nostalgia, Arab Nationalism, and the Andalusian *Chronotope* in the Evolution of the Modern Arabic Novel', *Journal of Arabic Literature* 36.1 (2005), 57–73.

[30] Granara, 'Nostalgia', 69.

al-Andalus featured in Ali's novel, the 1994 novel *Gharnāṭa* by the Egyptian author Raḍwa 'Ashour, and Egyptian filmmaker Youssef Chahine's 1997 film *al-Masir* (*Destiny*), which focuses on the philosopher Ibn Rushd (Averroes) in Córdoba.[31] Alongside these fictionalizations, innumerable allusions can be found in public discussions of contemporary East-West relations at that time and since.[32] It has continued to attract novelistic treatments in the twenty-first century in texts such as Diana Abu-Jaber's *Crescent* (2003).[33] By invoking Ibero-Arabic conviviality as part of the novel's exploration of Arab-American identity in contemporary Los Angeles, *Crescent* seeks, in the words of Nouri Gana, 'to reinvent Arabness in tandem with rethinking the multicultural under the auspices of the powerful metaphor of Andalusia'.[34]

Ali's novel follows the final months of an established Muslim family's life on their ancestral estate outside of Granada. Their estate, the Banu Hudayl, and its attached village, al-Hudayl, are not only abundant in rice fields and orange, lime, pomegranate, and date orchards (77) due to inherited Arab cultivation and irrigation methods, but are a remaining oasis of liberality in matters intellectual, political, and sexual. The family, descended from the fictional celebrated warrior Ibn Farid, is cultured and urbane, including its female members, but also prone to forbidden love affairs that lead to banishments. Although the defeat of Granada has scattered the family—some have pragmatically converted to Catholicism, while others leave for a safer life in North Africa—strong devotion in conditions of adversity brings lost members back to the fold at the estate before the family's massacre at the hands of Christian forces. Having begun with Cisneros's book burning, the novel concludes with the family's one remaining son, Zuhayr, joining the Alpujarras rebellions that have formed the story's backdrop, to fight bravely but fruitlessly for the survival of his people in al-Andalus.

[31] Raḍwa 'Ashour, *Granada: A Novel*, trans. William Granara, foreword by Maria Rosa Menocal (Syracuse, New York: Syracuse University Press, 2003); Youssef Chahine, *al-Masir* (Pyramide/MSR International Films, 1997).

[32] Richard Phillips, 'Remembering Islamic Empires: Speaking of Imperialism and Islamophobia', *New Formations* 70 (2010), 94–112.

[33] Diana Abu-Jaber, *Crescent* (New York: W. W. Norton and Company, 2003).

[34] Nouri Gana, 'In Search of Andalusia: Reconfiguring Arabness in Diana Abu-Jaber's *Crescent*', *Comparative Literature Studies* 45.2 (2008), 228–46.

The novel does not offer an exact parallel or historical allegory of contemporary events. According to Gana's eloquent and insightful assessment, this is partly because al-Andalus itself generates an inherently ambivalent legacy that does not offer a single coherent 'lesson' for the present:

> In the history of Arab consciousness, Al-Andalus reverberates like a melancholic wound, fissuring chiastically between narcissistic cultivation and elegiac vulnerability. On the one hand, it is a distant utopia of inimitable Arab Muslim achievement...—an exemplum of a cherished cultural poetics of conviviality. On the other hand, it persists as an unjustly but irrecoverably lost key to a rightful home, a not-so-distant legacy of cultural and political devastation.[35]

While this ambivalence is also present in *Pomegranate Tree*, which oscillates between celebration and mournful valediction, Ali does extract one salient (and arguably predictable for him) lesson modern readers can draw from the story: that occupation, oppression, and dispossession by the West have long been the conditions endured by peoples across the Islamicate world, and that occupation, oppression, and dispossession breed resentment and incite the will to defend land and way of life. The novel's chief objective is to trace the lives of Andalusian Islamic people under conditions of increasingly brutal occupation, as they not only endure ever more encroachments on their freedom to worship and conduct their business, but also, at a more brutal level of *Realpolitik*, fall victim to the flagrant (and literal) scorched-earth confiscation by church and crown of Muslim-held lands. The Muslim characters fret with mounting anxiety over the escalation of Christian control in Granada, which one of them explicitly describes as 'an occupied city' (75). Ali's focalization of the thoughts of Cisneros confirms this description, as the inquisitor vows to eradicate Islam from this last stronghold with the help of the Castilian armed forces stationed there.

The conquest and expansion of Muslim power throughout the Iberian Peninsula across the eighth century, conversely, is not narrated in terms of invasion or occupation, but rather as a legitimate act of liberation. In a community debate at al-Hudayl, the village's weaver

---

[35] Gana, 'In Search of Andalusia', 234.

describes the history of Islam's spread through Iberia as a legitimate programme of 'sav[ing] this land for the Prophet' (143), narrating this history using a spiritual-militaristic language of conflict, confrontation, victory, and defeat, in which the taking of territory is necessary to the securing of souls. Such a narration corresponds to Granara's point that al-Andalus has come to represent for modern authors and readers 'the expanding boundaries of the Islamic jihad, of spreading the faith and bringing order to a chaotic world'.[36] In a view that would have been grist to the mill of the French Islamophobes discussed in the previous chapter, the weaver cites Charles Martel's 732 defeat of Muslim forces as the end of the aspiration to create a truly Islamic Europe, the decisive event of which would have been 'to construct a mosque in Notre Dame' (143). The mandate for religious colonization is not queried in the world of the novel; indeed, the weaver's view of Islam's righteous expansion is held even by Christian characters whose own origins in Iberia predate the coming of Islam. Granada's Captain-General Don Inigo Lopez de Mendoza, despite being the scion of a royal Visigothic family, defends the Muslim presence on the premises that Muslims are now Spanish by right of lengthy and widespread rule and because their takeover was comparatively benevolent. He says to Cisneros:

[m]ost of the people we call Moors are our own people.... They have ruled over a very large portion of our peninsula. They did so without burning too many books or tearing down all our churches or setting synagogues alight to build their mesquitas.   (67)

It is tempting to ponder whether such defences, that is of length and relative benevolence of rule (not 'too many books' burnt;[37] not 'all our churches' torn down), would ordinarily pass muster for Ali in his capacity as an anti-colonial activist; and indeed critics such as Richard Phillips warn against a defensive tendency to be 'convenient and simplistic' in claims that al-Andalus was an 'empire without imperialism'.[38]

---

[36] Granara, 'Nostalgia', 58.

[37] Janina M. Safran and others have demonstrated that the book burnings took place in Muslim-ruled Andalusia were in fact directed at Islamic texts, but this is not an argument of which Ali avails himself. See Safran, 'The Politics of Book Burning in Al-Andalus', *Journal of Medieval Iberian Studies* 6.2 (2014), 148–68.

[38] Phillips, 'Remembering Islamic Empires', 103.

Nevertheless, Phillips argues that the novel's more generous assessment of the Andalusian empire is consistent with the critique Ali advances against modern imperialism as the most pernicious form because, unlike earlier imperial formations, its collusion with capitalism has concentrated the world's wealth and military power in the West.[39] Without disputing this, it is also the case that Ali's political emphasis in *Pomegranate Tree* lies elsewhere, in his commitment to countering the idea that Islamic or 'Arab' history is dominated by religious zealotry rather than an understanding of effective governance.

In emphasizing the relative benevolence of Islamic rule in Spain, Ali's novel exhibits his deep investment in the influential idea of the Andalusian *convivencia*, the putative long past of diasporic Islamic rule that produced an enlightened and moderate society of interfaith cohabitation. Attributed to the philologist Américo Castro (although Ryan Szpiech points out that the idea preceded the term in scholarly discussion)[40] *convivencia* has appealed not just to popular historians, and scholars looking to query the nationalist, Eurocentric frameworks medieval studies has inherited from nineteenth-century historiography and philology, but also to Islamic activists and modernists looking to strategically refigure Islamic medieval history as a time of East-West encounters, critical reflections, and multiple truths.[41] In what might be the quintessential description of the *convivencia*, María Rosa Menocal, one of the most influential Anglophone scholars of the medieval Western Islamic diaspora, says:

> ...especially in al-Andalus, a new, symbiotic European culture developed, a uniquely rich tripartite culture based on the relatively peaceful and often prosperous cohabitation, for a time, of the offspring of Abraham, the children of Ishmael and Isaac alike...al-Andalus created an atmosphere within which the inherited learning

---

[39] Phillips, 'Remembering Islamic Empires', 104; Ali, *Clash*, 3.

[40] Ryan Szpiech, 'The Convivencia Wars: Decoding Historiography's Polemic with Philology', in *A Sea of Languages: Rethinking the Arabic Role in Medieval Literary History*, ed. Suzanne Akbari and Karla Mallette (Toronto: University of Toronto Press, 2013), 135–61.

[41] My thanks to Sahar Amer for her observations in conversation about the valency of the medieval past for Islamic queer activists.

of all three separate cultures had come together and were actively and in many cases fruitfully exposed to each other.[42]

As Szpiech has demonstrated in a thorough account of what he ironically calls 'the convivencia wars',[43] the scholarly prosecution of what is now generally regarded as a sanguine account of Iberian-Muslim society has been mitigated by more cautious accounts from Iberianists in a range of languages tracing the tensions, ambivalences, and fragilities not just between faiths but between the *taifas* (smaller principalities) of the Western diaspora, as well as between Arab and Berber dynasties on the peninsula. Notwithstanding these accounts, the idea of the Islamic-ruled *convivencia* has proven robustly popular and ideologically serviceable especially beyond academia.[44] *Pomegranate Tree* is the epitome of this. To take just one example, in al-Hudayl the local imam preaches to the village mosque's congregation, which is tri-faith, that 'in this village we have lived in peace for five hundred years. Jews have been tormented elsewhere, but never here. Christians have bathed in the same baths as Jews and Muslims' (123), going on to lead them in a recitation of a Quranic *surá*, the final line of which appears to advocate religious pluralism: 'Ye have your religion and I have my religion' (124). Ali does not identify the much-debated surá, but it is the *Sūrat al-Kāfirūn*/'The Unbelievers', to which he gives a recognizably liberal interpretation in support of his historical-ideological portrait of 'tolerant' Andalusian Islam. By the standards of contemporary historiography, Ali's depiction of perfect peace under Muslim rule courts accusations of being utopian, even denialist. The novel's conspicuous presentism, however, seems strategically central to its avowedly anti-Islamophobic purpose. In Phillips' words, al-Andalus functions in Ali's post-first Gulf War context as 'a reference point for moving forward in positive ways, such as in contesting and proactively negotiating

---

[42] María Rosa Menocal, *The Arabic Role in Medieval Literary History: A Forgotten Heritage* (Philadelphia: University of Pennsylvania Press, 1987), 65. See also Menocal, *The Ornament of the World: How Muslims, Jews, and Christians Created a Culture of Tolerance in Medieval Spain* (Boston and New York: Little, Brown and Company, 2003).

[43] Szpiech, 'Convivencia Wars'. See also David Nirenberg, *Communities of Violence: Persecution of Minorities in the Middle Ages* (Princeton, NJ: Princeton University Press, 1996).

[44] See Phillips, 'Remembering Islamic Empires', for examples in the trans-Atlantic media.

tolerance as a Muslim value, which contributes to—doesn't just fit in with—Western/European values'.[45]

In Ali's novel, the interfaith cohabitation of al-Andalus has inevitably led to a society of miscegenation, whose members have fused culturally, religiously, and sexually. The village of al-Hudayl contains generations of Jewish and Christian 'natural sons' of the Muslim heads of the Banu Hudayl, whose filial and political loyalties lie with their trusted Muslim protectors. The novel dwells on the anxieties this generates in Cisneros, making extensive use of interior monologue. Despite his obsession with attaining uniformity of religion throughout Spain by forced conversion, Cisneros must also bear grudging witness to the extent to which this has produced what he most reviles: a culture of 'passing', in which outward religious affiliation is no guarantee of faith, and it is this that fuels his ferocity as an inquisitor. His encounters with Granada's Moriscos, whom he always suspects are crypto-Muslims, leave him unsteadied, a feeling he instantly converts into revulsion at 'Mahometan' perfidy (137). Just as the Grand Inquisitor Torquemada had fanatically hunted down crypto-Judaism, so too Cisneros aims to root out and punish any covert adherence to Islam among Granada's Moriscos. In the novel's prologue, we witness his disdain for both Talavera and the 'imbecile Dominicans' (xii), who he represents as lenient in matters of conversion and religious co-habitation, notwithstanding the fact that the zealously orthodox Torquemada was a Dominican. He attributes this order's apparent laxness to what he takes to be the Morisco pasts of many Dominicans, as though it is an atavism of the blood, concluding 'what else could be expected from a clergy whose abbots, only a few hundred years ago, were named Mohammed, Umar, Uthman, and so on?' (xiii).

Ali's novel implies that Cisneros's dread of atavism is driven by fears about his own lineage. Although Cisneros willingly insists that Torquemada's Jewish ancestry fuelled the Grand Inquisitor's zealous displays of loyalty to the Church (68), he is horrified at the prospect of any similar background in himself. Brooding over his dark skin and eyes and his long hooked nose, features that Sara Lipton and others have shown to have been physiognomic markers of Jewishness in late medieval

---

[45] Phillips, 'Remembering Islamic Empires', 112.

caricatures,[46] his flurry of anxious denials is telling: 'I am sure, yes sure, that my blood is without taint... There is no Jewish blood in me. Not one tiny drop. No. On this I have no doubts.' (206). Cisneros's assertion of his pre-Visogothic Old Christian ancestry suggests Ali is aware of Spain's fifteenth-century *limpieza de sangre* (purity of blood) statutes. David Graizbord's account of how

> ... unstable, tightly criss-crossing notions of genealogical cleanness (Sp. *limpieza*), defectiveness (*mácula*, and the like), race (*raza*), stock (*casta*), lineage (*linaje*), origin (*generación*), nation or ethnicity (*nación*), nativeness (*naturaleza*), nature (*natura*), and local civic membership (*vecindad*), emerged in Iberia as key elements of popular and learned discourse of community and human difference.[47]

illuminates the extent to which physiological, moral, and communal fitness were intimately linked, and gives historical solidity to Ali's depiction of racism as both motivating and perpetuating political conquest.

Given Ali's ongoing critique of colonialism, it is not surprising that his novel presents a continuity between the eradication of the Andalusian Muslims and the destruction of the indigenous cultures of Central and South America at the hands of the Spanish *conquistadores*. Earlier in the story, the more sanguine characters treat the trans-Atlantic conquests as a potential distraction from domestic reconquest (147). By the end of the novel, however, domestic and foreign subjugation have become two sides of the one coin. In order to make this link, Ali avails himself of a favoured trope in the historical novel, in which larger historical forces are concentrated into known historical characters, who interact with the fictional characters created by the author. In a devastating culmination that echoes the famous statement in Heinrich Heine's 1821 Granadan tragedy *Almansor* that 'where they burn

[46] Sara Lipton, *Dark Mirror: The Medieval Origins of Anti-Jewish Iconography* (New York: Metropolitan Books, 2014), 172–97.

[47] David Graizbord, 'Pauline Christianity and Jewish "Race": The Case of João Baptista D'Este', in *Race and Blood in the Iberian World*, ed. Max S. Hering Torres, María Elena Martínez, and David Nirenberg (Münster etc.: LIT Verlag, 2012), 62; see also David Nirenberg, 'Was There Race before Modernity? The example of "Jewish" Blood in Late Medieval Spain', in *The Origins of Racism in the West*, ed. Miriam Eliav-Feldon, Benjamin Isaac, and Joseph Ziegler (Cambridge: Cambridge University Press), 232–64.

books, they will end by burning men',[48] the entire village and estate of the Banu Hudayl is slaughtered and put to the torch, under the leadership of an adolescent Spanish captain whose youth is overcompensated by his cruelty (258–66). In the novel's epilogue the reader meets this young captain twenty years later, as he is escorted to the palace of Tenochtitlan to meet the Aztec king Moctezuma; the final lines chillingly reveal that he is none other than Hernán Cortés (273). Ali inventively exploits a small gap in what is known of Cortés's youth around 1500 to suggest that al-Andalus provided a training ground for the notorious conquistador's later depredations in the New World. In this respect Ali's text goes beyond the Islamic diaspora and, uniquely among his medievalist novels, reaches into the western and southern hemispheres, pointing forward to a global history of colonialisms and neocolonialisms to come. In this respect his novel concurs with the accounts of scholars such as Abbas Hamdani who have argued that the plundering of al-Andalus provided the wealth the Spanish crown needed to embark on its trans-Atlantic voyages.[49]

By the end of the novel the European south has begun its transformation into a power of the Global North, an entity whose force, implacable self-interest, and will to enslave and expropriate on a mass scale have enriched it at the expense of those places and peoples whose resources it claims as its own. While Ali does not assert a direct link between Spanish reconquest and U.S.-European presence in the Middle East, the novel's conclusion suggests the analogy. This same link is made soon afterwards in *Gharnāṭa* by Raḍwa Ashour, Part 1 of her Granada Trilogy (1994–5), in which the inhabitants of post-capitulation Granada are subjected to a procession in which Christopher Columbus displays his New World plunder. Although the event is initially celebratory, its mood darkens as captive indigenous South Americans are paraded before jeering Castilians. A young Muslim man, Saad, finds himself comparing these peoples' captivity to that of the Muslim inhabitants of Málaga, who had been sold into slavery after being starved into capitulation in 1487. He wonders:

---

[48] Heinrich Heine, *Almansor*, in *Gesamtausgabe der Werke*, ed. Manfred Windfuhr (Hamburg, 1973–97), Bild 5, 16.

[49] Abbas Hamdani, 'An Islamic Background to the Voyages of Discovery', in *The Legacy of Muslim Spain*, ed. Salma Khadra Jayyusi (Boston: Brill, 1994), 289–93.

> ...whether [the Spaniards] attacked them by land and sea the way
> they did to the people of Malaga. Did they starve them to the point of
> forcing them to eat their own horses? Or did they raze their homes
> and pounce on them before taking them away as prisoners?[50]

Ashour's novel is ultimately more optimistic about the possibilities
offered by these newly opened modern horizons, even having one of
her characters (in seeming defiance of *limpieza de sangre* laws) reach
the New World where he lives with an indigenous woman. Like Ali,
however, she offers an ominous interpretation of the expansion of the
West at the expense of the European Islamosphere. Ashour has stated
expressly that *Gharnāṭa* is a response to the First Gulf War.[51] It is also
impossible to overlook the fact that in 1992 the aftermath of the First
Gulf War coincided with the very public commemoration of five
hundred years since Columbus's journey to the Americas. Ashour's
novel, like Ali's, astutely exposes the anti-Islamic violence that underpins and links the colonial past and the neocolonial present.

The Book of Saladin

Ali's stated purpose of revealing the sophistication of Islamicate political history would seem naturally to lead him to the celebrated Crusade-
era military and political leader Ṣalāḥ al-Dīn Yūsuf ibn Ayyūb, or, as he
is called in English, Saladin (1138–1193) in the second novel of the
quintet. Because of his famed routing of the Christians at the Battle of
Hattin and his recapture of Jerusalem in October 1187, Saladin's story
would have been broadly familiar to both the initial Anglophone
readership of Ali's *The Book of Saladin* (1998), as well as to his readers
in translation. His reputation in the West, dating back to the thirteenth
century[52] as not just a formidable opponent but the ultimate 'chival-
rous Saracen', was amplified exponentially by Sir Walter Scott's portrayal of him in the popular Crusade romance *The Talisman* (1825).[53]

---

[50] Ashour, *Granada*, 28.
[51] María Costanza Guzmán, 'Reviewed Work: *Granada: A Novel* by Radwa 'Ashour,
William Granara, María Rosa Menocal', *The Arab Studies Journal* 13/14 (2005/6), 129.
[52] Carole Hillenbrand, 'The Evolution of the Saladin Legend in the West', in *Crusades:
Medieval Worlds in Conflict*, ed. T. Madden (Aldershot: Ashgate, 2011), 9–23.
[53] *The Talisman*, Penn State Electronic Classics, (file:///D:/Users/mq20160735/
Documents/crusades/talisman.pdf).

Scott's influential characterization of Saladin, which featured the sultan's humility and clemency, has recurred repeatedly with minor variations in Western literary and cinematic iterations up to the present, including in Cecil B. De Mille's 1935 film *The Crusades* and, in the wake of Ali's novel, in Ridley Scott's Second Gulf War-era Crusade epic *Kingdom of Heaven* (2005), where he is again an appealing embodiment of austere dignity who, through his mercy toward the conquered inhabitants of Jerusalem, 'out-Christians' the Crusaders.[54] Ali leverages Saladin's prestigious Western legacy in his novel, which retains some of its key tropes such as the sultan's simplicity and generosity. As I will show, however, he does this in a way that does not deliver up Saladin yet again as exemplary non-Christian, but ultimately reclaims his significance for the medieval Islamicate world.

This reorientation depends mostly, and most simply, on narrative content and structure. The novel gives far greater attention to the turbulent events surrounding Saladin's rise to power, removal of the decadent Egyptian Fatimid dynasty, and consolidation of the Islamicate Levant under his rule, than it does to Muslim-Christian conflicts. Much of the story takes place before Saladin's victory at Hattin and recapture of Jerusalem, so these famous events, which have been subject to compulsive retelling in Western accounts, come late into the tale and are the culmination of the novel's larger Islam-focused story in which the Holy City (referred to throughout by the Arabic name al-Kuds) is not lost but won. The crusaders' presence in Palestine, furthermore, is not explored in terms of a Christian mandate or rationale, but is instead depicted as the result of a divided Arab-Islamic *ummah* that has through political in-fighting made itself vulnerable to invasion and the occupation it now endures.

In offering this account, Ali participates in a longer non-Western practice of portraying Saladin. According to eminent Crusades scholar Carole Hillebrand, Saladin being Kurdish yet from a Turkish military elite, a leader of Arab lands, and a unifier of Sunni Muslims, means he has been 'well placed to become a hero to many different groups in the

---

[54] Ridley Scott, *Kingdom of Heaven* (Twentieth Century Fox, 2005); Cecile B. De Mille, *The Crusades* (Paramount Pictures, 1935).

Middle East in the modern world.'[55] Jurji Zaidan again offers a striking precedent, in his Riwayat, *Saladin and the Assassins* (1913), which devotes even less space than Ali's novel to Saladin's clashes with crusaders, focusing instead on political intrigues in the Fatimid court and tensions between Saladin and Rashīd ad-Dīn Sinān 'the Old Man of the Mountain', the leader of the Assassin (Nizari Ismaili) sect in Syria.[56] Zaidan's reclamation of Saladin's story as a narrative of the East is especially significant considering how the consumption of Walter Scott's novels in the occupied nineteenth-century cultures of the Middle East, including wide reading of *The Talisman*, exerted a vital influence on the development of the Arabic historical novel. Ali's narrative, like Zaidan's before him, displaces Western political perspectives on Saladin via a strategy of narrative minimization. It is true that the crusaders' occupation of Palestine is returned to throughout the novel, but this is only in so far as it forms the backdrop and the primary motive for Saladin's rise and his centralization of Muslim rule, and then fuels his avenging might at Hattin and Jerusalem. Whereas the Western historical imaginary has been preoccupied with the crusaders' interests in the Levant, with Saracens appearing only in so far as they thwart or fulfil Western ambitions, the only Christians who feature long enough to receive dialogue in Ali's novel are Balian of Ibelin, the defeated protector of Jerusalem (who receives a few lines after the fall of the city) and a character called Bertrand of Toulouse—not the Bertrand who had been Count of Tripoli decades before the novels' events, but a fictional humble Cathar and Templar deserter who divulges his Order's military plans in exchange for refuge in Saladin's court. Bertrand, whose pursuit of spiritual truth extends to Muslim theology, exists in the novel only to generate a debate on the effectiveness of *Hadith* (the sayings of the Prophet) for Islamic governance (117), so in the end even his Christianity is largely irrelevant.

Ali's reduction of the Christian presence means that his novel goes further than his other famous Middle Eastern precedent, Egyptian director Youssef Chahine's 1963 film *Al Nasser Salah Ad-Din* (*Saladin*

[55] *The Crusades: Islamic Perspectives* (Edinbugh: Edinburgh University Press, 1999), 594.
[56] Zaidan, *Saladin and the Assassins*.

the Victorious).[57] Chahine also places Saladin in a broader Eastern political context, and privileges the Arab perspective on the Third Crusade by emphasizing the Arabs' legitimate *in situ* ownership of Palestine over Christendom's claim. For Saladin and his followers, 'Jerusalem has always been an Arab land,' and the Crusaders' 1099 capture of the city has rendered the Arabs of Jerusalem 'mere refugees, driven from their lands, which they've inhabited for generations'. At the heart of Chahine's account, however, is the homosocial narrative of Saladin and King Richard the Lionheart's admiring rivalry, which is inherited from Scott (Saladin and Richard never met in life), and again reveals the cross-cultural reach of 'the *Talisman* effect'. Ali's novel, conversely, devotes little space to Richard. Although its epistolary coda relates a number of the same events as Chahine's film, Ali refuses the director's romanticization of Richard as the 'exceptional infidel' and downplays any regard between Saladin and the English king. In narrating Richard's execution of 2700 Islamic prisoners, Ali's narrator goes so far as to change the king's moniker 'Lionheart' to 'Lionarse' (353), repeating the conventional insults about Richard's putative homosexuality.

The novel's Levantine setting distinguishes it from Ali's other two medieval novels, which both take place in Islamo-Mediterranean societies. This means that the dominant Christian-Muslim conflict it portrays is not due to the overturning of centuries of benign cohabitation, as in *Pomegranate Tree*, but is unambiguously the result of invasion and brutal occupation by Church-mandated overseas forces. The Crusaders, or Franj as they are called, are nothing other than violent usurpers, 'the barbarians from the West...who came across the water' (7). This is not to say, however, that a longer story of interfaith cohabitation is entirely absent from the novel: Cairo, dominantly Muslim, is also home to Coptic Christians and to a flourishing Jewish community, who are presented as respected and integral to the city's cultural life, living in a protected Juderia. Indeed, one of the most striking elements of *The Book of Saladin* is its portrayal of Jewish-Muslim cooperation in the medieval Middle East. Ali strongly emphasizes Saladin's sense of fellowship with Jews, in particular with his

---

[57] Youssef Chahine, *Al Nasser Salah Ad-Din* (*Saladin the Victorious*) (Assia, 1963).

physician Maimonides (called by the Arabic name Musa Ibn Maymun in the novel) and his biographer, the fictional character Isaac Ibn Yakub who also narrates the novel. The Sultan repeatedly includes Jews with Muslims in his category of the 'people of the book' (Christians are admitted to this category only once), and speaks of the crusaders' 1099 massacre in Jerusalem as a shared tragedy suffered by Jews and Muslims equally:

> The barbarians had decided to kill all the Believers. All of your people, Ibn Yakub, I'm sure you know better than I, were collected in the Temple of Suleiman. The exits were blocked, and the Franj set the holy sanctuary on fire. They wished to wipe out the past, and rewrite the future of al-Kuds, which once belonged to all of us, the People of the Book. (33)

The novel does concede that Jews were not universally well-treated under Muslim rule, as Ibn Maymun/Maimonides recounts his own tale of forced conversion and exile from Almohad Córdoba. But the novel's greater emphasis on the shared suffering of these Semitic peoples under Christian rule reflects, in Bishnupriya Ghosh's words, Ali's narration of 'intensively networked historical relations that were always mixed, always entangled—and often in painful and inextricable ways.'[58]

For Ghosh, Ali's medieval Palestine in The Book of Saladin clearly addresses itself to the geopolitical moment of its writing, and: 'unravels the commonly-held contemporary perception of Jews and Muslims as eternally opposed forces caught in never-ending wars over [Jerusalem].'[59] Ghosh's assertion is corroborated when one considers that Ali was writing the novel during the rocky period of the Oslo Peace Process, in which Israel and the Palestinian authority undertook, with little success, to work toward a two-state solution that acknowledged Palestinian sovereignty. Suicide attacks, assassinations, asymmetrical power relations, and mutual obduracy in the years up to the novel's publication in 1998 were among the circumstances that led to a stalemate that served to reinforce, in Ali's view, his vocal and abiding advocacy of a one-state solution.[60] He has

---

[58] Bishnupriya Ghosh, 'Once There Was Cosmopolitanism: Enchanted Pasts as Global History in the Contemporary Novel', *Ariel: A Review of International English Literature* 42.1 (2011), 18.

[59] Ghosh, 'Cosmopolitanism', 25.

[60] Tariq Ali, 'From the Ashes of Gaza', *The Guardian*, 30 December 2008.

stated in interview that the novel—his only one to be translated into Hebrew—is intended to offer historical proof and a model of peaceful cohabitation and a protected Jewry under benevolent Arab-Islamic leadership.[61] In this respect Ali's utilization of the historical novel genre goes beyond the goal of phenomenological world disclosure to engage in what Ghosh calls 'world making', a future-orientated practice that she claims is '*the* project' for postcolonial writers, for whom 'the contemporary Middle East as a locus of conflict has been a central preoccupation', with Palestine as the 'paradigmatic postcolony'.[62] Ghosh's point here about postcolonial and diasporic literatures resonates with Cheah's argument about world literature being driven by a normative ethical project to 'remake the world as a hospitable place...that is *open* to the emergence of peoples...deprive[d] of world' by the forces of colonialism and globalization.[63]

Beyond the compass of the Israel-Palestine conflict, Saladin's tale resonates with Ali's broader condemnation of the West's political, military, and economic interference in the Arab world. The significance of the novel's events to Ali's views of contemporary Middle Eastern politics is evident in the fact that its narrative is reprised in compressed form in *Clash of Fundamentalisms*, after which he concludes that 'the Crusades left a deep mark on European and Arab consciousness',[64] a wound in the political psyche that continues to manifest in the West's repeated neocolonial interventions in the East. Writing in the early days of the U.S.-led invasion of Afghanistan he draws a direct parallel between it and the Crusades, saying '[r]eason [is] once again usurped by military might'.[65] Saladin's story has proven serviceable for a range of Middle Eastern cultural projects with decolonizing aims. Zaidan's emphasis on the sultan's reinvigoration of an Arab Caliphate under a crumbling dynasty provided a recognizable historical precursor to underwrite the accelerating quest for self-determination among the Arab provinces of the late Ottoman empire. Chahine's film also uses the Crusades to promote a later form of pan-Arabism, in particular the political agenda of the Egyptian president Gamal Abdel Nasser (1956–70), in which the Arab people unite under one charismatic leader. Made in the years after the 1956 Suez Crisis, in which Nasser's

---

[61] Talat Ahmed, 'Interview: Tariq Ali'.   [62] Ghosh, 'Cosmopolitanism', 19–20.
[63] Cheah, 'World against Globe', 326.   [64] Ali, *Clash*, 42.   [65] Ali, *Clash*, 42.

newly independent Egypt was invaded by France and the United Kingdom among others, it is not difficult to recognize the parallel being drawn between contemporary events and an historical conflict in which Arabs of all faiths band together to expel the Western aggressors, with their English king and his French offsider, Philip II. Ali's use of the Crusades as a political parallel is broader than Zaidan's and Chahine's. Although readers familiar with his critical views on the rise of Saudi Arabia and its dealings with the U.S.[66] will recognize parallels in the enfeebled Fatimids, who betray their fellow Muslims through opportunistic pacts with the Crusaders (100–1), the novel overall could allude to any or all of the West's interventions in Middle Eastern and North African geopolitics in the years and decades leading up to *The Book of Saladin*. Nevertheless, it reiterates Zaidan's and Chahine's gesture of making Saladin's victories speak to the challenges of the modern Islamicate world.

The focus on the political complexion of the medieval Levant creates a conundrum for the atheist Ali, which is how to represent religion in the novel (and indeed throughout in the entire Quintet). The Islamic faith is completely central to the cultural, demographic, and political dynamics of the twelfth-century Levant, and is implicitly foundational of the characters' personal identities and to their claim to ownership of the lands they inhabit and, in the case of Saladin, rule. And yet there is little evidence of the characters engaging in active forms of worship: on the few occasions in *Pomegranate Tree* when the characters attend mosques, the content of the Imam's sermon is explicitly political, concerned with the survival of the community, while in *Saladin* there is even less evidence of any kind of religious ritual or observance. Islam is transmuted into a phenomenon of philosophical-political identity and, eventually, of resistance, rather than a system of belief per se, although characters frequently refer to Allah and the Prophet. The extent to which interfaith conflict is presented as a symptom or a by-product of territorial politics is apparent in the novel's coda, where Saladin is reported as pondering 'is it our fate as inhabitants of an area which gave birth to Moses, Jesus, and Mohammed, to be always at war' (352). His moniker throughout the novel of 'Defender of the Loyal' thus

---

[66] Ali, *Clash*, 74–5.

seems to refer more to cultural and territorial allegiance than to devotion to a deity. Ali's discomfort with the role of religion in Arab-Islamic history, and his stated wish to refute contemporary caricatures of Muslims as religious fanatics, are also evident in the novel's insistent emphasis on the strains of scepticism and rationalism within the Judeo-Arabic cultures of both the East and the Western diaspora. In addition to Saladin's physician being the celebrated Jewish polymath Ibn Maymun (Maimonides), throughout the novel one encounters a roll-call of scientists, jurists, philosophers, poets, astronomers, and cartographers who together constituted what is often called the Golden Age of Islamic thought. Among the most celebrated are Ibn Sina/Avicenna (86) Abu Ala al-Maari (125), Mohammed al-Idrisi (129), Ibn Rushd/Averroes (189), Ibn Hazm (215), and al-Farabi (221). The appeal of this disputatious tradition for the non-religious Ali is also apparent in *Clash of Fundamentalisms*, where many of these same thinkers' ideas are condensed into a chapter called 'The Joys of Heresy', which celebrates how they 'expanded the frontiers of debate and dissent in the search for knowledge and thus enriched Islamic civilisation' (52). The substance of their writings is not dwelt on in detail in the novel; what is most important is that they embody a robust tradition within Islam that, in the words of Saladin's sultana Jamila, 'never allowed any authority to set limits to the kingdom of reason' (125).

It is a striking feature of the novel that Sultana Jamila is its boldest and staunchest advocate of scepticism, to the point where she dismisses religion as a pursuit of the timid and weak-minded. Despite the presence in Saladin's court of Ibn Maymun and the famed historian and poet Imad al-Din, the narrator Ibn Yakub regards her as the most brilliant mind among them. Although men are the main bearers of action in Ali's novels, the female characters, all of whom are fictional creations, feature prominently, not just as figures of romantic and sexual fascination, but as proud custodians of familial and cultural tradition. Nisreen Yousef interestingly does not interpret this as a feminist gesture, but rather as a 'postcolonial revisionist' act of world-making, because it 'defies [presumably Western] assumptions that Islam is a patriarchal religion'.[67] The combination of historical fact

---

[67] Nisreen T. Yousef, 'Historiographic Metafiction and Renarrating History', *Routledge Companion to Pakistani Anglophone Writing*, ed. Aroosa Kanwal and Saiyma Aslam (London: Routledge, 2018), 121. Text in parantheses is mine.

and romantic fantasy is not only a staple of Western historical fiction, but in fact has an early precedent in the fictions of Zaidan, although Zaidan's romances are far more chaste than Ali's occasionally lurid erotic scenarios. What Ali shares with Zaidan, who was Christian, is a representation of historical Islam as humanist, and of historical Muslim women as possessing powerful intellectual, emotional, and (in Ali's case) sexual agency, though they have little official autonomy. They take clandestine lovers, read philosophical and even heretical works, and are fully apprised of the *Realpolitik* of the courts, estates, and kingdoms in which they live. Although all three novels include such female characters, this is most pronounced in *The Book of Saladin*, in Jamila's daring and erudite disputations with Ibn Yakub and her lesbian liaisons within the harem. Ali's libertarian portrait of free female sexual agency is reinforced by a 'don't ask, don't tell' approach to homosexuality, male and female. Together these enable Ali to convey to readers what he has called 'the bulging vein of dissent and eroticism' in the Islamicate historical body politic.[68]

The Book of Saladin shows that the Crusades era continues to attract modern writers and filmmakers of the modern Islamicate diaspora because of its capacity to offer commentary on larger geopolitical events while also exploring intimate portraits of cross-cultural enmity and friendship. Its appeal for Ali lies in its sweeping public story of war, invasion, and religious intolerance, and its compelling characters facing dilemmas about territory, ambition, and the ethics of occupation, all issues that continue to haunt the present with their seemingly inexhaustible significance.

A Sultan in Palermo

Moving back to the European area of the Mediterranean, Ali turns his attention to the Islamic culture of Norman Sicily in his 2005 novel *A Sultan in Palermo*. Set in 1153–4, the year leading up to the death of the Islamophilic but infirm Norman king Roger II, the novel focuses on the Siculo-Normans who are facing the imminent end of their centuries-long habitation of the island, where they have lived first as rulers in

---

[68] Ali, *Clash*, ix.

their own right and then as the majority population of the Norman Kingdom of Sicily.[69] Palermo's Muslims live in fear that the city, with its many mosques, is about to enter a new era of Christian despotism and forced conversions, in which the Norman bishops and barons will manipulate Roger's successor, his son William, who is presented as weak and uninterested in rule. As with *Shadows of the Pomegranate Tree*, the novel is suffused with a mood of precarity as it tracks the escalating fear that the ailing Roger will capitulate to these groups as well as to the Lombards who had taken up residence in Sicily as part of King Roger's father's attempts to latinize the island. This fear is realized when Roger agrees to the execution of Philip al-Mahdia, his trusted adviser and a covert Muslim, at which point he loses the fragile goodwill of his Muslim allies. Anti-Norman rebellion is fomenting in the provinces, under the leadership of an opaque but charismatic figure known only as the Trusted One, and toward the end of the novel one town fights back and slaughters the Lombards who attempt to take it. Meanwhile the emirs of Syracuse, Catania, and other Southern Italian cities prepare themselves to resist the now untrammelled power of the barons. The novel's central narrative culminates in a Norman massacre in Palermo, and ends on a note of unresolved threat and danger, with the promise of more Christian depredation to come. Its coda, titled 'Lucera 1250–1300', recounts what came later: the expulsion of the Muslims from the island in 1224 to Lucera in Apulia at the hands of that famous cultural Islamophile, Frederick II. Despite bringing Lucera into prosperity, after Frederick's death they are massacred, with only a few escaping to elsewhere in the Islamicate diaspora, either to North Africa or to Palestine, where 'the Franks had been defeated by Salah al-Din and driven out' (246). As will be discussed later, this mixture of despair, resistance, and hope is as much a response to the historical moment in which Ali is writing as it is to the one he is portraying.

Ali is not the only modern Anglophone writer over whom Siculo-Norman culture has exerted a fascination. After a trickle of novels in the second half of the twentieth century, the first decade of the twenty-first century witnessed a renewal of interest in this setting. To name just a few, in the years surrounding Ali's novel, Maria R. Bordihn's *The*

[69] Alex Metcalfe, *The Muslims of Medieval Italy* (Edinburgh: Edinburgh University Press, 2009).

Falcon of Palermo (2005), Barry Unsworth's *The Ruby in her Navel* (2006), and Jack Ludlow's *Conquest* Trilogy (2009–10) were published, possibly prompting the 2010 republication of Cecelia Holland's 1974 novel of Norman Sicily, *Great Maria.*[70] In addition to the novelizations, the high-profile popular historian John Julius Norwich (1929–2018), to take just one example, published several books across his long career dedicated to Norman Sicily, all of which stress the uniqueness of its 'kaleidoscopic' cross-cultural past.[71] Beyond the Anglophone world and much closer to the source, the influential Sicilian novelist and essayist Leonardo Sciascia (1921–89) was indefatigable throughout his career in his search to identify how Sicily's long history of serial habitation and colonization by different cultures set it apart from the Italian mainland and elsewhere. Central to this distinctiveness is the idea of Sicily as a cosmopolitan crossroads, a terraqueous and quintessentially Mediterranean hybrid culture. Because of its long history of colonizations, Sicily has, Sciascia claims, long been subsumed under the culture of others, but he makes an exception of the period of medieval Muslim presence which he regards as, in the words of Salvatore Pappalardo, 'a familiar otherness, a domestic alterity'[72] that created a syncretic culture that was the essence of 'Sicilianness'. In a number of his works, Sciascia seizes on the romantic orientalist idea of an abiding 'Arab *Sicilitudine*' that goes back to the times of the Sicilian Emirate and later the Norman Kingdom of Sicily. For Sciascia this is personal, as he regards himself, despite seven centuries having elapsed since the expulsion of Muslims from Sicily, as an Arab Sicilian, claiming in *La Sicilia come metafore* (*Sicily as Metaphor*) that his very name, once spelled Xaxa, has fallen victim to the orthographic elision imposed by the Tuscanization of Italian.[73] Notwithstanding the nostalgic impetus

---

[70] Maria R. Bordihn, *The Falcon of Palermo* (New York: Atlantic Monthly Press, 2005); Barry Unsworth, *The Ruby in her Navel* (London: Hamish Hamilton, 2006); Jack Ludlow, *Conquest Trilogy* (London: Allison & Busby, 2009–10); Cecelia Holland, *Great Maria* (Naperville, IL: Sourcebooks Landmark, 1974/2010).

[71] See, for instance, John Julius Norwich, *The Kingdom in the Sun, 1130–1194* (London: Longman, 1970), which was also re-printed in 2011; and *Sicily: An Island at the Crossroads of History* (New York: Random House, 2015).

[72] Salvatore Pappalardo, 'From Ibn Ḥamdīs to Giufà: Leonardo Sciascia and the Writing of a Siculo-Arab Literary History', *Italian Culture* 36.1 (2018), 33.

[73] Leonardo Sciascia, *La Sicilia come metafore: Intervista di Marcelle Padovani* (Milan: Arnoldo Mondadori, 1979).

of Sciascia's excavation of Sicily's Arab past, his observations accord with medieval scholars such as Kinoshita, who regards the persistence of Arab culture in Norman Sicily as paradigmatic of 'the historical layering underpinning cultural production in the "European" Middle Ages'.[74]

As the extensive research of Karla Mallette and others has shown, Sicily's Islamic and Norman-Islamic past had been a point of cultural preoccupation for some time before Sciascia's time, in the writings of a number of nineteenth-century Sicilian philologists, historians, and orientalists whose work responded closely to the volatile politics of Italy's move toward national unification (Mallette, 2005, 2010).[75] Sciascia's argument for the centrality of Islamic culture to Sicily's history was deeply influenced by the work of the most famous of these nineteenth-century scholars, Michele Amari, whose 1854 account of Siculo-Arab history, *Storia dei Musulmani di Sicilia* remains the best-known study in the concerted historiographic attempt to give account of the impact of '*I nostri saracini*' on the island's history and character. Amari's voluminous study explores both the period of Islamic rule from the ninth to the eleventh century, with its the hybrid Byzantine-Islamic culture, and the period under the rule of the Norman kings, who despite their Northern European provenance and nominal Christianity were deeply immersed in the island's Muslim culture. The two kings who have received most attention in this respect are King Frederick II and his grandfather King Roger II, the 'baptized sultan'[76] at the centre of Ali's novel, whose self-presentation was deeply imbued with the iconography of Islamic rulers[77] and who presided over a court in which Arabic poetry flourished along with Islamic medicine and geography.

---

[74] Sharon Kinoshita, 'Translatio/n, Empire, and the Worlding of Medieval Literature: The Travels of *Kalila wa Dimna*', *Postcolonial Studies* 11.4 (2008), 372.

[75] Karla Mallette, 'Orientalism and the Nineteenth-Century Nationalist: Michele Amari, Ernest Renan, and 1848', *The Romanic Review* 96.2 (2005), 233–52; Mallette, '*I nostri saracini*: Writing the History of the Arabs of Sicily', *California Italian Studies* 1.1 (2010), 1027.

[76] Menocal, *Arabic Role*, 49.

[77] Karen C. Britt, 'Roger II of Sicily: Rex, Basileus, and Khalif? Identity, Politics, and Propaganda in the Cappella Palatina', *Mediterranean Studies* 16 (2007), 21–45.

In her study, *The Arabic Role in Medieval Literary History*, Menocal offers a vivid reconstruction of the Norman Sicilian court, which she describes as a 'virtuously incestuous'[78] extension of the Andalusian *convivencia*. Although control over the island had been 'lost by the Arabs to the Normans in the eleventh century' after two centuries of Muslim dominance, she argues that under Norman rule it was nevertheless 'an even more vibrant center of Arabic learning'.[79] In focusing on Sicily's Norman-Islamic culture, *A Sultan in Palermo* also elaborates on the portrayal of al-Andalus in *Shadows of the Pomegranate Tree*, depicting Sicily as a twin culture whose flourishing interfaith *convivencia* is nevertheless a fatally imperilled arrangement. In its broadening of the diasporic canvas, the novel offers a challenge to what Ross Brann and others have described as 'Andalusi exceptionalism'.[80]

One condition that distinguishes this third medievalist novel from Ali's previous two is the immediacy and intensity of the geopolitical context surrounding its production, and its visibility within the text. While *Shadows of the Pomegranate Tree* was written in the aftermath of the First Gulf War, and the fragile Israel-Palestine peace process was the general backdrop at the time *The Book of Saladin* was produced, *A Sultan in Palermo* was written during a period of open East-West conflict and in a climate of intensified Western suspicion toward the Islamicate world in the wake of the 11 September 2001 attack on the U.S.A. Produced in the early stages of the military occupation of Afghanistan and later of Iraq by the U.S. and its allies, the novel is less veiled than its predecessors in its allusions to contemporary events. It is difficult, for instance, not to see a parallel between the U.S.-led so-called 'Coalition of the Willing' who invaded Iraq and the novel's presentation of the Christian barons, bishops, and Lombards as a thuggish mass united only by mutual self-interest and anti-Muslim sentiment. This evocation of the Normans as models for and precursors of modern colonial violence is not new; as Clare Simmons, Reginald Horsman, and others have shown, it was regularly evoked in novels and commentary throughout the nineteenth-century Anglosphere, where it conversely served as a historical mandate and ennobling for the British

---

[78] Menocal, *Arabic Role*, 49.   [79] Menocal, *Arabic Role*, 64.
[80] Ross Brann, 'Andalusi "Exceptionalism"', in *A Sea of Languages*, 119–34.

Imperialism.[81] Ali's novel adds to the literature that represents the medieval past in such a way as to condemn what the Normans did and what they have come to stand for in the long history of colonial conquest and neocolonial incursion. It is also tempting to see the increasingly morally compromised Roger as a premodern avatar of western leaders like the British Prime Minister Tony Blair, whose hawkish turn during the Iraq War disillusioned many of his erstwhile supporters (Ali would so far as to call Blair a 'war criminal' in 2016 after the release of the Chilcot report on Britain's involvement in the Iraq War).[82] Ali ends his novel as his protagonist, the cartographer Muhammad al-Idrisi (who will be discussed below), sets out from Sicily seeking safe haven elsewhere in the Islamosphere. Recalling the dramatic television news footage coming out of Iraq at the time when Ali must have been writing or at least formulating the novel, it is hard not to be chilled by the novel's closing lines: 'He would go to Baghdad, the city that will always be ours. The city that will never fall. The city that will never fall' (239). In terms of Baghdad's 'medieval' history this could refer to the fall of Abbasid Baghdad, then the world's largest city, to the Mongol Empire in 1258; but it can safely be surmised that it is also evoking the more recent fall of Baghdad in 2003 to Western forces. And, finally, by foreshadowing a near future of Muslim displacement, statelessness, and devastation, Ali alludes proleptically and soberingly to the present moment of the novel's writing—and indeed to the decade and more beyond, the events of which have tragically confirmed its pessimistic vision.

As mentioned above, the novel focalizes this larger story through its protagonist al-Idrisi, the brilliant geographer, cartographer, and physician who in 1154 completed one of the medieval period's most famous world maps as part of the larger *Tabula Rogeriana/al-Kitab al-Rujari* (long title 'The Book of Pleasant Journeys into Faraway Lands'), a compendium of geographical knowledge compiled over the course of eighteen years with court patronage from Roger II. When the project is

---

[81] Clare Simmons, *Reversing the Conquest: History and Myth in Nineteenth-Century British Literature* (New Brunswick: Rutgers University Press, 1990); Reginald Horsman, *Race and Manifest Destiny: The Origins of American Racial Anglo-Saxonism* (Harvard: Harvard University Press, 1981).

[82] Democracy Now, interview with Tariq Ali: https://www.democracynow.org/2016/7/6/tariq_ali_on_chilcot_iraq_report.

proposed in the novel, al-Idrisi underlines to Roger that Sicily is ideal for the collection of travellers' knowledge because of its position at the 'centre of the world', as a stopping point for people travelling both east and west. Indeed, al-Idrisi himself comes to embody the cosmopolitan mobility of the Western Islamic intelligentsia, who circulated throughout its Western diaspora. Born in Ceuta on the North African coast, which was then part of the Andalusian *taifa* of Málaga, he was educated in Córdoba and travelled extensively around and beyond the Islamicate world, making it as far as central Europe, the Eastern Mediterranean, and even the Viking town of Jorvik. He lived in Sicily from young manhood until late in life, and is known to have died in Ceuta, his birthplace. Ali's technique in the Quintet of taking historical figures and rendering them allegorical is clearly visible in the case in his portrayal of the intellectual alliance between Roger and al-Idrisi. On the one hand it produces this astonishing work of cartography; on the other it brings both of them under suspicion in their respective faith communities, with al-Idrisi losing cherished friendships over accepting Norman patronage. Al-Idrisi's relationship with Roger raises the broader question of the ethics of living under occupation. Throughout the novel he questions what it means to have remained in Sicily when his best friend, a fictitious minor poet Ibn Hamid, has left for al-Andalus. Although al-Idrisi has always felt safe under the patronage of Roger, whose devotion to the interfaith pursuit of knowledge is never in doubt, he is nevertheless increasingly plagued by a recognition of his complicity, and as the Normans become more menacing, he becomes actively involved in organizing resistance among the people of his estate.

The benefits he enjoys as a result of his protected cooperation are, moreover, repeatedly contrasted throughout the novel with the life of Muslim Sicily's other famous son, the poet Ibn Ḥamdīs. Arabic poetry from the Islamicate diaspora is cited or directly quoted throughout Ali's quintet, but it is in *Sultan* that it takes on the status of pointed commentary, with Ibn Ḥamdīs being the most significant voice. Born in 1056 into a Sicily that was still Muslim but weakened by internecine strife between rival Emirs, Ibn Ḥamdīs's reaction to the Norman conquest in Sicily was to leave the island in the 1070s, seeking both fame and refuge in al-Andalus. His career took him around the Western Islamic diaspora from Seville to Tunisia and Morocco, and eventually to Majorca, where he died. Like many another medieval poet, he is partly so famous today because of the survival of his compiled verses (*diwan*). Menocal points out that while we know that extensive composition took place in Sicily—for instance, she mentions a now-lost eleventh-century anthology of 20,000 Siculo-Arabic verses by 170 poets—Ibn Ḥamdīs's *diwan* is one of only two extant and is available in only two manuscripts.[83] What has made him equally if not more famous, however, is his *ṣiqilliyyas*—his Sicilian poems of exile in which he yearns nostalgically for both lost homeland and lost youth. Granara's excellent work on Ibn Ḥamdīs discusses the poet's incorporation of the classical, pre-Islamic Arabic verse form the *qaṣīda* and how this same reverence for the Arabic tradition informs his use of nostalgic motifs.[84] None of this is directly germane, however, to Ali's use of the poet in the novel. Rather, when Ibn Ḥamdīs's verses are quoted, it is to meditate on the contradiction of a figure who chose exile as a kind of conscientious objection, but can never let go of the thought of Sicily, writing 'Chain yourself to your beloved homeland / Die in your own abode / And as the mind refuses to try out poison / Reject the thought of exile' (75). Ibn Ḥamdīs functions as a prick to al-Idrisi's conscience, making the latter feel like a collaborator and causing him to accuse the poems of sentimentality and excessive harshness toward the Norman kings (77). But by the end of the novel, as al-Idrisi readies himself to depart for Baghdad after Roger's death, he quotes the following lines from the poet approvingly: 'I exhausted the energies of war / I carried on my shoulders the burdens of peace' (226). The choice to seek asylum from a brutally occupied territory rather than stay and fight to no avail is ultimately accepted. Again, given the political backdrop of composition, in which millions of people in the Islamicate East were seeking asylum from warfare and occupation, this is a pointed conclusion at which to arrive.

Ali is far from the first to champion Ibn Ḥamdīs as a conscientious objector and anti-colonial figure. The philologist Amari, who was

<hr />

[83] Menocal, *Arabic Role*, 118; see also Mallette, 'Poetries of the Norman Courts', in *The Literature of Al-Andalus*, ed. María Rosa Menocal, Raymond P. Scheindlin, and Michael Sells (Cambridge: Cambridge University Press, 2000), 377–87.

[84] Granara, William, 'Ibn Ḥamdīs and the Poetry of Nostalgia', in *The Literature of Al-Andalus*, 390.

forced into exile from Sicily because of the Bourbon regime's negative response to his book on the Sicilian Vespers—a book described by Mallette as 'a revolutionary *manifesto à clef*'[85]—identified powerfully with the medieval poet as a political exile of conscience. Papallardo further points out that Ibn Ḥamdīs's rejection of Norman rule in Sicily also made him a forceful figure for Sciascia, whose interest in Islamic and Norman-Islamic Sicily grew as he followed the process of decolonization taking place across from Sicily in the Maghreb.[86] It is in this politicized vein that Ibn Ḥamdīs is also taken up by Ali: his contribution to medieval Arabic poetics is of little to no concern.

The other poet who is frequently cited in the novel is not Sicilian, but, rather, the single most famous Arabic poet of al-Andalus, Ibn Quzman. Among scholars of Arabic verse, Ibn Quzman is renowned for his innovative use of the *zajal*, a strophic verse form with established rhyme schemes which he rendered in a colloquial Hispano-Arabic that for scholars offers a valuable repository of the spoken Arabic of eleventh- and twelfth-century Muslim Spain.[87] But, again, this not the reason Ali includes him. Rather, Ibn Quzman's *diwan*, which celebrates everything from drunkenness to adultery and sodomy, encapsulates for Ali a medieval Islamic bon vivantism that he wishes to emphasize in order to counter the negative orientalism underpinning post-9/11 Western perceptions of Islam as fanatically fundamentalist and life-denying. In fact, as with the other two novels, despite the narrative pivoting on interfaith conflict, there is little actual religiosity in the world of the novel, apart from people's speech being sprinkled with standard religious phrases. As noted earlier in this chapter, Ali himself is open about wanting as an atheist to understand Islamic history, so it is unsurprising that the twelfth-century Sicily he gives his readers is, like his other portraits of medieval Islam, a sophisticated and permissive secular society that might at most be called 'culturally Muslim'. In this vein, al-Idrisi, about whose personal life historians know very little, has been gifted by Ali, like the family of the Banu Hudayl and Saladin in the earlier novels, with a compelling and convoluted love life. Not only does he have a wife and family on his estate

---

[85] Mallette, 'Orientalism and the Nineteenth-Century Nationalist', 235.
[86] Pappalardo, 'From Ibn Ḥamdīs to Giufà', 35.
[87] Menocal, *The Arabic Role*, 21.

in Noto (with his meddling arranged wife conveniently dying off-stage before readers can meet her), but also a long-time lover in King Roger's harem, Mayya, and then another lover, Mayya's younger sister Balkis, who is the wife of the Emir of Syracuse. The emir is infertile but al-Idrisi helpfully continues his line by impregnating Balkis and allowing the emir to believe that the son she bears is his rightful heir.

Al-Idrisi, who does heavy allegorical lifting throughout the novel, is also emblematic of medieval Islam's dazzling scientific rationalism. While Sicily might not have matched places like Córdoba, which gave birth to vital continuers of Aristotelian natural philosophy such as Ibn Rushd/Averroes, Ali makes much throughout the narrative of Idrisi's polymathic pursuit of geographical and physiological knowledge. In some ways this operates as a counterbalance to the potential for Ali's novel, notwithstanding the author's early life in the Islamic diaspora, to lapse into an alternative orientalism, with its sexual permissiveness and its voluptuous, knowing women echoing the tropes of earlier portraiture of 'oriental women'.[88] As discussed earlier in this chapter, the text's medieval setting makes it all the more vulnerable to a premodern exoticizing that reinforces the orientalism.

Ali's novels flirt with romantic orientalism in an attempt to forestall the negative kind in his readers. With its broad-brush and openly ideological approach to medieval Sicily, indeed to what Leonardo Sciascia's would call 'Sicily as a metaphor', Ali's novel forges a conceptual Islamic Sicily, as a precursor and a parallel to rehabilitate twenty-first century Islam in the eyes of his Anglophone readers, and to argue for the vision of a future geopolitical *convivencia*. In a world that seems more polarized than ever, it is not an unwelcome aspiration.

[88] See Mohja Kahf, *Western Representations of the Muslim Woman: From Termagant to Odalisque* (Austin: University of Texas Press, 1999).

| 3 |

The Name of the Hobbit

Halflings, Hominins, and Deep Time

On 11 December 2012, three days before the scheduled premiere of
Peter Jackson's much-anticipated *The Hobbit: An Unexpected
Journey*, the Asylum film company was poised for online and DVD
release of its 'mockbuster' film *Age of the Hobbits* until it was blocked
by a restraining order. The plaintiffs, Warner Bros, New Line Cinema,
MGM, and the producer Paul Zaentz Co, argued not only that the as-
yet unreleased film cashed in shamelessly on the global advertising
campaign for Jackson's film, but, more importantly, that Asylum's
film title constituted an infringement of their trademarked right to
the name 'Hobbit'.[1] This argument was accepted by the judge of the
United States District Court of California, who also concurred that it
constituted 'trademark dilution: which would in turn generate con-
sumer confusion'. The complainant made detailed objections to Asylum's initial use of a font that veered dangerously close to the legitimate
franchise's distinctive serifed gold lettering; but even when the poster
was revised to feature a more blockish font, it was still deemed to be in

---

[1] Warner Bros Entertainment Inc., New Line Cinema LLC, New Line Productions Inc.,
Metro-Goldwyn-Meyer Studios Inc., and the Paul Zaentz Company, Plaintiffs v The
Global Asylum Inc., Defendant, 2012, Complaint, United States District Court, Central
District of California.

World Medievalism: The Middle Ages in Modern Textual Culture. Louise D'Arcens, Oxford University Press.
© Louise D'Arcens 2021. DOI: 10.1093/oso/9780198825944.003.0004

violation because of Asylum's refusal to stop using the word 'Hobbit'. Asylum, a notorious mockbuster factory whose catalogue of cut-price piggybacking classics boasted in 2012 such almost-familiar titles as *Snakes on a Train*, *The Da Vinci Treasure*, *Sunday School Musical*, *The Day The Earth Stopped*, and *Transmorphers*, had never before had a film blocked on the basis of trademark violation or dilution, although they had been threatened with litigation before. It is telling that only their trespass into the legal minefield of Tolkien trademarking put them onto the wrong side of U.S. copyright law. The film was finally released in the U.S. in February 2013 under the new title *Clash of the Empires* [Figure 1], while its UK title was the more clearly Tolkienesque *Lord of the Elves*.[2]

A plot summary of *Clash of the Empires* would, arguably even more than its title, appear to support a case for intellectual property infringement: in it, as its plot synopsis attests, a diminutive, peaceful 'ancient people' must unite with humans to defend their freedom against an oppressive warlord and his dragon-riding minions. Upon watching the self-proclaimed 'epic fantasy adventure', however, all sense of familiarity abruptly drops away, as the viewer discovers that its hobbits are not Tolkien's Halflings. Rather—and this was the crux of Asylum's defence in the copyright infringement case—they are *homo floresiensis*, the short, large-footed hominin species from the Late Pleistocene era which had been unearthed in 2003 on the Indonesian island of Flores by a team of Indonesian and Australian archaeologists, palaeontologists, and geochronologists.[3] Despite the fact that in the film's pre-release campaign on Netflix Asylum explicitly mentioned that it was re-interpreting Tolkien's *Lord of the Rings*, the company responded to the first cease and desist letters from Warner Bros et al. by replacing their first poster caption 'Before there was Man', which might still be seen to be obliquely alluding to the early stages of Middle Earth's First Age, with the caption 'They're not Tolkien's Hobbits; They're Real'. Such demurrals notwithstanding, the film's narrative can be seen as a

---

[2] Joseph J. Lawson, *Clash of the Empires* (Asylum Pictures, 2012).

[3] For an account of the process from the perspective of one of the Australian Lead Investigators, see Mike Morwood and Penny van Oosterzee, *A New Human: The Startling Discovery and Strange Story of the 'Hobbits' of Flores, Indonesia* (Walnut Creek, CA: Left Coast Press, 2007).

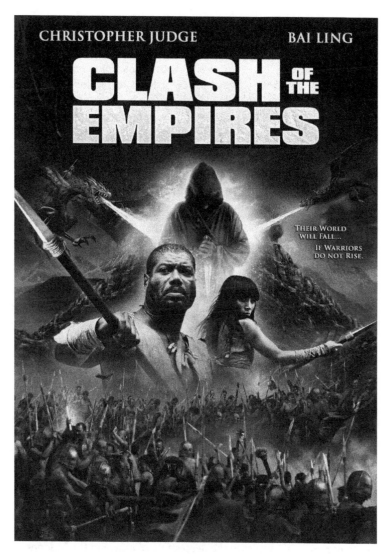

FIGURE 1   A revised poster for *Age of the Hobbit/Lord of the Elves/Clash of the Empires*. Reproduced with the permission of Asylum.

loose transposition of Tolkien's Middle Earth quest tale onto an imagined paleolithic Indonesia (though it was shot in Cambodia). Across its 87 minutes, a group of *homo floresiensis*, played by amateur Cambodian actors, forge a fellowship with 'giant' *homo sapiens* (represented here by former *Stargate SG-1* star Christopher Judge and Chinese-American actress Bai Ling) to rescue enslaved hobbits and fend off the army of the evil invading *homo erectus*, Java Man. The film gives a medievalizing nod to Flores's eastern neighbour, the island of Komodo, in the form of the giant airborne komodo dragons ridden by the cannibalistic Java Men.

In this chapter I wish to show that the convergence of fantastic medievalism and imaginative paleoanthropology in *Clash of the Empires* is in fact not at all an isolated phenomenon, but rather part of a larger story of world medievalism that has unfolded for over a decade now. For all its avowed status as a Z-grade cash-in, the film merely gives narrative form and schlock value to an intriguing convergence that has emerged directly out of the scientific, anthropological, and archaeological communities in the wake of the discovery of *homo floresiensis*. Ever since the Australian-Indonesian archaeological team came across this hominin's remains in a cave in Flores, the individual to which the bones belong has gone informally by the name of 'the hobbit'. However seemingly the naming might have come about, this chapter will explore its hardening into a trope, showing how this name came to shape the hominin's scientific and popular reception, and how it has given a very specific complexion to its embodiment of the global deep past. The story of the Flores hobbit would thus seem to be a *nonpareil* example of the centrifugal energy of medievalism, exposing the seemingly endless byways down which it can stray as it moves ever further from Europe, colliding with, absorbing, and transforming other stories as it goes. I have elsewhere described this as medievalism's 'feral' quality—its capacity 'to range wide, menacing our historical, cultural and ideological categories [and] to connect rhizomatically to different "regimes of signs"'.[4] Emanating from the philologically trained imagination of a British novelist to the deep strata of a cave in the Indonesian archipelago, where it sounds as a faint but distinct echo, the Flores

---

[4] Louise D'Arcens, 'Response to Bruce Holsinger: In Praise of Feral Medievalism', *Postmedieval* 1.3 (2010), 345.

hobbit takes us to the outer discursive, material, and geo-locational edges of medievalism as a phenomenon.

Having described this Indonesian-based exemplar as 'the outer edge' of medievalism, it should be emphasized that the region today called Southeast Asia was of course highly significant for medieval Eurasia, a point acknowledged widely at least since Abu-Lughod called for greater recognition of the region's place in the medieval world system.[5] For several centuries before its more widely known exploitation by European colonial powers from the sixteenth century on, the Indo-Malay region was an increasingly thriving part of a maritime mercantile and cultural network connected to China, East Africa, the Asian subcontinent, and Islamicate Eurasia. Prior to the island of Flores's colonization by the Portuguese, it sat within the region's archipelagic circuit of entrepôts and emerging Sunni sultanates. These sultanates, which developed from the thirteenth and fourteenth centuries and reflect the vital role of trade as a conduit for the spread of religion,[6] operated alongside, and in some cases displaced, what Geok Yian Goh has called the 'Buddhist ecumene', as well as the Hindu cultures that spanned the Southeast Asian mainland and the Indian subcontinent.[7] Marco Polo (1254–1374), Ibn Battuta (1304–69), and Niccolò de' Conti (1396–1469) were the most famous of the non-Asian medieval travel writers to describe (albeit with dubious reliability in Polo's case) the vigorous mercantile activity in this region and the pursuit of its sought-after goods, in particular spices and camphor. The subsequent entry of these exotic commodities into the diplomatic circuits of the medieval Mediterranean is attested in numerous inventories, and arrestingly captured in a recent study of the gifting by the Sultan of Egypt of an 'Australasian' (probably Indonesian) sulphur-crested cockatoo to the Sicilian court of Frederick II.[8] Alex J. West has suggestively called

[5] Abu-Lughod, *Before European Hegemony*.

[6] Geoff Wade, 'Early Muslim Expansion in South East Asia, Eighth to Fifteenth Centuries', in *The New Cambridge History of Islam*, vol. 3, ed. David O. Morgan and Anthony Reid (Cambridge: Cambridge University Press, 2010), 366–408.

[7] Geok Yian Goh, 'Beyond the World-System: A Buddhist Ecumene', *Journal of World History* 25.4 (2014), 493–513.

[8] Heather Dalton, Jukka Salo, Pekka Niemelä, and Simo Örmä, 'Australasian Cockatoo: Symbol of Détente between East and West and Evidence of the Ayyubids' Global Reach', *Parergon* 35.1 (2018), 35–60.

this region 'the medieval tropics', and has argued persuasively for its inclusion as a flourishing part of the world in the Middle Ages.[9]

Although, as Michael Laffan points out, the 'interlocking tradition of Buddhist, Muslim, and Sinic cultures would be further complicated by European engagements and Christianity',[10] Southeast Asian cultures' memory of their precolonial past has continued to be a source of regional pride, and has inspired heritage programmes that were not just equivalent to the medievalist restoration efforts undertaken in Europe but in fact were the product of a complex intersection with European practices. One revealing instance of this is the recent restoration of Borobudur, the ninth-century Buddhist temple in central Java. Despite being undertaken significantly during the period of decolonization in the second half of the twentieth century, and engaging with Indonesia's complex national cultural heritage politics, it also drew on aspects of archaeological method introduced by its former Dutch colonizers.[11] Another domain where the culture of the early Southeast Asian sultanates has been recovered and transmitted cross-culturally is literary studies. One fascinating instance of this is the 2010 English translation of the fifteenth-century Malay epic *Hikayat Hang Tuah* (*The Epic of Hang Tuah*) by poet and scholar Muhammad Haji Salleh. Salleh, who decades earlier had abandoned English to write poetry in Malay only, makes a twofold postcolonial gesture in this creative-scholarly translation. Not only does he recover the precolonial literature of the Malaccan court, but in so doing he borrows on and purposefully redirects the chivalric idiom of European romance and its nineteenth-century revisitation, combining frequent allusions to 'knights' (a term translating several Malay terms for warrior and leader) with Malay

---

[9] Alex J. West, 'Manuscripts and the Medieval Tropics', in *Toward a Global Middle Ages: Encountering the World through Illuminated Manuscripts*, ed. Bryan C. Keene (Los Angeles: The J. Paul Getty Museum, 2019), 94–8.

[10] Michael Laffan, 'Crossroads Region: Southeast Asia', in *The Cambridge World History*, vol. 6, ed. Jerry H. Bentley, Sanjay Subrahmanyam, and Merry E. Wiesner-Hanks (Cambridge: Cambridge University Press, 2017), 374.

[11] Marieke Bloembergen and Martijn Eickhoff, 'Decolonizing Borobudur: Moral Engagements and the Fear of Loss. The Netherlands, Japan, and (Post)Colonial Heritage Politics in Indonesia', in *Sites, Bodies and Stories: Imagining Indonesian History*, ed. Susan Legêne, Bambang Purwanto, and Henk Schulte Nordholt (Singapore: NUS Press, 2015), 33–66.

terms and honorifics.[12] The significance of Salleh's translation as a recovery of Malay classical literature is reflected in its publication by the Malaysian National Institute of Translation with, to quote Harry Aveling, 'an imitation leather cover, traditional illustrations and frequent lettering in the Jawi (Arabic-Malay script), which made it look like a venerable tome (a *kitab*) rather than a mere book'.[13]

I evoke the Indo-Malay region's rich involvement in the medieval world system, and its later celebrations of its precolonial past, not because these play a large role in the story of the Flores hobbit; indeed, the only link seems to be that the late Professor Raden Pandji Soejono, a senior Indonesian archaeologist involved in its excavation, was descended from the rulers of the Javan Majapahit empire.[14] Conversely, Southeast Asia's dynamic history is mentioned here to throw into relief the rich local past that has been occluded in the 'Tolkienizing' process through which *homo floresiensis* has come to be understood, a process which removes it from its Southeast Asian provenance, placing it instead within a fantastic medieval imaginary that is famously Anglo-Nordic in flavour. If, as I suggested above, this story reflects medievalism's 'feral' qualities, in which the medieval is promiscuously entangled with other cultural forms, it can equally be said to expose medievalism's capacity to domesticate: to take that which unsettles categories, and refashion it using an iteration of the medieval that is comforting, even homey in the case of Tolkien's placid halflings. The unearthing of *homo floresiensis* added an important missing chapter to the history of humans' migration around the planet; indeed, for several years, as I will go on to discuss, it was believed to challenge the prevailing story of human evolution itself. But the nature of this story as world medievalism is less to do with planetary migration and more to do with the forces of global capitalism to shape an unfamiliar Asian narrative

---

[12] Muhammad Haji Salleh, 'A Malay Knight Speaks the White Man's Tongue: Notes on Translating the *Hikayat Hang Tuah*', *Indonesia and the Malay World* 34.100 (2006), 395–405.

[13] Harry Aveling, 'A Malay Knight Speaks the White Man's Tongue', *Indonesia and the Malay World* 44.130 (2016), 401. The syncretism evident in Salleh's translation is symptomatic of what Su Fang Ng has called the 'accretionary globalism' of Malay epic, which carries in it 'souvenirs' of its journey of *translatio* across Europe, the Islamicate world, and Southeast Asia. See 'Global Souvenirs: Bridging East and West in the Malay Alexander Romance', *Literature Compass* 11.7 (2014), 395–408.

[14] Morwood, *A New Human*, 1–2.

into a familiar Western one. Despite, moreover, the global span of the Tolkien industry, which reaches from the author's birthplace of Bloemfontain, South Africa, to Hobbiton in Matamata, New Zealand, via Hollywood and cinemas across the world, it is still marked by the essentially nationalist imaginary of Tolkien and nineteenth-century medievalism. This reveals the capacity for Anglo-European medievalism to not just domesticate but in fact colonize narratives, and even material histories, that lie beyond its cultural, historical, and spatial remit.

The medievalizing of the Flores hominin is also revealing of the extent to which medievalism's domesticating capacity is extended not just across space but also through time. Again, even if *homo floresiensis*'s hobbit identity started off as an amusing shorthand, this chapter will explore how the traction it gained in the media and the scientific community reveals the potency of the medieval for channelling our understanding of the earth's deep historical past. On the one hand I wish to suggest that the discursive field that grew up around *homo floresiensis* discloses how medievalism's often mythic or legendary vision of the past allows 'the medieval' to function as the hinge into a kind of non-specific 'pre', a space that appears to have the urgency of history but also the scale of prehistory. On the other hand, it is important to register how the Flores hobbit exposes the potential of fantasy medievalism to obscure the depth of the past it purports to stand in for. The sentiment expressed by Jeffrey Jerome Cohen and Linda Elkins-Tanton in their book *Earth*, that '[t]he Earth is too large, too old, too inaccessible to our senses for us to fully apprehend it all [or] to contend with global-scale issues and events',[15] is clearly reflected in the imaginative folding of the prehistoric into the medieval. Asylum's *Clash of the Empires* pursues this logic ad absurdum by literally creating a paleolithic Indonesia modelled on Tolkien's medievalist mythography; but, as will become clear, this medievalist impulse is detectable throughout the decade and a half of *homo floriensis*'s representation in both popular and scientific reporting. In examining these representations, this chapter will also consider recent arguments which have claimed that medieval studies is complicit

---

[15] Jeffrey Jerome Cohen and Linda Elkins-Tanton, *Earth* (New York etc.: Bloomsbury, 2017), 11.

in the 'provincializing' of prehistory, and in the failure to imagine the lives of prehistoric humans as properly 'human'.[16]

The Flores Hobbit and the story of world humanity

Before going further into the detail of its medievalization, it is necessary to offer a brief account of *homo floresiensis*'s dramatic entrance into the world of paleoanthropology. In 2001 a joint Australian-Indonesian archaeological team led by the late Mike Morwood, a seasoned researcher in Australian Aboriginal archaeology, and researchers from the Indonesian National Centre for Archaeology headed to Indonesia looking for evidence of how people came to migrate from the Asian mainland to the Australian continent. The prevalent view that prompted the excavation, according to Morwood, is that the ancestors of Australia's indigenous people reached the continent's northern coast by crossing 'the deep, enigmatic Wallace Line, a moat separating mainland Asia and the world of islands between Asia and Australia' and then travelling south via the islands of Indonesia.[17] The team's pursuit of this migration history, which dates back tens of thousands of years, took them to the island of Flores, one of the Lesser Sunda Islands east of Java, about halfway between Australia and mainland Southeast Asia. Most specifically it took them to the giant cave of Liang Bua ('cool cave') on the western side of Flores, the elevation and dry, cool conditions of which were deemed to be ideal for human habitation, and hence propitious to the team's proposed research.

After working in the cave for two years, finding skeletons of komodo dragons, extinct giant rats, and storks and pygmy stegodons, they decided to excavate down to six metres, into the cave's Pleistocene

---

[16] See Daniel Lord Smail, *On Deep History and the Brain* (Berkeley and Los Angeles: University of California Press, 2008); and Daniel Lord Smail and Andrew Shryock, 'History and the "Pre"', *American Historical Review* 118.3 (2013), 709–37.

[17] Morwood, *A New Human*, xi. It should be noted that this migration theory has met with objections from some indigenous [change to 'Aboriginal'] Australians who argue that it fails to acknowledge their immemorial ancestral habitation of the continent known as Australia, and gives succour to those who wish to cast them as Australia's first wave of 'migrants'.

layer. Here they found bones that they soon determined to be a relatively complete skeleton of a small (106 cm tall) adult female human. The team initially gave this skeleton the unmemorable name of 'LB1' (that is, Liang Bua 1). With its tiny size, in particular its tiny brain cavity, and what were believed to be longish arms, short legs, and strikingly long, curved feet,[18] LB1 had the appearance of a very early hominin, not unlike some three-million-year-old skeletons unearthed in Africa. The thing that made it particularly remarkable to the excavation team, however, and to many in the palaeoarchaeological community, was that the sediment surrounding the skeletal remains turned out to be carbon dated to a very recent *c.*17,000 or 18,000 years. Because this post-dated the arrival of *homo sapiens* on Flores by around 30,000 years or more, the bones were inferred to be possible evidence of a human species that had not, like other early humans, been summarily wiped out by its later-arriving cousins, but instead experienced a 'significant overlap' with them before becoming extinct.[19] This potentially game-changing inference has since been found to be incorrect: a 2016 article by the team announced that their revised stratigraphic analyses of the cave floor had identified anomalous conditions in which younger sediment had come to overlay much deeper sediment. Because the younger sediment had been used to inferentially date the skeletal remains, this revised chronology led to a subsequent redating of the bones as being from between 100,000–60,000 years ago.[20] But it is important for this chapter's analysis of the hominin's reception that for over a decade the date of 17,000–18,000 years was the prevalent understanding of its age.

In the months and years after the publication of the team's results in *Nature* on 28 October 2004, debate raged over the identity and significance of these bones. This debate was high-stakes, for it was over nothing less than what was currently understood to constitute the human. This debate, which resembled in its vehemence those that have broken out each time a small early human has been found over

[18] William Jungers and Karen Baab, 'The Geometry of Hobbits: *Homo Floresiensis* and Human Evolution', *Significance*, December 2009, 159–64.

[19] M. J. Morwood, R. P. Soejono, et al., 'Archaeology and Age of a New Hominin from Flores in Eastern Indonesia', *Nature* 431, 28 October 2004, 1087–91.

[20] Thomas Sutikna et al., 'Revised Stratigraphy and Chronology for *Homo Floresiensis* at Liang Bua in Indonesia', *Nature* 532.21 (April 2016), 366–9, plus appendix.

the past century or so,[21] has revolved predominantly around the diminutive size and shape of the hominin, which have fuelled several conflicting hypotheses. The contours of this debate are as follows. On one side are adherents of what team members Bert Roberts and Thomas Sutikna called the 'sick hobbit hypothesis',[22] who argued, based on the belief that the bones were c.18,000 years old, that these were simply the remains of a pathological modern *homo sapiens* suffering from some kind of growth disorder which would account for its diminutive stature, and in particular for its tiny skull, which they believed to suffer from microcephaly (its brain was only a third of the size of *homo sapiens*'s). While the diagnosis of the underlying pathology has varied and continues to do so, this was the key argument that the bones constitute an interesting but not highly significant find, especially since the modern-day Flores population has a shorter average stature than many other places.

Those on the other side of the debate argued that *homo floresiensis* was in fact a separate and hitherto unknown species of human, possibly descended from *homo erectus*, known to have been in the Java area for up to 1.6 million years (this thesis now seems to be in abeyance), or, more controversially, descended from some other hominin that had migrated out of Africa—perhaps *homo habilis* or even some kind of australopithecene species.[23] Regarding the hobbit's small stature, a number of defenders have hypothesized that it might be due to the same insular effect that shrank the local stegodon down to less than a third of their former size.[24] Despite the tininess of the hobbit's skull, endocasts taken of it demonstrate that its brain morphology, along with other artefacts and fossil deposits found in the same strata, including knapped stone tools, animal bones with cuts and burnt hearth stones, point to a being with language, the capacity to plan, and the ability to

---

[21] John De Vos, 'Receiving an Ancestor in the Phylogenetic Tree: Neanderthal Man, Homo Erectus, and Homo Floresiensis: *L'histoire se Répète*', *Journal of the History of Biology* 42 (2009), 361–79.

[22] Richard 'Bert' Roberts and Thomas Sutikna, 'A Decade On and the Hobbit Still Holds Secrets', *The Conversation*, 30 October 2014, https://theconversation.com/a-decade-on-and-the-hobbit-still-holds-secrets-33454.

[23] Jungers and Baab, 'The Geometry of Hobbits', 161.

[24] Rex Dalton, 'More Evidence for Hobbit Unearthed as Diggers Are Refused Access to Cave', *Nature* 437.13 (2005), 934–5.

hunt cooperatively, butcher, and cook food. In other words, despite its brain size being well below the threshold of what has been believed to constitute the human, it ticks the key 'human' behavioural boxes. The recent redating of *homo floresiensis* now points with much greater certainty toward these features being species characteristics of an early human rather than evidence of a pathological modern human. At the time of the present chapter's writing, there is a strong consensus arguing that the hobbit is in fact a separate early human species, although as recently as 2018 some were still arguing for its status as a pathological modern human. Ironically, the Asylum Company unwittingly (though also insensitively) edged into the 'sick hobbit' debate in its decision to use a cast in *Clash of the Empires* made up significantly of actors with dwarfism to play the 'tree people', although these performers are mixed in with children and adult Cambodians whose small stature is not medically caused.

For many following the story of *homo floresiensis*'s re-emergence across the first decade or so, the establishing of the hobbit as a separate species was explosively significant. This was not just because it potentially offers a new account of the hominin migration out of Africa, but, more broadly, because its existence has been taken as further confirmation of the idea of the tree of human evolution being 'branchy', or even a 'bush' of differing and even contemporaneous species, rather than the triumphalist story of one species *Homo sapiens*'s inevitable evolutionary conquest over all others. This idea is most famously associated with evolutionary biologist Stephen Jay Gould, who in his much-cited early essay 'Bushes and Ladders in Human Evolution' challenges the unilinear 'ladder' model of Darwinian gradualism.[25] Although Gould died a year before the Liang Bua excavation got underway, his considerable Left-wing following linked his 'bush' theory posthumously to *homo floresienses*, arguing, in the words of Richard York, that the hobbit shows how the 'evolutionary development of our species was not a linear march to our current form, but rather a process of diversification of hominin species and subsequent pruning of lineages through extinction, with the present time, where we are the only extant hominin,

[25] Stephen Jay Gould, 'Bushes and Ladders in Human Evolution', in *Ever Since Darwin: Reflections in Natural History* (New York and London: W. W. Norton, 1977), 56–62.

being historically atypical'.[26] The 2007 location of hominin remains in the Philippines, which in 2019 were attributed to the new species *Homo luzonensis*, points to Asia as a fertile proving ground for Gould's theory.[27]

The 17,000–18,000 timeframe placed around *homo floresiensis* up until the redating in 2016 was also believed to potentially alter the story of *homo sapiens*'s theorized role in the demise of other early humans. Although there is contestation of the narrative wherein *homo sapiens* survived at the expense of its cousin species, it has become a customary belief based on our supposed supersession of Neanderthal humans, who went extinct around 39,000 ago. Because *homo sapiens* is believed to have been in the Indonesian region for *c.*45,000 years, and the fragments of thirteen *homo floresiensis* individuals were until 2016 believed to have been found in deposits ranging from 95,000 to as recently as 12,000 years ago, this was taken to be evidence of contemporaneous existence of the two human species. This contemporaneity, moreover, was arresting because it was much more recent than that between *homo sapiens* and Neanderthals. While the Liang Bua site has not yielded evidence that *homo floriensis* and *homo sapiens* could have met, it is not the only site on Flores with evidence of early human life, and Mike Morwood was optimistic before his death in 2013 that more solid evidence of contemporaneity might be found either in Flores or the surrounding islands of Sulawesi, Java, or Timor. Now that the hypothesized likelihood of any contemporaneity between *homo floresiensis* and *homo sapiens* has been drastically scaled back, it could seem redundant, at least from a scientific point of view, to dwell on this period of mistaken inferences. But it is precisely these early years between 2003 and 2016 that are of interest for an analysis of the medievalization process: for it was these years, when simultaneous existence seemed a genuine possibility, which gave rise to the narrative of the tenacious little Indonesian Hobbit.

[26] Richard York, '*Homo Floresiensis* and Human Equality: Enduring Lessons from Stephen Jay Gould', *Monthly Review* 56.10 (2005), 16.

[27] F. Détroit, A. S. Mijares, J. Corny, G. Daver, C. Zanolli, E. Dizon, E. Robles, R. Grün, and P. J. Piper, 'A New Species of *Homo* from the Late Pleistocene of the Philippines', *Nature* 568.7751 (2019): 181–6.

Medievalizing the prehistoric

Returning to the mockbuster *Clash of the Empires*, the contemporaneity between modern humans and the 'real' hobbits (as the film's publicity called them) is rendered not just temporally, but spatially, as cheek-by-jowl cohabitation. Here the community of *homo floresiensis*, called 'tree people' and 'half-men', live in territory immediately adjacent to that occupied by the 'giant' *homo sapiens*, while the looming mountain of the 'rock men', Java Man, lies further off. This cohabitation quickly develops into cooperation as the humans Amthar (Judge) and Laylan (Ling) join with the Bilbo/Frodo-equivalent character Goben (Sun Korng) to free his people from the threat of Java Man. Given inter-species cooperation is a feature of *The Hobbit* and *Lord of the Rings*, it is difficult to disentangle whether such cooperation in the film is mod-elled solely on Tolkien, or also to some extent on the speculations in the scientific literature about possible encounters between earlier and later *homo* species. Statements from Asylum at the time are confusing: screen writer Eric Forsberg, a self-proclaimed Tolkien fan, insisted there was 'no connection' between the film and the Flores hominin,[28] but this is contradicted by statements from the company defending the film against Warner Bros et al.'s legal injunction, which in fact reveal the producers' awareness of the scientific literature, even if this has been gained through the filter of its popular media reportage. As will become apparent, Asylum's claim that *Clash of the Empires* is based on 'the real-life human subspecies, Homo Floresiensis, discovered in 2003 in Indonesia, which have been uniformly referred to as "Hobbits" in the scientific community' does have a basis in fact, as does its statement that 'a simple Google search of Hobbits and archaeology reveals dozens of articles containing the term "Hobbit(s)" in the title'.[29] Despite the fact that the company's statements were deemed spurious in the con-text of their trademark violation defence, it is certainly the case that

[28] James Handel, '"Age of the Hobbits" Is Now "Clash of the Empires"', *The Holly-wood Reporter*, 12 December 2012, https://www.hollywoodreporter.com/thr-esq/age-hobbits-is-clash-empires-401897.
[29] Matthew Belloni, '"Hobbit" Lawyers Threaten "Age of the Hobbits" Movie', *The Hollywood Reporter*, 17 October 2012, https://www.hollywoodreporter.com/thr-esq/hobbit-lawyers-threaten-age-hobbits-377892.

there existed by 2012 a considerable body of refereed archaeological literature, published in some of the most prestigious scientific journals, which not only had '"Hobbits" in the title' but proved to be an unexpected and fertile site for fantastic medievalism, cultivating an intimate relationship between the hominin and Tolkien's famous Halfling.

One fact that emerges clearly in the literature around the archaeological find is that *homo floresiensis*'s medievalist career has been tied from the very beginning to the global phenomenon of Tolkien cinema, with the 2012 mockbuster skirmish being only a late episode in the longer story. In September 2003, when the discovery was made, the enormous box-office success of the first two films in Peter Jackson's *Lord of the Rings* trilogy meant that Tolkien's hobbits and their medievalesque Middle Earth occupied people's thoughts worldwide, with much anticipation building toward the release in December 2003 of the final instalment, *The Return of the King*. At the instigation of Mike Morwood, the project's lead palaeoarchaeologist, and his young Indonesian colleagues, LB1 has gone informally by the name of 'the hobbit' or just 'Hobbit'. In *A New Human*, Morwood's account of the team's discovery, he recounts floating the taxonomic name *Homo hobbitus* with the team, saying that at the time 'the main appeal of using it as a species name . . . was the thought of learned types at conferences having to seriously discuss the attributes and evolutionary history of *Homo hobbitus*'.[30] He was also, he says, keenly conscious of providing a hook for the public to recall and envisage the hominin, using as his model the 1973 naming of the African hominin *Australopithecus afarensis* 'Lucy', which he believed made her famous, while such spectacular recent finds as the 7 million-year-old *Sahelanthropus tchadensis* have remained anonymous, he suggests, due to the unpronounceability of their scientific names. Nevertheless, some in the team were scandalized, and felt that this was 'trivializing' of the find and its significance. In what is possibly a revealing commentary on Tolkien fans and even medievalismists in general, team member Peter Brown was also concerned that once the news was public the name would attract 'the lunatic fringe', and 'result in every loon on the planet phoning me' (something he

---

[30] Morwood, *A New Human*, 152.

claims did happen).[31] In terms of the scientific nomenclature, Morwood says '[i]n the end commonsense prevailed' and the team agreed to use *homo floresiensis*; but several years later he expressed some lingering regret about this, and still believed the hobbit moniker to be 'singularly appropriate', pointing out that the little hominin had nestled in a cosy hole and had run from komodo dragons, 'the Flores version of the fire-breathing dragon, Smaug'.[32] In any case, the young Indonesian field archaeologists' affectionate name for the hominin stuck, regardless of scientific naming. The team's geochronologist Bert Roberts has stated that his main concern at the time was that the 'stroppy' Tolkien estate would take action against them for using 'their trademarked words'.[33] This was not an unreasonable concern, as would later become clear when volcanologist Brent Alloway was prevented by the estate from giving the name 'The Other Hobbit' to a public lecture he was to deliver in Wellington, New Zealand, in December 2012, just a week before Asylum films was also restricted by Warner Bros et al.[34] In response to Roberts's fear, Morwood settled on dropping the definite article so they would not seem to be claiming the hominin was *the* Hobbit, as in Tolkien's creation.[35] But the article also stuck, and to this day the petite hominin is universally and stubbornly known as 'the Hobbit'.

The name 'hobbit' appears in an article in the very first issue of *Nature* in which the news was officially broken to the scientific community.[36] This would certainly have captured the imagination (and might even have been at the urging) of the journal's senior editor Henry Gee, himself an avid Tolkienist who, by sheer coincidence, was in the late stages of completing his 2004 book *The Science of Middle Earth* when the investigating team sent their explosive draft articles to the journal for refereeing. Gee mentions in a footnote of the book's 2014 revised edition that *The Science of Middle Earth* was published just

---

[31] In Ewen Callaway, 'Tales of the Hobbit', *Nature* 514, 23 October 2014, 424.
[32] Morwood, *A New Human*, 152.
[33] Callaway, 'Tales of the Hobbit', 424.
[34] Justin Lee, 'Hobbit Makers Ban Uni from Using "Hobbit"', *Newshub*, 24 October 2012, https://www.newshub.co.nz/nznews/hobbit-makers-ban-uni-from-using-hobbit-2012102417.
[35] Callaway, 'Tales of the Hobbit', 424.
[36] Dalton, 'More Evidence for Hobbit', 1029.

one week before the game-changing news about *homo floresiensis* broke, adding '[i]t is another delicious circumstance that the creature, being very small and living in caves, was christened the Hobbit'.[37] While the timing might have been coincidental, there is a striking convergence between Gee's interpretation of Middle Earth, as an environment hosting human and nonhuman-adjacent creatures, and the 'bushy' multi-species paleolithic Flores conjured up by the early interpretation of the Liang Bua discovery (and later depicted in Asylum's *Clash of the Empires*). The influence of Gould's evolutionary paradigm is clearly evident in Gee's parallel account of Earth and Middle Earth:

> it has become more and more apparent that human evolution, like the evolution of any other species, is quite unlike a ladder and more like a bush, in which collateral lines of human-like species evolved in parallel, with the implication that many different species of human or human-like creatures coexisted on the Earth at any given time in the past several million years. To have one single species of human in possession of the whole planet—as is the case at the present day—is extremely unusual.... Men, in Middle Earth as in the Real World, remain largely unaware that for most of their history they were unaccompanied by other, similar species—in Tolkien's terms, other 'speaking peoples'.[38]

Gee goes on to take the comparison further. Claiming that in Tolkien's created world Elves, Dwarves, and other beings that are now fairy-tale creatures 'need not have been idle fancies, but the natural end-products of a process of decay leading to disappearance', he reminds readers that Neanderthals and *homo erectus* were more real than might be suggested by such figures as the 'the orang pendek of Malay folklore'.[39] Taking into account that Gee was writing the first edition of his book at the same time as he was shepherding the first *homo floresiensis* articles through *Nature*'s publication process, one can recognize an oblique allusion to the then-still-confidential Flores hobbit in the reference to the hominoid *orang pendek* ['short person'] of Sumatran (not Malay) folklore.

---

[37] Henry Gee, *The Science of Middle Earth*, rev. 2nd ed. (Golden, CO: Reanimu Press, 2014), 198 n. 87.

[38] Gee, *Science of Middle Earth*, 197.   [39] Gee, *Science of Middle Earth*, 197–8.

Gee's last comment is also of note because, as a number of cultural anthropologists have pointed out, the naming of *homo floresiensis* after Tolkien's decidedly Western Halfling is noteworthy not just for its timely alignment with Jackson's *Lord of the Rings* films in the first decade of the twenty-first century, but for its avoidance of linking the hominin to indigenous Flores folklore, in particular to the figure of the *ebu gogo* (which means 'ravenous grandmother' because of her habit of stealing food and even children from human settlements) or its cognate figure *lae ho'a*. In the folklore of Flores, the *ebu gogo* is a small hairy apelike/hominoid creature with pendulous breasts said to dwell in the forest and make murmuring sounds. Although the name comes from another part of the island, the area around where the Hobbit was found has its own cognate figure which goes by several names, and which some have speculated might be related to *homo floresiensis*, especially because this figure is believed by locals either to be still alive or to have survived recently enough to be in living memory.[40] Gregory Forth, anthropologist and author of the studies *Beneath the Volcano: Religion, Cosmology and Spirit Classification among the Nage of Eastern Indonesia* (1998) and *Images of the Wildman in Southeast Asia* (2008), claims that for the purposes (as discussed earlier) of fixing the hominin's identity in the mind of the public, the name *ebu gogo* was canvassed by the team as a possible name for it, but was ultimately rejected. Morwood later mentions that it was in fact Forth's own *Beneath the Volcano* that had inspired the team's interest in *ebu gogo*. Forth, however, in an article contemplating the meaning of the recent find for anthropologists, expresses relief that the name was rejected; he felt it would be stretching the *ebu gogo* legend too far, since the creature's morphology in the local legends is not an exact fit with *homo floresiensis*. Nevertheless, he regrets the 'hobbit' appellation more:

> [C]asting *Homo floresiensis* as 'hobbits' potentially obscures the essential difference between an empirical species, designated a member of the genus *Homo* like ourselves, and the images of literary fiction. Like hobbits, both *Homo floresiensis* and *ebu gogo* are

---

[40] Gregory Forth, 'Hominids, Hairy Hominoids, and the Science of Humanity', *Anthropology Today* 12.3 (2005), 15.

products of human imagination, but the images have different bases: tangible, skeletal and archaeological evidence in one case, and the testimony and traditions of local people in the other. Rather than simply assuming that these traditions are as fantastical as Tolkien's fiction, the challenge for social anthropologists is to discover the correct relationship between the palaeontological and ethnographic images and the true source of their resemblance.[41]

It is clear here from his objections that although Forth was partly concerned that the 'hobbit' naming, which he believed was 'evidently to communicate effectively to a wider public',[42] would distance the hominin from its Southeast Asian locale and hence from Flores's indigenous folklore, he was more troubled that the find's significance would be 'trivialized' by it being named after a fictional character, especially since that character had been the subject of recent block-buster movies.[43] Even before *Homo floresiensis* was unearthed, Forth had been suggesting that *ebu gogo*-type creatures 'may well have some empirical basis in a former component of the human population of Flores'.[44] This belief was granted more solidity when the hominin was believed to be 13,000–18,000 years old; writing in 2005, when the shock of this initial dating was still being processed, Forth tentatively explored the idea, not just that the relatively young hominin might be related to *ebu gogo*, but that *ebu gogo* or its cousins might be the hominin's still-living descendants, hidden in the island's dense forests. He feared that this possibly still extant creature would be caught up, like the komodo dragons that live on Flores as well on the neighbouring island of Komodo, in a touristic frenzy all due to the fantasy medievalization now imposed upon them. Although the subsequent redating of the Liang Bua remains would appear to deliver a blow to survival theses such as Forth's, his prediction about tourism has proven at least partly correct. The representation of the cave on the Flores Tourism website not only features the excavation site as an attraction, but calls it 'The Hobbit Liang Bua'. Moreover, despite the 2016 redating, which

---

[41] Forth, 'Hominids', 16.   [42] Forth, 'Hominids', 16.
[43] Forth, 'Hominids', 16.
[44] Forth, *Beneath the Volcano: Religion, Cosmology and Spirit Classification among the Nage of Eastern Indonesia* (Leiden: KITLV Press, 1998), 109.

refutes former excitement about significant coexistence between *homo floresiensis* and *homo sapiens*, the site continues in 2019 to tantalize would-be visitors with the question 'Did modern humans cross with the hobbit?'[45]

It appears ultimately that the name of *ebu gogo* was not taken up at least partly because of the team's unwillingness to instrumentalize the folklore of their Flores colleagues, a number of whom have now gone on to receive training from them as archaeologists and tour guides. It is equally true, though, that the researchers also did not wish to compromise the credibility of their find by appearing to resemble cryptozoologists—people who make claims about the survival of apparently prehistoric creatures such as the Sasquatch and the Loch Ness Monster. The otherwise troubling fantasy-medievalization of *homo floresiensis* in this case was less compromising, precisely because it was so culturally and historically distant from Pleistocene Flores, unlike the local folkloric creatures whose names were canvassed as alternative monikers.

Nevertheless, another troubling effect emerged as an unanticipated by-product of the naming. The issue of *Nature* in 2004 in which the research was first announced to the world featured a portrait of *homo floresiensis* by the Australian nature artist Peter Schouten in which the hominin is presented as unmistakably male—Morwood wryly remarks that 'the penis and testicles were a dead giveaway'[46]—despite descriptions of the bones specifying that the 'pelvic anatomy strongly supports the skeleton being a female'.[47] Although Morwood relates being surprised by the image, which gained an iconic status for a while, he concluded that it was probably knowledge that the hominin was a hunter that led Schouten to gender it male, and dwelt no further on the matter. An alternative reading is that this masculinization is tied in with the racializing of the hobbit as white: the 'hobbit' nomenclature served to link the hominid to the conspicuous homosociality of Tolkien hobbit narratives, in which female hobbits, while mentioned (ironically

---

[45] Flores Tourism website, 'The Hobbit Liang Bua': http://florestourism.com/places/the-hobbit-liang-bua/.

[46] Morwood, *A New Human*, 193.

[47] P. Brown, T. Sutikna, et al., 'A Small-Bodied Hominin from the Late Pleistocene of Flores, Indonesia', *Nature* 431.28 (2004), 1055.

mostly as ancestors) are kept firmly in the background, while male characters joined forces with males of other species to save Middle Earth. The 'gender deficiency' of Schouten's portrait, to use Morwood's phrase[48] was later corrected in a bust by American palaeo-artist John Gurche[49] and in a full body reconstruction by French palaeo-sculptor Elisabeth Daynès[50] which emphasized the breasts of the stocky hominin [Figure 2]. Later still, members of the original team created a digital

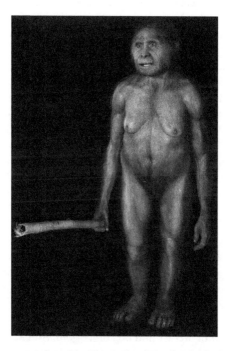

FIGURE 2   Reconstructed model of *homo floresiensis* by Elisabeth Daynès. Reproduced with the permission of S. Plailly/E. Daynès/Science Photo Library.

[48] Morwood, *A New Human*, 193.
[49] John Gurche, reconstruction of *homo floresiensis*, http://gurche.com/homo-floresiensis.
[50] Atelier Daynès, reconstruction of *homo floresiensis*, https://www.elisabethdaynes.com/paleoart-reconstructions/.

facial reconstruction that was also female.[51] Nevertheless, artists continue to produce masculine iterations of the female hominin for consumption by a public accustomed to thinking of hobbits as male creatures.

While the original naming might have been jovial, with a slightly opportunistic dimension of fame-grabbing to it, it gave rise irresistibly to a notable Tolkienism in the reporting of the Flores discovery. This is arguably to be expected in non-specialized media reporting: Carmelo Amalfi and Leigh Dayton's 2005 article 'Hobbits May Be Earliest Australians' in the national broadsheet *The Australian*[52] came early into a fifteen-year-long avalanche of articles relating sensationalized versions of the research to a global public with a seemingly inexhaustible appetite for scientific Tolkienisms. But what is more surprising is that these fantasy motifs are also conspicuous in the academic and refereed scientific reporting, especially in recent years when the status of the hominin as a separate human species has come to be widely accepted, and a lighter note has been permissible in the reportage. This Tolkienism far exceeds the isolated and somewhat coy use of the word 'hobbit'. From about five years after the first article in *Nature*, we begin to find articles such as the one published in the *Journal of Biogeography* called 'Fellowship of the Hobbit: The Fauna Surrounding *Homo Floresiensis*'.[53] This same motif then trickled out to the more populist palaeontology podcast website *PASTTIME*, which in January 2014 released a program whose title 'The Hobbit—An Unexpected Discovery' clearly plays on the title of Peter Jackson's *The Hobbit: An Unexpected Journey*. The convergence of Tolkien, his cinematic afterlife, and palaeontology is evident both in the opening lines of the podcast description: 'Hobbits! Dragons! Weird elephants and ancient mysteries! It's the stuff of literary and box office gold. And it turns out it's the stuff of prehistory, too!', and in a map showing the migration of early humans, which is not only called 'An Unexpected Journey' but uses a

[51] Susan Hayes, Thomas Sutikna, and Mike Morwood, 'Faces of *Homo Floresiensis* (LB1)', *Journal of Archaeological Science* 40 (2013), 4400–10.

[52] Carmelo Amalfi and Leigh Dayton, 'Hobbits May Be Earliest Australians', *The Australian*, 8 December 2005.

[53] Hanneke J. M. Meijer, Lars van den Hock Ostende, Gert van den Bergh, and John de Vos, 'The Fellowship of the Hobbit: The Fauna Surrounding *Homo Floresiensis*', *Journal of Biogeography* 37 (2010), 995–1006.

font reminiscent of the distinctive insular-style font found on Tolkien's famous maps of Middle Earth.[54] In *The Conversation* in October 2014 we even find team members Bert Roberts and Thoma Sutikna themselves mobilizing Tolkienisms when discussing plans for future excavations on Flores, saying 'It is not beyond reason to think that another new species of human might be discovered in the years ahead, and a new companion welcomed into the palaeoanthropological Fellowship of the Ring'.[55]

The most arresting instance of this genre is Ewen Callaway's 2014 article in *Nature* called 'Tales of the Hobbit'. A retrospective on the discovery, it features a two-page illustration of the research team by artist Señor Salme in which they are arranged in a configuration reminiscent of the cinematic depictions of the Fellowship of the Ring in Peter Jackson's trilogy. In another instance of feral medievalism, lead investigator Mike Morwood is drawn as a kind of fusion of Bilbo Baggins and Indiana Jones from the famous adventure films, holding aloft the hominin skull, which gleams brightly like a cross between Tolkien's coveted ring and the crystal skull in the Indiana Jones film of that name.[56] This alludes to the tale of international intrigue and literal skulduggery that developed in the wake of the bones' discovery, as narrated by Morwood and the Australian members of the team. By the team's account Teuku Jacob, head of the paleoanthropology laboratory at Gadjah Mada University, claimed the bones for his own laboratory, literally walking off with them in a leather case (Salme's illustration depicts Jacob hiding the coveted hobbit skull in his luggage among his clothes), later refusing the others access to both the bones and purportedly interfering in their access to Liang Bua.[57] Meanwhile he took clandestine silicone casts that broke the hominin's fragile jaw and destroyed its pelvis.[58] This was partly scientific rivalry—Jacob was a vehement advocate of the 'sick hobbit thesis', and did not believe it to be a distinct species of *Homo*—and partly symptomatic of cross-cultural

---

[54] PASTTIME podcast, 'Episode 10 Field Guide: The Hobbit—An Unexpected Discovery', http://www.pasttime.org/2014/01/episode-10-field-guide-the-hobbit-an-unexpected-discovery/.
[55] Roberts and Sutikna, 'A decade on', n.p.
[56] Callaway, *Fellowship of the Hobbit*, 424.
[57] Morwood, *A New Human*, 223–35.
[58] Dalton, 'More Evidence for Hobbit', 934–5; Callaway, *Fellowship of the Hobbit*, 425.

proprietorialism: Jacob was not on the team and the Australians wanted their own bone analyst, whereas among Indonesian paleo-anthropologists Jacob was a revered senior figure and it was customary to seek his opinion, although the decision to hand the bones over to him without consultation seems to exceed this. Local and international opinion on this ranged from condemnation of Jacob for reckless interference to censure of the Australian team for Western arrogance and playing the role of 'sheriffs'.[59]

This dispute did not fall neatly along national lines—both Austra-lians and Indonesians had critics among their own compatriots. But the 'sheriff' comment was pointed: it was commonly used in Indonesia to describe Australia's role in supporting Timor Leste's independence from Indonesia and the perception of it as a self-appointed 'sheriff' of the Asia-Pacific region. It reflects the fact that the ownership of the hobbit, and the friction around its Western medievalization, also need to be contextualized in terms of the particularly strained relations between Indonesia and Australia in the first decade of the twenty-first century. In addition to Timor Leste, tensions had also developed between the two nations over Australia's treatment of asylum seekers in its Indian Ocean territorial waters close to Indonesia, and in the wake of the October 2002 Bali bombings perpetrated by the Southeast Asian extremist group Jamaah Islamiyah which killed eighty-eight Aus-tralian nationals. Although Morwood's account mostly focuses on the scientific and institutional politics of the scandal, he does allude to the larger political situation: the meaning of Jacob's 'sheriff' barb is not lost on him. Forth, furthermore, reports that the Australian archaeologists are apparently called 'scientific terrorists' by the people of Flores, whose sense of ownership of the hominin Forth describes as nationalistic[60]—again, a loaded word in the wake of the Bali bombing. All of this lies behind the hybrid medievalism of the Callaway article and its illustrations: here Tolkienian medievalism, like the medievalisms discussed in this book's previous chapters, becomes a lightning rod that channels complex inter-personal, institutional, and regional politics.

[59] Morwood, *A New Human*, 215.
[60] Forth, 'Flores after *Floresiensis*: Implications of Local Reaction to Recent Palaeoanthropological Discoveries on an Eastern Indonesian Island', *Bijdragen tot de Taal-, Land- en Volkenkunde* 162.2/3 (2006), 339.

Medievalism and containment of the deep global past

Although it is clear that the hobbit analogies were originally intended to be used lightly, this convergence of palaeontology with Tolkienesque medievalism is, as I will go on to suggest, not simply serendipitous but highly apposite. For just as the Flores discovery was widely interpreted for over a decade as offering tantalizing evidence for a Gould-esque evolutionary 'bush' characterized by the coexistence of multiple human species, so too, as Gee has pointed out in *The Science of Middle Earth*, Tolkien's legendarium features a world in which Man, itself a category consisting of earlier and later types, coexists through a series of lengthy ages with a range of related species such as Hobbits, Elves, Wizards, and others. In an excellent essay on prehistory in Tolkien's corpus, John D. Rateliff argues that Tolkien depicts 'a plural humanity sharing the Earth (Elves and Dwarves and Men and Hobbits) ... as they did historically during the period when Neanderthals and Cro-Magnons shared the earth'.[61] Although the later ages are ruled by Man, the species is portrayed by Tolkien as flawed and frail in a way that resists both human exceptionalism and progress as a historical trajectory. Rateliff points out, rather, that Tolkien's world of gradual extinction, which moves from 'a multiplicity of wonders and speaking races ... to a world in which we find ourselves profoundly alone', is in fact deeply elegiac in its overarching tone and arc.[62] Like similar conservative English thinkers of his time such as G. K. Chesterton, Tolkien was prepared to acknowledge evolution as a plausible account of physiological development; but considering the importance of Catholicism to his worldview, and in particular his belief that modern secular culture represents a lapse from the teleological guarantees offered by Christianity, it is not surprising that his fantasy world reflects a degree of scepticism toward the progressivist claims of evolutionary biology and scientific palaeontology. Philip Irving Mitchell summarizes Tolkien's view of time,

---

[61] John D. Rateliff, ' "And All the Days of her Life Are Forgotten": *The Lord of the Rings* as Mythic Prehistory', in *The Lord of the Rings 1954–2004: Scholarship in Honor of Richard E. Blackwelder*, ed. Wayne G. Hammond and Christina Scull (Milwaukee: Marquette University Press, 2006), 86.

[62] Rateliff, 'All the Days of her Life', 71.

arguing that his writings can be described as combining Christian eschatology with a limited 'accommodation of evolution'.[63] This is captured in the oft-quoted lines from his 1931 poem 'Mythopoeia':

> I will not walk with your progressive apes
> Erect and sapient. Before them gapes
> The dark abyss to which their progress tends....[64]

While the allusion to 'erect and sapient' apes marks an acceptance of human evolution from hominid ancestors as biological fact, the image of a 'dark abyss' as the ultimate destination of modern human progress marks a decisive rejection of Darwinian triumphalism, which in its modern arrogance creates the self-aggrandizing idea of 'the primitive' and derides earlier humans as infantile precursors to modern man. In this respect Tolkien seems to offer both a fitting precedent to the *homo floresiensis* researchers, and an apt mythic world for their prehistoric Hobbit.

'Mythopoeia' also expresses Tolkien's belief in the necessity of myth-making to bestow significance and depth on the ancient physical and cultural past currently being uncovered in a spirit of dry, scientific demystification:

> Blessed are the legend-makers with their rhyme
> Of things not found within recorded time.[65]

This sceptical accommodation of the positivistic method of earth sciences is also present in the deep temporal complexion of his medie-valesque Middle Earth. Gee, Mitchell, Deborah Sabo,[66] and Gerard Hynes[67] have all traced the impact of the deep-time sciences, in par-ticular geology and archaeology, on Tolkien's world-building. In most cases the traces of the deep past of Middle Earth seem more neolithic in form (such as standing stones on the Barrow-Downs); but the

---

[63] Philip Irving Mitchell, '"Legend and History Have Met and Fused": The Interlocution of Anthropology, Historiography, and Incarnation in J. J. R Tolkien's "On Fairy Stories"', *Tolkien Studies* 8 (2011), 2.

[64] J. R. R. Tolkien, *Tree and Leaf, Including the Poem Mythopoeia* (Boston: Houghton Mifflin, 1989), pp. 83–90, ll. 119–21.

[65] Tolkien, *Tree and Leaf*, ll. 91–2.

[66] Deborah Sabo, 'Archaeology and the Sense of History in J. R. R. Tolkien's Middle-Earth', *Mythlore* 99/100 (2007), 91–112.

[67] Gerard Hynes, '"Beneath the Earth's Deep Keel"', *Tolkien Studies* 9 (2012), 21–36.

primordial societies of the Drúedain/Woses/Wild Men, who built the megalithic Púkel-men statues, appear to hark back to a remnant palaeolithic past lurking beneath the medieval surface of the novels' world. Additionally, *Lord of the Rings* also, as Hynes points out, contains passing remarks that register the growing scientific consensus around the profound timescales of geological change, with ancient characters such as Gandalf/Olórin attesting to the forces behind mountain and landmass formation.[68] A closer look at deep time in Tolkien's work reveals, then, that however incidental the archaeologists' allusions to his hobbits might have been, they fortuitously illuminate the significance of the Flores hominin for contemporary discussions about the being of humans, past and present.

It is not the key aim of this chapter, though, to pursue a detailed comparative study of Tolkien's time-and-species-dense legendarium with contemporary archaeology's account of the developmental courses of human evolution. Rather, what I wish to discuss in this final section of the chapter is what this convergence of the Middle Ages and prehistory can tell us about the suggestive but also the suppressive power of 'the medieval' within the contemporary global-temporal imaginary. Speaking specifically of Tolkien, Rateliff argues that even if Tolkien intended to develop an imaginary deep past that was specifically English (as opposed to, say, the broader Britishness of the Arthurian legends), '[his] deliberate vagueness about specific one-on-one correlations...grants his myth transcendence and "applicability"'.[69] But this same point can be made of a very large number of medievalist texts which avail themselves of the plasticity of the Middle Ages as an imaginative rather than an historical category that is both inside and outside of history. It is true that the 'applicability' Rateliff identifies in the 'timeless' medieval is generally assumed to point forward to modernity: the politics in the fantasy television series *Game of Thrones* would be an obvious example, alluding, for instance, to twenty-first-century attitudes toward gender and religious extremism. My argument here is that this image of pastness is also able, conversely, to fold the prehistoric into the historical imaginary so that the unimaginable, deep past is made imaginable under the sign of the medieval. The

---

[68] Hynes, 'Beneath', 26–7.   [69] Rateliff, 'All the Days of her Life', 90.

non-specificity of this kind of Middle Ages fuses, to borrow the temporal taxonomy deployed by Gilles Deleuze, the urgency of *chronos* or measurable time with the scale of *aeon*, immeasurable time, paraphrased by Deleuze scholar Anna Powell as duration, the 'pure, empty form of time'.[70] The Middle Ages becomes then an image of pastness itself.

Voluminous textual evidence from the scientific and popular media shows that this was registered intuitively, though not necessarily reflectively, in the repeated transposition of the medieval onto the palaeolithic in the wake of *homo floresiensis*'s uncovering. The extent of this is visible in Warner Bros' litigation case against Asylum over the DVD cover for *Clash of the Empires*, in their claim that the image on the Asylum film's DVD cover features 'medieval battles', when it in fact it depicts loin-clothed Asian male figures armed with spears alone—no armour, helmets, swords, shields, or other medieval battle paraphernalia in sight. Even taking into account the plaintiff's vested interest in identifying plagiarism of their Hobbit brand, this claim demonstrates the extent to which the medieval visual idiom has come to determine how the deep past is understood in contemporary popular culture.

But this phenomenon is not limited to the case of the Flores hobbit and its reception. Just a few years earlier the 1999 film *The 13th Warrior*, directed by John McTiernan and based on the American author Michael Crichton's 1976 novel *Eaters of the Dead*, had offered another instance of medievalism in which the deep human past is folded into a mythicized medieval setting.[71] The story is presented in the novel's faux-scholarly Introduction as an historical account, an annotated version of a translated collated edition of the writings of the renowned tenth-century Arab traveller, Ahmad Ibn Fadlān, and is narrated by him. Both novel and film start, notably, with a famous historical scene of medieval intercultural contact in which Fadlān (played in the film by Antonio Banderas), encounters a group of Rus Vikings on the banks of the Volga.[72] Although this meeting is attested in Fadlān's writings, which describe the appearance and habits of the

---

[70] Anna Powell, *Deleuze, Altered States, and Film* (Edinburgh: Edinburgh University Press, 2007), 141.

[71] John McTiernan, *The 13th Warrior* (Touchstone Pictures, 1999).

[72] It is this cross-cultural encounter that inspired the painting that appears on the cover of this book. "Funeral of an old Rus nobleman" by Henryk Siemiradzki.

Rus, the story soon breaks free from its historical source and takes Fadlān on a journey that fuses recorded history with a historic-mythic version of the Norse past in which the deep prehistoric past continues to exist in the present. Accompanying the Vikings back to their homeland in his prophesied capacity as the eponymous '13th warrior' on an undisclosed heroic mission, Fadlān arrives in a Northern country closely modelled on the scene and narrative of the Old English heroic poem *Beowulf*: its king Rothgar, warrior Buliwyf, and great hall Hurot all closely echo major names in the poem. In this Northern setting the humans contend with a hominid population called the Wendol (a name combining *Beowulf*'s monstrous adversary Grendel and the Wendlas, the tribe of the herald Wulfgar), who inhabit the same time-space, lurking at the edges of medieval society and threatening its order with murderous nightly raids.

This interspecies hostility is, of course, already a feature of the medieval poem on which this part of the story is based. But the novelization, using what Hugh Magennis calls 'Crichton's rationalist approach, which seeks always to "explain" the marvellous in logical terms',[73] explores the idea that a lifeform that is depicted as monstrous in *Beowulf* might in fact point to evidence of the historical coexistence of different *homo* species. The Wendol are described as follows by Fadlān, when he finally gets a proper look at one of their corpses:

> [T]hey appeared to be manlike in every respect, but not as any man upon the face of the earth. They were short creatures, and broad and squat, and hairy on all parts of their bodies save their palms, the soles of their feet, and their faces. Their faces were very large, with mouth and jaws large and prominent, and of an ugly aspect; also their heads were larger than the heads of normal men. Their eyes were sunk deep in their heads; the brows were large, and not by virtue of hairy brows, but of bone; also their teeth were large and sharp, although it is true the teeth of many were ground down and flattened. In other respects of their bodily features and as to the organs of sex and the several orifices, they were also as men.[74]

---

[73] Hugh Magennis, 'Michael Crichton, Ibn Fadlan, Fantasy Cinema: *Beowulf* at the Movies', *OEN* 35.1 (2001), 34. Magennis also notes that, significantly, Crichton dedicated *Eaters of the Dead* to the pioneering palaeoanthropologist William W. Howells.

[74] Michael Crichton, *Eaters of the Dead* (New York: Knopf, 1976), 91.

These standard 'Neanderthal' tropes (heavy brows and jaws, broad hirsute bodies) are followed by a description that makes them seem even more ancient: they are 'like enough to men as monkeys are also like men'.[75] The film, possibly in response to growing archaeological consensus by 1999 that Neanderthals cannot have survived into the Viking Age, is more circumspect. It depicts the Wendol as anatomically modern but culturally primitive, using a mélange of well-worn tropes that sit uncomfortably between ideas of the prehistoric and the indigenous, including face paint, animal skins, drumming, and skilled horsemanship. But the novel, published some twenty-three years earlier, is more ready to entertain a theory of a multi-*homo* Middle Ages: its faux scholarly frame reinforces Fadlān's description by including an Appendix in which scholars debate whether the Wendol as described by the Arab traveller are modern humans or in fact 'remnant Neanderthals', citing evidence from modern palaeontology about whether, despite an absence in the fossil record, there could have been such a lengthy period of overlap between that species and modern 'Cro-Magnon' humans. The novel's preoccupation with transtemporal cohabitation of species should not surprise anyone familiar with Crichton's later more famous novel *Jurassic Park* (1990), although in the latter case the cohabitation results from the modern scientific regeneration of prehistoric species rather than their survival into the historical era. What is distinct between these two novels' depiction of cohabitation, though, is that in *Eaters of the Dead* Crichton settles on the Middle Ages as the period in which early human survival and a continuing deep past can plausibly be imagined.

It is true that in *Eaters of the Dead/The 13th Warrior*, the prehistoric human past being portrayed is more limited in its reach, as the Neanderthal were a human species whose remains have not been found beyond the Eurasian continent and British Isles. In this respect the book and film differ from the Tolkienizing of the Flores Hobbit. By imagining medieval Scandinavia harbouring an in situ prehistoric population, Crichton's and McTiernan's texts stop short of replacing Southeast Asian prehistory, and the global migratory past it potentially signifies, with a fantasized Western Middle Ages. And even though the

---

[75] Crichton, *Eaters*, 93.

texts' Arab narrative perspective on medieval Scandinavia is the product of Crichton's own creative continuation of Fadlān's much shorter
text, this is a medieval world characterized by cross-cultural and interfaith camaraderie, which complicates the global hegemony of the
Anglo-European medievalist imaginary inherited from Tolkien. Nevertheless, the untimely prehistoric realm the Wendol inhabit is, like that
of the Flores hobbit, only imaginable via a modern recreation of a
medieval perspective. These early humans' being in the world is not
disclosed through their linguistic self-representation or cultural expression, but rather through the traces of grotesque violence left behind
after their nightly raids and their behaviour in battle, which, although
no more bloodthirsty than that of the Vikings, is narrated by Fadlān as
more evidence of their savagery. When they retreat from the climactic
battle in fatal disarray, leaving behind their dead, their demise is met
with jubilation by the modern humans,[76] and the reader is invited to
share in that triumph.

This would appear to exemplify perfectly the view of historian Daniel
Lord Smail, who both alone and in co-authored work with anthropologist Andrew Shryock, has argued that as a legacy of the now discredited
paradigm of sacred history, the medieval has come to stand in as the
'origin' of civilization in a way that occludes the prehistoric past and
those deeply ancient peoples who can no longer speak for themselves.
In *On Deep History and the Brain*, moreover, he singles out early
medieval Europe as a period that has been 'so thoroughly barbarized'
within the modern historical imaginary 'that it could stand in for the
Paleolithic past'. Within this logic of historical displacement, the European Middle Ages become an 'epistemological veil that screens us from
the speechless past',[77] speaking on its behalf in an act of deep historical
colonization. This is even more explicit in an article in *postmedieval*
that reprises his claims in *On Deep History and the Brain*, where he
argues that the rise of the discipline of medieval history in the nineteenth century was 'founded on the exclusion of a deeper past' and in
particular on an exclusion of 'the peoples of the Palaeolithic [who] are
the original subaltern'.[78] He, in conjunction with Shryock, attributes
the continuation of this exclusion of the prehistoric to what he sees to

---

[76] Crichton, *Eaters*, 94.   [77] Smail, *Deep History and the Brain*, 13.
[78] Smail, 'The Original Subaltern', *Postmedieval* 1–2 (2010), 180–6.

be medievalists' disciplinary and institutional vested interests in claiming the medieval as the emergence of the modern, as well as to a
generalized attitude in which the deeper past is 'subservient to the
demands of modernity, whether our attitudes toward modernity are
adulatory or insurgent'.[79]

He does temper this account further into his essay with Shryock;[80]
but Smail's argument about medievalists making unreflective claims for
the medieval as 'the origin of the modern' requires further qualification
from the perspective of medievalism studies. Scholars of medievalism
are far more accustomed to engaging with non-academic texts and
social discourses in which the medieval, far from being understood as
proto-modern, is cast as the amorphous antithesis of an equally
amorphously formulated 'modern'. And, moreover, it is common to
see this 'premodernizing' account being mobilized ideologically in a
way that has been negative, with the medieval signifying, as studies of
medievalism have frequently and rightly noted, as an 'abjected other',
a primitive and 'discredited obverse' vis-à-vis the triumphally conceived
modern. As the 'premodern', it is the repository of all that has been
superseded. Even those more nostalgically positive representations of it
as a period of plenitude, moral consensus, and long tradition still
situate it as the opposite of the modern. Medievalism studies is a field
which, far from regarding the modern as an uncontested term, or as a
legitimating horizon for the medieval, explores rather the exceptionalist
tendency of modernity to define itself against an unspecified 'pre' to
which the Middle Ages is a gateway, but which stretches from the
premodern to the prehistoric. So while Smail and Shryock are right to
raise concerns about the 'othering' gesture involved in designating an
arbitrary point in history 'pre', it is possible to reformulate their claim
by suggesting that the medieval has been the victim of this gesture at
least as often, or more often, than it has been complicit in it.

To recognize the ways in which the medieval has been stigmatized in
relation to modernity is not to deny the Eurocentrism that has shaped
medievalism, which features throughout this book as an assumption
which is now in need of exposure and overturning. I want to end by
suggesting, however, that the question of historical colonization in

---

[79] Smail and Shryock, 'History and the "Pre"', 711.
[80] Smail and Shryock, 'History and the "Pre"', 715.

instances such as the Hobbitizing of *homo floresiensis* needs also to be considered as partly symptomatic of the restricted scope of the modern historical imagination. There is no doubt that when contemplating the vast tracts of time ushered in by geological and palaeontological under-standings of world history, the modern Western mind is brought up short against the limitations of its historical imagination: in *On Deep History and the Brain*, Smail argues 'while historians gradually came to accept the long chronology as a geological fact . . . we have not yet found a persuasive way to plot history along the long chronology'.[81] What the naming and reception of the Flores hobbit shows is how the 'premo-dern' medieval has come to stand in for the deep past not only insofar as it simply replaces and occludes it, but also insofar as the medieval has itself been designated the gateway to the long 'pre-'. By a kind of logic of historical substitution, the unimaginable 'original' face of deep time is replaced by something which offers an orientation even though it is widely understood to be a substitution. As this chapter has shown, it is an imperfect substitution, especially because it places earlier humans, especially non-European humans, outside of history. Smail mentions this threatened oversight in terms of Africa, a vital source of human history's 'long chronology';[82] the story of the Flores hobbit shows that the deep history of Asia is also vulnerable to occlusion under the star of the Europeanized, premodernized medieval. The name of the hobbit, with all its imperfections, thus allows but also prevents us from seeing the face of the deep human past.

[81] Smail, *Deep History and the Brain*, 13.   [82] Smail, *Deep History and the Brain*, 14.

| 4 |

Ten Canoes and 1066

Aboriginal Time and the Limits of Medievalism

The medieval and the coeval

Australian archaeologist Billy Griffiths ends his award-winning study of Australian archaeology, *Deep Time Dreaming: Uncovering Ancient Australia*, with an anecdote summarizing 'the dissonance at the heart of Australian cultural life'.[1] Driving back from Lake Mungo in the far inland of New South Wales, where Australia's oldest known Aboriginal human remains revealed themselves in 1968 and 1974, he encounters 'a different vision of the deep past': an enormous plaster statue of an Egyptian pharaoh towering over the carpark of a stopover called Tutankhamun's Bistro. For Griffiths, the jarring incongruity of this symbol in the middle of rural Australia has an ideological significance, crystallizing 'the anxieties of a settler nation still struggling to come to terms with its deep Indigenous history, fumbling for foreign symbols to fill an unfamiliar land'.[2] He argues that the difficulty non-Aboriginal Australians have absorbing the vast age of Mungo Woman

---

[1] Billy Griffiths, *Deep Time Dreaming: Uncovering Ancient Australia* (Melbourne: Black Inc., 2018), 291.

[2] Griffiths, *Deep Time Dreaming*, 291.

World Medievalism: The Middle Ages in Modern Textual Culture. Louise D'Arcens, Oxford University Press.
© Louise D'Arcens 2021. DOI: 10.1093/oso/9780198825944.003.0005

and Mungo Man, dated to 40,000 years, is reflected in their readier grasp of the less confounding antiquity of Egyptian burial remains. It is 'the pharaoh's hollow gaze' Griffiths wishes to challenge, by exposing readers to the unmatched depth of the Aboriginal past of the continent now known as Australia. And yet despite this declared mission, he provocatively concludes his book by calling Aboriginal culture 'the classical culture of this continent'.[3] In so doing, he invokes a conflicted legacy. On the one hand he repeats Claude Lévi-Strauss's laudatory but also Europeanizing gesture of describing Australian Aboriginal people as the 'intellectual aristocrats' of early humanity;[4] on the other, he heeds Aboriginal leader Noel Pearson's call for Aboriginal song cycles and mythic stories to be considered 'the Iliad and Odyssey of Australia',[5] revered testaments to the continent's deep and complex human history.

The classicizing trope corresponds closely to the medievalist trope I discussed in the previous chapter on *homo floresiensis*. It carries with it the same capacity to both illuminate and obscure the past outside Europe, as well as running the same risk of diminishing the vast depth and scale of that past in order to communicate its significance to the Eurocentric world. This chapter continues the meditation on the ways in which medievalism operates as a global discourse beyond Europe, but in this case the focus will be on complicating medievalism's relationship to the world-encircling yet also exclusionary phenomenon of British settler colonialism as it has manifested in Australia. This relationship, as I will show, has been largely, and unsurprisingly, one of complicity, in which medievalism has operated as a reinforcing discourse of colonial Anglocentrism. But the 'worlding' of medievalism will not stop there; I will also examine the surprising potential, in the hands of Aboriginal agents, for invocations of a 'Middle Age' that troubles and even displaces the Western timeline on which the idea of the medieval depends. The chapter will examine this through a discussion of the 2006 film *Ten Canoes*, an acclaimed Aboriginal

---

[3] Griffiths, *Deep Time Dreaming*, 296.

[4] Josephine Flood, *Archaeology of the Dreamtime*, rev. edn (Sydney: Collins, 2004); cited in Billy Griffiths and Lynette Russell, 'What We Were Told: Responses to 65,000 Years of Aboriginal History', *Aboriginal History* 42 (2018), 44.

[5] Noel Pearson, 'A Rightful Place: Race, Recognition, and a More Complete Commonwealth', *Quarterly Essay* 55 (Melbourne: Black Inc., 2014), 36; Griffiths, *Deep Time Dreaming*, 292.

cross-cultural text co-produced by the Yolŋu people of Arnhem Land in Northern Australia, in which a 'Middle Age' is both invoked and portrayed in an entirely defamiliarizing way. It is widely acknowledged that 'the Middle Ages' is itself a temporally relative term, signalling an era whose identity is shaped by its designated position between the more 'absolute' eras of the classical and modern West; a major purpose of this book has been to show how medievalist texts also often end up exposing the cultural relativity, and indeed the limitations, of the term. As I will show, nowhere is the temporal and cultural relativity of the 'Middle Ages' more apparent than in *Ten Canoes*.

The chapter will also continue to explore the multi-faceted implications of contemporary texts' folding of pasts from outside of Europe into the Western concept of 'the medieval', or into concepts of coevalness with the European Middle Ages, as well as considering the implications of calling this 'medievalism'. On the one hand, I will consider how it can seem potentially valuable to understand a text like *Ten Canoes*'s engagement with local and Southeast Asian pasts in the period 500–1500 CE in terms of its relationship to medievalism, because to do so brings the indigenous past into the realm of the global-historical rather than situating that past in the domain of 'timeless' or fossilized prehistory to which colonial culture has relegated it. As I have discussed elsewhere, descriptions of pre-contact Aboriginal pasts as 'timeless' have been troubling in their misattribution of primitive, ahistorical changelessness to non-European cultures—a misattribution, moreover, that has mandated the imposition of European culture and *chronos* over indigenous 'nature' and its apparently limitless *aeon*.[6] The gesture of 'denying coevalness' to non-Europeans, and in particular to colonized peoples, is now widely recognized as a symptom of European colonization, as a result of Johannes Fabian's critique of anthropology in *Time and the Other*,[7] and its uptake in cultural histories of colonialist mentalité, including Anne McClintock's *Imperial Leather: Race, Gender, and Sexuality in the Colonial Contest*. McClintock describes the

---

[6] Louise D'Arcens, *Old Songs in the Timeless Land* (Cawley/Turnhout: University of Western Australia Press/Brepols, 2011), 4.

[7] Johannes Fabian, *Time and the Other: How Anthropology Makes its Object* (New York: Columbia University Press, 1983).

emergence under British imperialism of a trope that she calls 'anachronistic space', in which:

> Imperial progress across the space of empire is figured as a journey
> back in time to an anachronistic moment of prehistory. By extension,
> the return journey to Europe is seen as rehearsing the evolutionary
> logic of historical progress, forward and upward to the apogee of the
> Enlightenment in the European metropolis.[8]

Within this paradigm, 'the agency of the colonized... [is] disavowed and projected onto anachronistic space: prehistoric, atavistic, and irrational, out of place in the historical time of modernity'.[9] Billy Griffiths and Lynette Russell, an anthropological historian and descendent of the Wotjabaluk people, argue that approaching Australia's pre-contact Aboriginal past as historical enables us to 'engag[e] with the deep past as a transformative human history'[10]—a human history, moreover, I will go on to discuss, whose transformations are at least in part tied up with Aboriginal Australia's relations to the global medieval, in particular with pre-European contact with Muslim Southeast Asia and the larger Islamicate world of the southern hemisphere. In this respect the chapter resonates with Wai-Chee Dimock's argument that conceptions of American history must undertake a Braudelian 'scale enlargement' to encompass the 'long history of America as a Native American habitat'.[11] On the other hand, the chapter raises the question of whether including pre-colonial-contact Aboriginal culture within the scope of world medievalism is itself an inescapably colonizing gesture that can only reinscribe Eurocentric epistemologies, or whether this problem can be ameliorated by bringing perceptions of the global medieval into dialogue with Aboriginal perceptions of time and history. The geo-temporal and ideological complexities of medievalism as a 'world' phenomenon are thrown into sharp relief, as I will show, by

---

[8] Anne McClintock, *Imperial Leather: Race, Gender, and Sexuality in the Colonial Context* (New York and London: Routledge, 1995), 40.

[9] McClintock, *Imperial Leather*, 40.

[10] Griffiths and Russell, 'What We Were Told', 31.

[11] Wai Chee Dimock, 'Introduction: Planet as Duration and Extension', in *Through Other Continents: American Literature across Deep Time* (Princeton, NJ and Oxford: Princeton University Press), 4.

Ten Canoes as a text that narrates pre-contact time in a way that simultaneously addresses itself to Western and Yolŋu audiences.

World and Country

Before turning to how the film exposes the limits of medievalism, we must again revisit the idea of 'world', which I have been finessing in each chapter of this book in response to the text being discussed. When applied to a film like *Ten Canoes*, the term 'world' needs to be used with some significant caveats. At the most fundamental level, its status as a cinematic work shaped by Yolŋu principles requires that any description of it as 'world cinema' must adopt the 'polycentric' model advocated by Lúcia Nagib, in which 'world cinema is simply the cinema of the world', rather than reproducing the liberal pluralist model that accommodates 'peripheral' cinemas but still takes the stylistic and narrative canons of Hollywood to be the norm.[12] Reaching beyond the question of its medium, however, is the broader phenomenological question of what 'world disclosure' *Ten Canoes* can be said to be undertaking; what world it invites viewers to apprehend. And it is here that the word 'world' seems an imperfect fit: its collocation with ideas of the 'global' means that it risks being paradoxically both too broad and too narrow. It captures neither precise locality nor how the local functions as an iteration of the cosmos, in the way this film demands. Marisol de la Cadena and Mario Blaser argue that when Western academic disciplines encounter unfamiliar indigenous phenomenologies, 'rather than resting on colonial world-making [they should be] in constant negotiation with worlding practices that might not—or might not only—reflect them'.[13] This corresponds to the argument by historians Caroline Dodds Pennock and Amanda Power that as a term, globalism bears in it a historical substrate that is

[12] Lúcia Nagib, 'Towards a Positive Definition of World Cinema', in *Remapping World Cinema: Identity, Culture and Politics in Film*, ed. Stephanie Dennison and Song Hwee Lim (London and New York: Wallflower Press, 2006), 30–7.
[13] Marisol de la Cadena and Mario Blaser (eds), *A World of Many Worlds* (Durham and London: Duke University Press, 2018), 18.

fundamentally exclusionary to those who have been subjected to globalizing processes:

> Thus, in the established narrative of intensifying 'global' integration, the 'globalizing' is done largely by Europeans and their empires; it is among them that the capacity for thinking and operating on a worldwide scale is concentrated, and their specific approaches and achievements are treated as archetypal. Communities and societies that are not seen as playing an active part in this particular process tend to be excluded by default: mere forerunners, spectators or victims of the progress of more advanced nations. Yet their exclusion does not seem to provoke doubt about whether the contemporary world is really 'globalized', or prompt reflection on whether employing the terminology of 'the global' is more ideologically driven than geographically accurate.[14]

To this end, I argue that any discussion of the 'world' *Ten Canoes* discloses must be expanded, yet also deepened and localized, by exploration of how it articulates the intricate and encompassing Aboriginal idea of 'Country'.

Simultaneously numinous and material, capacious yet specific, Country is at the very heart of Australian Aboriginal ontology and cosmology. A group of Aboriginal and non-Aboriginal researchers known as the Bawaka Collective, working on and with Yolŋu Bawaka Country, have defined it thus:

> Country is the Aboriginal English word which encompasses [a] vibrant and sentient understanding of space/place which becomes bounded through its interconnectivity. Country and everything it encompasses is an active participant in the world, shaping and creating it. It is far from a passive backdrop to human experience, a scene in which humans live their lives, a place in which to embed academics' research.[15]

---

[14] Caroline Dodds Pennock and Amanda Power, 'Globalizing Cosmologies', *Past and Present* 238, Supplement 13 (2018), 88.

[15] Bawaka Country, Sarah Wright, Sandie Suchet-Pearson, Kate Lloyd, Laklak Burrarwanga, Ritjilili Ganambarr, Merrkiyawuy Ganambarr-Stubbs, Banbapuy Ganambarr, and Djawundil Maynuru, 'Working With and Learning From Country: Decentring Human Author-ity', *Cultural Geographies* 22.2 (2015), 270.

This group, who also write under the name Gay'wu group of women (Gay'wumirr Miyalk Mala), preface their award-winning 2019 book *Song Spirals* by elaborating further that Country:

> means not just land, but also the waters, the people, the winds, animals, plants, stories, songs and feelings, that becomes together to make up place. Country is alive for us, it cares for us, communicates with us, and we are part of it.[16]

Murri researcher Brooke Collins-Gearing et al., discussing Country as a concept common to Aboriginal people throughout Australia, describe it as 'the energy and agency of the lands around us and not just a physical setting'.[17] From these explanations it is clear that Country's foundation on an ethos of reciprocity between the human and the more-than-human reflects its profound difference from the instrumentalist impetus underlying the world-encompassing geopolitical phenomena of colonialism and globalization. The expansionist ambitions of these phenomena, moreover, contrast with Country's groundedness in specific topographies which have their own ancestral stories (or Dreaming), from which issue law and knowledges that shape the identities and practices of the people belonging to that Country. So, although an examination of *Ten Canoes* might point to it as 'world medievalism' insofar as it illuminates how medievalism is transformed by its uptake by cultures around the world, it is more apposite to describe the film as offering a medievalism 'of Country'. Another culturally attuned phrasing would be 'medievalism *on* Country', as used by Jenna Mead in her meticulous analysis of a doctoral degree conferral that took place in 2015 on Yolŋu Country.[18] Mead's use of the widely recognized Aboriginal English phrase 'on Country' has the virtue of firmly anchoring the medievalism she explores in the specific locality where it occurred, thereby offering a counterpoint to the

---

[16] Gay'wu Group of Women, *Song Spirals: Sharing Women's Wisdom of Country through Songlines* (Sydney: Allen & Unwin, 2019), ix.

[17] Brooke Collins-Gearing et al., 'Listenin' Up: ReImagining Ourselves through Stories of and from Country', *M/C Journal* 18.6, December 2015, 1, ezproxy.newcastle.edu.au/login? url=http://search.ebscohost.com/login.aspx?direct=true&db=ufh&AN=111814601&site=edslive.

[18] Jenna Mead, 'Medievalism on Country', in *The Global South and Literature*, ed. Russell West-Pavlov (Cambridge: Cambridge University Press, 2018), 264–306.

assumption that medievalisms appearing outside of Europe are produced solely by the flows of global mobility.

Ten Canoes

Ten Canoes, the winner of the *Un Certain Regard* jury prize at the 2006
Cannes Film Festival, is the result of a collaboration between Dutch-
born *balanda* (non-Aboriginal) Australian director Rolf de Heer and
members of the Yolŋu community of Ramingining in North-East
Arnhem Land.[19] De Heer's key collaborators were his co-director
Peter Djigirr and the acclaimed veteran actor and ceremonial dancer
David Gulpilil. The film's intertwining plots, which will be discussed
below, were developed collaboratively between de Heer and the people
of Ramingining. Gulpilil, a Yolŋu man who initially brokered the
relationship between de Heer and the Yolŋu, provides the film's voiceover narration. Although as storyteller he goes unseen and unnamed
throughout the film, to many Australian viewers his voice is instantly
recognizable, especially his distinctive laugh, which first featured in
Nicholas Roeg's cult film *Walkabout* (1971). Filmed on location in the
Arafura Swamp and its environs, *Ten Canoes* is the first Australian film
to include dialogue entirely in the languages of the Yolŋu Matha group.
It exists in three different versions, which reflects its aim to speak to
both global and local audiences: one version is in Yolŋu Matha with
English subtitles and voiceover narration, one includes Yolŋu Matha
dialogue but with no narration, and the third features both dialogue and
narration in Yolŋu Matha. This production of different versions is part of
an approach aimed at managing carefully the selective release and
withholding of protected Yolŋu knowledges. This practice is approved
by Screen Australia's Pathways and Protocols guide, which states that
filmmakers must respect Aboriginal people's right to 'maintain the
secrecy of Indigenous knowledge and other cultural practices'.[20] Jennifer

---

[19] *Ten Canoes*, dir. Rolf de Heer and Peter Djigirr (Palace Films, 2006). All future
references are to this version of the film.
[20] Terri Janke, *Pathways and Protocols: A Filmmaker's Guide to Working with
Indigenous People, Culture, and Concepts* (Australian Government: Screen Australia,
2009), 12.

Deger has argued that this 'dynamic interplay between revealing and concealing gives local cultural productions a specific kind of ontological charge and political potency'.[21] The version discussed in this chapter is the cinematic release version; that is the one with English subtitles and voiceover.

Language is just one element in the film's broader attempt to present audiences with a Yolŋu perspective. Although it is not the first to do so—the 1997 video *Gularri: That Brings Unity* by Bangana Wunung-murra is an earlier instance[22]—*Ten Canoes* is ground-breaking in its communication of a specifically Aboriginal feature-length story to a worldwide audience. The film offers a filmic representation of what might be described as a distant Aboriginal past and also an ancestral tale set in the Yolŋu Dreamtime, a past that the storyteller underlines is 'true'. In focusing on this deep past, the film differs markedly from the representation of Aboriginal people and cultures in the historical films of twenty-first-century Australian cinema, which are often set in the colonial period or the early twentieth century and document the deleterious effects of European contact on Aboriginal culture. These comprise a majority of films by non-Aboriginal directors such as Philip Noyce's *Rabbit-Proof Fence* (2002) about Aboriginal children removed from their parents by the State in the 1930s; De Heer's own earlier film *The Tracker* (2002), also starring David Gulpilil, about an Aboriginal tracker working for the frontier police force in outback Australia; and Jennifer Kent's harrowing *The Nightingale* (2019), which links the sexual violation of an Irish convict woman with the dispossession of Tasmania's Aboriginal people. This corpus of *balanda* historical cinema has recently been supplemented by a film with an Aboriginal director: *Sweet Country* (2017) by Kaytetye man and Cannes award-winning director Warwick Thornton offers a story of colonial brutality and injustice in which an Aboriginal man is pursued by the police after killing a white man in self-defence. *Ten Canoes* moves from the gener-alized postcolonial position expressed in these films, which expose the

---

[21] Jennifer Deger, 'Seeing the Invisible: Yolngu Video as Revelatory Ritual', *Visual Anthropology* 20.2–3 (2007), 105.

[22] *Gularri: That Brings Unity*, dir. Bangana Wunungmurra, produced by CAAMA Productions and Wankwarrpuyngu Yolŋu Media (Australia, 1997).

systemic racism of Australian settler colonialism, to offer instead what is more properly a decolonizing perspective. By presenting us with a story that displaces colonial contact as its constitutive historical reference point for portraying Yolŋu culture, it challenges Western audiences to reflect on their customary viewing of Aboriginal people as, to quote Torres Strait Islander theorist Martin Nakata, 'co-opted into another history, another narrative that is not really about them but about their relation to it'.[23]

Looking at its narrative structure, *Ten Canoes* explores performatively the challenges of representing, linking, and cinematically differentiating the Yolŋu present, distant history, and an ancestral past folding into this history. It does this by placing the narrative within what appear to be three timeframes. First, we encounter the prologue, which is in a present-tense frame shared by the audience and the Storyteller, who invites viewers to listen to his tale as an aerial camera sweeps over the vivid Arafura wetlands to a soundscape of thriving birdlife. In the cinematic release version, in which the voiceover is in English, the Storyteller's opening words constitute a surprising flirtation with the medievalist narrative tropes of the Western fairy-tale genre: Gulpilil begins 'One upon a time in a land far, far away', before bursting into his characteristic laughter and saying:

> Nah, not like that—I'm only joking. But I *am* going to tell you a story. This story is my story; it's not your story. A story like you've never seen before. But you want a proper story, huh? Then I must tell you something of my people and my land. Then you can see the story and know it.

When the film was released in 2006, a very similar opening line had recently been used in the first two films in the *Shrek* franchise (*Shrek*, 2001 and *Shrek 2*, 2004), which are not only known for their parodic engagement with medievalist tropes, but feature an endearing main character who lives in a swamp. The extent to which this might be coincidental is difficult to confirm, but also difficult to rule out, because

---

[23] Martin Nakata, *Disciplining the Savages, Savaging the Disciplines* (Canberra: Aboriginal Studies Press, 2007).

notwithstanding its deep engagement with Yolŋu culture, the cinematic version of *Ten Canoes* consistently exhibits a fine attunement to its reception by non-Aboriginal audiences. The wry knowingness of the film's prologue is a perfect example of this. Initially broaching a Eurocentric, metropolitan perception of Arnhem Land as 'remote' by way of a medievalist trope ('far, far away'), it disrupts this with laughter and immediately relocates the story in an intimate articulation of Country ('my people and my land') and an Aboriginal narratology ('my story...not your story'). This negotiation, and undercutting, of Western narratological expectations reflects the film's finely balanced status as a cross-cultural product, a point which will be explored more fully later on.

At the end of its overtly present-tense prologue, the film moves into its main narrative, which begins in a second, earlier timeframe described by the Gulpilil-Storyteller as 'back a long time...the time of my ancestors'. This story unfolds during the magpie goose egg hunting season, as we witness the elder Minygululu teaching his younger brother Dayindi (Jamie Gulpilil) how to make and pole a bark canoe, all the while telling Dayindi, who desires Minygululu's youngest wife, a cautionary story from the Dreamtime 'to help him live the proper way'. The telling of this tale takes the film into a third timeframe, which the Storyteller calls 'the time after the beginning, when my fathers were waiting to be born'. This tale parallels that of Minygululu and Dayindi, narrating how the young man Yeeralparil comes to regret coveting the youngest wife of his older brother, the warrior Ridjimiraril. Despite the story's tragic culmination, in which Ridjimiraril is speared to death in a *Makkarata* (conflict resolution ritual), it ends on a comic note in which Yeeralpiril, having inherited all three of his brother's wives, soon finds himself out of his depth. The film is then bookended by a genial epilogue that echoes the ruptured fairy tale of the prologue, as the Storyteller interrupts his own formulaic 'and they all lived happily ever after' with another peal of laughter, followed by:

> No, I don't know what happened after that—maybe that Dayindi find a wife, maybe he don't; it was like that for my people. But now you've seen my story. It's a good story. Not like your story, but a good story all the same.

Ten Canoes and Arnhem Land's 'medieval' time

While this Aboriginal deflation of popular medievalism is worthy of attention, it is not the reason why *Ten Canoes* is being explored here for the limits it presents to the notion of global medievalism. It is, rather, because its multi-temporal structure, and in particular its 'Middle Age'—the age of Minygululu and Dayindi, between the Storyteller's time and the Dreamtime—presents an interpretative and ethical conundrum. In the film's Press Kit, authored by the film's *balanda* co-director de Heer,[24] and in later interviews with him, the timeframe that the Storyteller calls 'the time of my ancestors' is described as having taken place 'a thousand years ago, tribal times in the North of Australia'.[25] From this the question arises: what does it mean to situate the long Yolŋu past within what by a Western reckoning would be the Middle Ages? Are we to take this part of the film as being set in eleventh-century Arnhem Land?

Responding to the question of history in the film, which arose among critics after the release of the Press Kit, de Heer has indicated that as a historical marker, 'a thousand years ago' was meant to have a more general ambit, meaning something closer to 'a long time ago';[26] he does, however, concede that it invokes a time that, although remote, is nevertheless historically imaginable. Indeed, from conversations with de Heer, it is apparent that his decision to nominate 'a thousand years' as the time setting was shaped by the historical and archaeological record, saying that he wanted the film's action to be understood to be taking place before any recorded Yolŋu contact with other cultures.[27] By 'before contact', he does not just mean before the arrival of the colonists who claimed the continent of Australia for the British empire, but also prior to earlier non-European contacts, in particular the

---

[24] My thanks to Lou Glover Nathan for contacting the Director on my behalf in order to verify his authorship of the Press Kit.

[25] *Ten Canoes* Press Kit, https://www.metromagazine.com.au/tencanoes/pdf/background.pdf, 4.

[26] Louise Hamby, 'Thomson Times and Ten Canoes (de Heer and Djigirr, 2006)', *Studies in Australasian Cinema* 1.2 (2007), 127–46.

[27] Therese Davis, 'Remembering our Ancestors: Cross-Cultural Collaboration and the Mediation of Aboriginal Culture and History in *Ten Canoes* (Rolf de Heer, 2006)', *Studies in Australasian Cinema* 1.1 (2007), 9.

well-known cross-cultural encounters between Islamicate Southeast Asian people and the peoples of Arnhem Land (including the Yolŋu but also stretching further west). The best known of these encounters is the long-standing relationship with Muslim Makassan traders from Sulawesi (a Greater Sunda island; Flores in the previous chapter is one of the Lesser Sunda) and from other islands in the Indonesian archipelago. This relationship developed as a result of the trade in *trepang* (also known as *bêche de mer* or sea cucumber), a culinary delicacy that was popular in Southeast Asia and especially valuable on the Chinese market. The harvesting and on-shore processing of northern Australia's abundant supply of *trepang* brought the Makassans into seasonal contact with Aboriginal communities on the north coast, especially the northwest,[28] where they would stay for months at a time. Important oral evidence of Makassan influence in Arnhem Land includes several hundred loanwords, including the word for white people, *balanda*, taken from 'Hollander',[29] and Islamic prayer fragments found in Yolŋu song cycles and rituals. Probably the best-known example of the latter is the inclusion of the name *Walitha' walitha*, derived from '*Lā 'ilāha 'illā llāh*' (there is no god but God) to designate a creation spirit in the *Wuramu* song cycle, a mourning ritual in East Arnhem Land.[30]

As Morgan Brigg has noted, in recent decades this centuries-long exchange has been more fully incorporated into mainstream Australian narratives of contact, and has been increasingly memorialized by 'Westerners engaged in the process of recuperating the Marege'-Makassar connection for the development of a revised national—or in some cases, regional—imaginary, perhaps to process and move

---

[28] Alistair Paterson, *A Millennium of Cultural Contact* (Walnut Creek, CA: Left Coast Press, 2011).

[29] Nicholas Evans, 'Macassan Loanwords in Top End Languages', *Australian Journal of Linguistics* 12.1 (1992), 45–91.

[30] Ian McIntosh, 'Islam and Australia's Aborigines? A Perspective from North-East Arnhem Land', *Journal of Religious History* 20.1 (1996), 53–77; Aaron Corn and Brian Djangirrawuy Garawirrtja, 'The Legacy of Yolŋu-Makassan Contact: Before the First Wave', in *The First Wave: Exploring Early Coastal Contact History in Australia*, ed. Gillian Dooley and Danielle Clode (Mile End, South Australia: Wakdefield Press, 2019), 112.

through the scars and wounding of violent settler past'.[31] One pointed example of this was the commissioning by historian Peter Spillet of the replica Makassan prau *Hati Merege* (Heart of Arnhem Land), which was sailed by Makassan sailors from Sulawesi to Galiwin'ku/Elcho Island of the Arnhem Land coast in 1988, the bicentenary of colonial settlement in Australia. In a year otherwise remembered for its conspicuous re-enactments of the arrival of the First Fleet of British convict ships at Sydney Cove, the sailing of the *Hati Merege* was a tribute to an older, more cooperative history of Aboriginal intercultural contact. The following decade saw the publication of Scottish-born Australian YA author Allan Baillie's novel *Songman* (1994), about a Yolŋu boy who travels to Sulawesi with Makassan traders. In addition to these *balanda* efforts, the *Trepang* opera project, performed several times between 1996 and 1999 on Elcho Island off the Arnhem Land coast, in Sulawesi, and in Darwin, was a Yolŋu-Makassan venture (with a *balanda* director) that enacted a story of first contact in the languages of the respective communities. Marcia Langton, activist, academic, and descendant of the Yiman and Bidjara nations, praised the production for its displacement of 'the Anglo preoccupation with presumed centrality in everything to do with Australian history'.[32]

The dating of Yolŋu-Makassan exchange varies not just within the community of Western archaeologists and historians, but between scholarly and Aboriginal accounts. According to scholars of Western history and archaeology, this relationship dates at least as far back as the seventeenth century and ended in the early twentieth. The earlier material record reveals such evidence as rock paintings of praus with distinctive Makassan sails[33] which some scholars have dated back as far as 1500. Yolŋu oral accounts, however, situate the earliest contact with Islamic Makassans and pre-Makassan people called the Baijini earlier

---

[31] Morgan Brigg, 'Old Cultures and New Possibilities: Marege'-Makassar Diplomacy in Southeast Asia', *The Pacific Review* 24.5 (2011), 614.

[32] Quoted in Peta Stephenson, 'Andrish St-Clare and the Trepang Project: The "Creative Intemediary" in an Indigenous-Asian Theatrical Production', *Journal of Australian Studies* 32.2 (2008), 71.

[33] Paul S. C. Taçon and Sally K. May, 'Rock Art Evidence for Macassan-Aboriginal Contact in Northwestern Arnhem Land', in *Macassan History and Heritage: Journeys, Encounters and Influences*, ed. Marshall Clark and Sally K. May (Canberra: ANU e-press, 2013).

still, up to 'five or six hundred years ago', in what would be coeval with the European late Middle Ages.[34] Earlier dates for contact appear to be corroborated by evidence from another part of Arnhem Land: Groote Eylandt, home to the Anindilyakwa people in the Gulf of Carpentaria. Here, archaeologist Anne Clarke identified in 1994 what she called 'an enigmatic fragment of evidence'[35]—a single pottery shard found at a level that tentatively dates its deposit on the island to over nine hundred years ago, and which has more recently been dated to between 1026 and 1264.[36] Although its provenance is not settled,[37] it is believed to come from beyond Arnhem Land, and as such offers tantalizing evidence of possible Aboriginal contact with cultures whose presence in the Indo-Malay region dates back to 'the global Middle Ages'.

This not only constitutes an important 'thickening' of the longer story of pre-European contact with the northern region of the Australian continent—a region deemed isolated in Euro-metropolitan terms—but is also highly relevant to a broader rewriting of trade and cultural networks across the global medieval world. It reminds us first of all, as mentioned in this book's previous chapter, that Southeast Asia was a vital hub of cross-cultural exchange with the larger Buddhist, Hindu, and Arab-Islamicate cultures of the Middle Ages, and through them to the Eurasian Middle Ages. But it goes further still, by linking this Southeast Asian sphere to the northernmost parts of a continent which, as Holmes and Standen have noted,[38] has generally been regarded as totally disconnected from the medieval world.

The northeast coast of Arnhem Land also offers tantalizing but currently inconclusive material evidence of possible contact with the

[34] Libby Tudball and Robert Lewis, *Ten Canoes: A Film by Rolf de Heer and the People of Ramingining* (Film Finance Corporation/Australian Teachers of Media, Inc., 2006), www.tencanoes.com.au, 10; Ian McIntosh, 'The Ancient African Coins of Arnhem Land', *Australasian Science*, May 2014, 20.
[35] Anne Clarke, 'Winds of Change: An Archaeology of Contact in the Groote Eylandt Archipelago, Northern Australia', 1994 PhD thesis, the Australian National University, 399.
[36] Anne Clarke and Ursula Frederick, 'Making a Sea Change: Rock Art, Archaeology and the Enduring Legacy of Frederick McCarthy's Research on Groote Eylandt', in *Exploring the Legacy of the 1948 Arnhem Land Expedition*, ed. Martin Thomas and Margo Neale (Canberra: ANU E Press, 2011), 151.
[37] Theories range from Indonesia to China; see, for instance, Angela Schottenhammer, 'China's Emergence as a Maritime Power', in *The Cambridge History of China*, ed. John W. Chaffee and Denis Twitchett (Cambridge: Cambridge University Press, 2015), 475.
[38] Holmes and Standen, 'Towards a Global Middle Ages', 13–14.

medieval Islamicate trade networks that linked Southeast Asia to India and the East African Coast. This evidence consists of five or possibly six copper coins from the East African sultanate of Kilwa Kisiwani which have been found on Yolŋu land, in the sands of the Wessel Island chain off the Arnhem Land coast (see Figure 3).

Five of these coins were found on Marchinbar Island, the Northern-most of the Wessels, in 1944 by an Australian airman stationed there to monitor potential Japanese threats to Northern Australia. The sixth coin, discovered on the more southern Elcho Island/Galiwin'ku in 2018, is as yet unconfirmed as a Kilwa coin but has the same dimensions as the five found on Marchinbar so is tentatively believed to be another; mineralogical tests are forthcoming.[39] Dated from *c.*900–1300 CE, they bear the names of identifiable rulers, such as Sulaiman ibn al-Hasan, the sultan between 1310 and 1333 whose court was visited by an admiring Ibn Battuta. Kilwa's significance as a Swahili-coast mercantile centre within a premodern Eurasian/African 'world system'[40] is well known, as is its sacking at the hands of the Portuguese in 1505. Less known, but of vital interest to understanding the place of Arnhem Land within a broadly conceived 'global medieval', is whether the presence of Kilwa coins on Yolŋu land 'implicate[s] Australia's Aboriginal peoples in the Maritime Silk Route, the ancient Indian Ocean trading network that linked such exotic ports as Kilwa and Zanzibar in East Africa with

FIGURE 3   Medieval coins from Kilwa, found on the Wessel Islands off the Arnhem Land coast. Reproduced with permission of the Museum of Applied Arts and Sciences, Sydney. Gift of M Isenberg, 1985. Photographer Sotha Bourne.

[39] Kylie Stevenson, '"It Could Change Everything": Coin Found off Northern Australia May Be from Pre-1400 Africa', *The Guardian*, 12 May 2019, https://www.theguardian.com/australia-news/2019/may/12/it-could-change-everything-coin-found-off-northern-australia-may-be-from-pre-1400-africa.

[40] Philippe Beaujard, 'The Indian Ocean in Eurasian and African World-Systems before the Sixteenth Century', *Journal of World History* 16.4 (2005), 411–65.

Arabia, Persia, India, China and Indonesia'.[41] There are several theories about how the coins might have reached the Wessels, with some favouring the idea that they washed up as booty from a later, probably Portuguese, shipwreck. Others believe that trade ships from medieval Kilwa could have reached the seas near Arnhem Land, since '[t]he Kilwa-Oman-Gudjerat-Malacca-Moluccas sea route was well established by the 1500s, and probably for many hundreds of years prior to that...', and Kilwa was known for its intrepid sailors.[42] While Ian McIntosh, who led a 2015 *balanda*-Yolŋu joint expedition to Marchinbar, favours a later date for the coins' arrival, he concedes that when one considers the long-standing trade relations between Arnhem Land and the Indo-Malay region, 'the link between [medieval] Africa and north Australia does not seem so extraordinary'.[43] Bryan C. Keene has cautioned against making over-reaching and senzationalizing claims about Australia's connection to medieval Europe that fail to take into account 'the numerous island civilizations that contributed to long-distance global trade throughout the premodern world';[44] the Kilwa coins and the Groote Eylandt shard offer a possible glimpse into Australia's connection to those civilizations. They also accord with Alex J. West's point about how material and archaeological evidence can potentially illuminate connections within the region in the absence of textual accounts, especially given the fragility of documents in the humid tropical climate.[45]

Having outlined how pre-colonial Arnhem Land connected to these two distant cultures in an expansive network, it should be reiterated that de Heer and the people of Ramingining sought to set *Ten Canoes* in a time where this Islamo-Asian late medieval culture has not yet had any shaping effect on Yolŋu culture or society. This is a knowing decision but should not be seen as a refusal of their coevalness with other neighbouring societies; the Yolŋu value deeply their long-shared history with the Makassans and are fully aware of the potential

[41] McIntosh, 'Ancient African Coins', 20.

[42] McIntosh, 'Ancient African Coins', 23–4.

[43] McIntosh, 'Ancient African Coins', 23–4.

[44] Bryan C. Keene, 'Introduction: Manuscripts and their Outlook on the World', in *Toward a Global Middle Ages: Encountering the World through Illuminated Manuscripts*, ed. Bryan C. Keene (Los Angeles: The J. Paul Getty Museum, 2019), 31.

[45] West, 'Manuscripts and The Medieval Tropics'.

implications of the Kilwa coins for the history of Arnhem Land as a site of cultural exchange. The 'thousand years ago' in the film is, therefore, that of Yolŋu Country alone, unchanged by any terraqueous contact. There are interactions, most of them hostile, between the groups in the film and 'strangers' who enter their terrain, but these strangers are from other Aboriginal groups, not from across the sea. The Country of the Yolŋu in *Ten Canoes*'s ancestral 'eleventh century' might be coeval with the global medieval world that is gradually being pieced together by archaeology, but, as I will elaborate later, it is determinedly not of it.

Ten Canoes and Australian colonial medievalism

Whatever its intentions, the film's avoidance of engagement with Anglo-European medieval timelines has the effect of sidelining attempts throughout the long nineteenth century to medievalize Australia in the name of colonialism. Medievalism in colonial Australia has been clearly implicated within the earlier 'global' phenomenon that was British imperialism, as a legitimating discourse for invasion and occupation, with the English Middle Ages in particular instrumentalized as historical proof of British greatness. De Heer's decentring is especially potent when we consider that the eleventh century had a particularly resonant meaning within this colonial medievalism, which cast the Norman conquest of 1066 as formative of the British tendency to invade and occupy. The instrumentalization of medieval histories of colonization was not limited to the Norman conquest; colonial Australian public culture, from the press and public addresses to popular fiction, presented the expansionism of the imperial age as an atavistic expression of the will-to-invasion attributed variously (or collectively) to Anglo-Australians' Saxon, Viking, and Norman forebears. But the preoccupation with the 'Norseness' of the Anglo-Australian character lent a deep historical complexion to racially inflected British triumphalism in colonial Australia. A 1907 article in the Sydney journal the *Lone Hand*, to take just one late example, attributed the British occupation of unceded Aboriginal land not to political or economic ambition, nor to the expediency of the penal system that transported convicts *en masse* to the Australian colonies, but rather to 'that roving instinct which bespeaks the unconquerable Norse element in the

British blood'.[46] As with its counterparts across the Anglosphere, the Australian notion of seafaring English 'Norseness' was subject to a range of inflections; but all instances of British greatness across the centuries were understood to have emerged as a result of it.

The fixation on Norseness was just one subgenre of the broader Australian use of Anglo-Saxonism as a discourse of British manifest destiny. Again, it was hardly unique to nineteenth-century Australia: Douglas Cole has argued that Victorian and Edwardian explorations of Anglo-Australian kinship 'lapsed easily into Anglo-Saxonism with scarcely a local twist'.[47] Looking at the bulk of Anglo-Saxonist discourse produced in colonial Australia, most of which appeared in metropolitan and regional periodicals, there is some basis to this claim. But Cole's assertion of mere imitation is disturbed when we unearth examples of Anglo-Saxonist triumphalism that attempt to adapt it to the particular circumstances of the Australian colonies. Looking at these more localized examples, we see that mythologies celebrating English continuity were placed under considerable discursive strain when used to characterize life in colonial Australia.

One conspicuous example of this can be found in Rolf Boldrewood's novels of the 1880s and 1890s, in particular *A Sydney-Side Saxon* (1894), which is striking for its portrayal of the long legacy of the Norman conquest in colonialist ideologies. In this pastoral novel, the Anglo-Irish-born Boldrewood portrays the landowning settlers of Australia's southeastern colonies as latter-day colonial Anglo-Normans, whose arrival in Australia enables them to overcome the atavistic 'Saxon' tendencies that stymied them in Britain and embrace instead their Norman drive for rightful domination in a new land. Its focus on Anglo-Australian settlers throwing off their former subjection sits uneasily alongside its emotional disavowal of Aboriginal dispossession (its narrative takes for granted the settlers' purchase of Aboriginal people as servants) and its uncomfortable courting of miscegenation only to ward it off (the 'Saxon' settler Jesse almost marries a biracial Aboriginal woman). Unlike the more straightforward iterations of

---

[46] Anon. (Frank Renar), 'Prolific Australia: The Continent of the British Race', *The Lone Hand* 1 (1907), 68.

[47] Douglas Cole, '"The Crimson Thread of Kinship": Ethnic Ideas in Australia, 1870–1914', *Historical Studies* 14 (1971), 511–25.

Anglo-Saxonist triumphalism, *A Sydney-Side Saxon*'s apparently blithe assertion of an ancient English instinct for land occupation labours under myriad barely acknowledged anxieties about colonial cohabitation and the racial destinies of settlers and the land's original owners.[48] Boldrewood's novels disclose the pressures placed on Anglo-Saxonist migration myths once they moved from the open seas to the shores of a land whose great age and ancient Aboriginal cultures threw into relief the relative youth of the settler culture, despite its attempt to narrate itself within a deep English past.

This creation of an ancestral complexion for colonial settler society was extended into the field of poetry. The historical self-consciousness of nineteenth-century Australian poetry took another, quite idiosyncratic, form that clearly demonstrates the plasticity of Anglo-Saxonism. Australian poets' perception that together they were founding Australian poetry led them to present themselves less as inheritors of a long Anglo-Saxon tradition and more as the Anglo-Saxons of Australia's future; that is, the writers of the *Ur*-texts of a glorious literary tradition that is yet to come. Their conviction that Australian settler culture lacked the historical depth of older European societies meant that the main historicizing gesture available to them was one in which they looked ahead to a distant Australian future when their own time would be regarded as a legendary chapter in the national story. The extreme age of the surviving Aboriginal culture around them did not figure in their sense of Australia's past or future.

Yet in the same decade that *A Sydney-Side Saxon* was written, and possibly in response to it, we find a poem parodying medievalism as a mandate for invasion. The 1897 poem 'An Australian Mummy' by Victor Daley demands attention for the way its description of Australian society lampoons the nostalgic nationalistic and racializing impulses of colonial Anglo-Saxonism.[49] Set three thousand years in the future, the poem purports to be written by a leading Australian poet of the fifth millennium, Alexander W. Mudlarque, in response to the

---

[48] Louise D'Arcens, 'Inverse Invasions: Medievalism and Colonialism in Rolf Boldrewood's *A Sydney-Side Saxon*', *Parergon* 22.2 (2005), 159–82.

[49] Victor Daley, 'An Australian Mummy', in *Creeve Roe: Poetry by Victor Daley*, ed. Muir Holburn and Marjorie Pizer, Foreword by E. J. Brady, drawings by Roderick Shaw (Sydney: Pinchgut Press), 128–32.

excavation of a mummy that had been buried in 1897 in 'the ancient city of Melbourne'. Gazing upon the mummy, Mudlarque is drawn into a historical reverie in which 'the Present fades' and he pictures life at 'the dawn / Of Austral history'. His romantic Anglo-Saxonism leads him naïvely to conjure up late nineteenth-century Melbourne as a utopian pre-modern paradise, including recasting its notoriously unstable colonial parliament in the image of the Anglo-Saxon folk-moot, with all of its connotations of wisdom and egalitarianism. Alongside its satiric use of popular Saxonizing motifs, Daley's invocation of the mummy alludes not just to the famous Egyptological finds made in the 1890s, but to the colonial antiquarian practice of collecting, swapping, and exhibiting evidence, including skeletal evidence, of the so-called 'timeless' culture of Australia's first inhabitants. Seen in this light, Daley's conceit of a local ancient mummy takes on a different complexion. Indeed, the poem's opening apostrophe, 'Brown, shrivelled Mummy!' could be taken to imply that the mummy is Aboriginal, though this is not definite. The ambiguity is sustained in the statement that the figure had 'lived *when* Austral history began', 'Austral history' here meaning colonial history. The 'when' does not clarify whether this is a relic of a 'timeless' Aboriginal human who came face to face with colonial history in the making, or of a 'bold forefather ... of the Austral Race [who] from Northern lands their wondrous voyage took'. Either way, the poem satirically exposes the overwriting of Aboriginal deep time with a fantasized Anglo-Saxon long history, and as such implicates medievalism in general, and Anglo-Saxonism in particular, within a widespread colonial project of historical denial in relation to prior Aboriginal possession.

Anglo-Australian settlers' use of the medieval past to underwrite competing territorial claims exemplifies what historian Tom Griffiths has described as the 'white noise' of dispossession in Australia. This practice has, he says, consisted not of 'a great Australian silence' about colonial theft so much as 'an obscuring and overlaying din of history-making ... to foster emotional possession of the land' for colonizers in the face of its prior Aboriginal occupation.[50] What Griffiths's argument points to, crucially for this chapter, are the ideological and ethical stakes

---

[50] Tom Griffiths, *Hunters and Collectors: The Antiquarian Imagination in Australia* (Cambridge: Cambridge University Press, 1996), 4.

of using the English or European Middle Ages, however fantastically rendered, in non-European spaces to signify deep time. The persistence of this historical 'overlaying din' and the nationalist-colonialist agenda it underwrites has been argued by Aileen Moreton-Robinson, academic and Goenpul woman from the Quandamooka Nation, in her book *The White Possessive: Property, Power and Indigenous Sovereignty* (2015). Moreton-Robinson has developed a forceful account of the 'logics of white possession'[51] to explain the intertwined historical, racial, and legal mandate that Anglo-European settlers continue to grant themselves in postcolonial societies. In Australia these possessive logics authorize the refusal of Aboriginal sovereignty and of Aboriginal people's enduring 'ontological connection to country',[52] and manifest in the ongoing disavowal of capitalist economies built on illegal dispossession. This invocation of the Anglo-European past is, as Adam Miyashiro has recently pointed out in a discussion of Hawai'i and the North American mainland, symptomatic of settler colonialism's global operation: 'White supremacy is transnational, deeply rooted in myths of white, "Anglo-Saxon" heritage, and structured in indigenous elimination.'[53]

Medievalism, temporality, and dreamtime

Considered in the light of a 250-year white possessive history, *Ten Canoes*'s portrayal of a supposed Yolŋu 'eleventh century' would appear to be a refusal of those colonial narratives discussed above that fetishize the Norman conquest as an eleventh-century mandate for colonization, and the assertion of a coeval Aboriginal history. Although this apparent reclamation is not as conspicuous as the African-American response to racist U.S. Anglo-Saxonism, as described by Matthew X. Vernon in *The Black Middle Ages: Race and*

---

[51] Aileen Moreton-Robinson, *The White Possessive: Property, Power and Indigenous Sovereignty* (Minneapolis: University of Minnesota Press, 2015), xxiv.

[52] Moreton-Robinson, *The White Possessive*, 11.

[53] Adam Miyashiro, 'Our Deeper Past: Race, Settler Colonialism, and Medieval Heritage Politics', *Literature Compass* 16.e12550 (2019), https://doi.org/10.1111/lic3.12550.

the Construction of the Middle Ages,[54] it is difficult not to register what it means to relocate this charged date in a pre-colonial environment. It should be remembered, however, that the 'thousand year' timeframe was specifically nominated by de Heer, the non-Aboriginal collaborator most responsible for the inclusion of Western elements within the film. It is true that *Ten Canoes* has been held up as an exemplar of consultative practice for its significant involvement of the people of Ramingining, who co-developed the film's content, determined the casting, acted in it, produced a number of its cultural objects that feature as costume and props, and had approval of its final content.[55] Nevertheless, it bears evidence of de Heer's input as a filmmaker in the Western tradition. A case in point is his devising of the film's central drama—a fictional plot founded on a younger brother's desire for his older brother's young wife, which is based on community input but also on a famous 1937 anthropological account of northeast Arnhem Land by William Lloyd Warner,[56] and shaped by the canons of Western storytelling. Despite its setting in pre-contact Arnhem Land, and its notably unhurried, often dialogue-free shooting of the magpie goose egg hunt, its triangulated central love plot carries echoes of narratives that are familiar to medievalists from such genres as romance and fabliau. De Heer introduced this narrative because he believed that a mainstream audience might not be engaged by his collaborators' original proposal to make a more fluid, non-plot-driven film. To that end his account of the film's temporal framing, and in particular, his situating of the film's 'middle' era a thousand years ago, is symptomatic of *Ten Canoes*'s nature not as a completely Yolŋu film but as a hybrid, cross-cultural product that aims to accommodate the radically different Western and Yolŋu perceptions of time and history, and to fuse these with an expectation that its largest audience is likely to be non-Aboriginal.

This cross-cultural element is also evident in the way the film's 'Middle Age' is represented visually. One of the most arresting features of this thousand-year-old 'age of ancestors', in which Minygululu

[54] Matthew X. Vernon, *The Black Middle Ages: Race and the Construction of the Middle Ages* (Basingstoke and New York: Palgrave Macmillan, 2018).

[55] Janke, *Pathways and Protocols*, 37–8.

[56] Anne Rutherford, '*Ten Canoes* as "Inter-Cultural Membrane"', *Studies in Australasian Cinema* 7.2–3 (2013), 137–51.

counsels Dayindi while gathering goose eggs, is that it is filmed in black and white. This differentiates it conspicuously from the film's 'modern' and 'Dreamtime' timeframes, which are in rich colour. Many viewers and critics have initially been puzzled by this, not just because it is an aesthetic rupture, but also because it uses a visual code evocative of twentieth-century modernity to signify pre-contact Aboriginal history. This decision, however, has a cultural foundation that is highly significant for the Yolŋu. De Heer has spoken of the dilemma he faced when, despite having committed himself contractually to shooting a film in colour, his Yolŋu collaborators explained that they were envisaging something more like a black-and-white documentary film. In his much-reported account of the project's early development, the co-director recounts the formative moment when David Gulpilil, in order to convey what the people of Ramingining had in mind, presented him with a black-and-white photograph of Yolŋu men fording bark canoes on the Arafura Swamp, saying 'we need ten canoes'. The photograph in question was one of a celebrated series of photographs taken in 1937 by the *balanda* anthropologist and activist Dr Donald Thomson, which documented Yolŋu life and featured numerous members of the grand-parental generation of de Heer's collaborators. It is this photographic series—held in the highest regard by the Yolŋu even today—that forms the visual basis for the black-and-white 'ancestral' sequences of the film, which often begin as posed scenes before coming into movement. Both the 'thousand years ago' story and the Dreamtime story nested within it self-consciously recreate and narrativize a large number of Thomson's still photos, in black and white and in colour respectively, weaving them as a visual archive into the film's story (see Figure 4).

Ten Canoes is, of course, far from the only film to evoke the pre-modern era by way of the trope of a 'surviving document' that functions to authorize, historicize, and verify the past being created in the text. Viewers of medievalist cinema will be familiar with an analogous trope, described by Bettina Bildhauer and others, whereby the film's narrative is framed by intertitles that take the form of images of a 'medieval' manuscript page which then dissolve into a cinematic recreation of the medieval past being represented in the film.[57] The framing image of the

---

[57] Bettina Bildhauer, *Filming the Middle Ages* (London: Reaktion Books, 2011), 99–114.

FIGURE 4 D. F. Thomson, 'Ganalbingu and Djinba Men Use Bark Canoes in the Arafura Swamp, Central Arnhem Land, Australia. May 1937' (4a); and the re-creation of Thomson's photograph in *Ten Canoes* (4b). 4a from the Donald Thomson Ethnohistory Collection, reproduced courtesy of the Thomson family and Museums Victoria; 4b reproduced with permission of Vertigo Productions.

FIGURE 4 CONTINUED.

manuscript page appears in everything from the 1939 version of *The Hunchback of Notre Dame* to animated classics such as the cartoon *Robin Hood* (1973) and, again, *Shrek* (2001), while medievalist maps of Middle Earth frame the *Lord of the Rings* blockbuster trilogy (2001, 2002, 2003). This visual trope has its parallel in medievalist literature, with one of the best-known examples being the discovery of Adzo of Melk's (fictional) framing text at the beginning of Umberto Eco's *The Name of the Rose* (1980), although Eco's text is highly reflexive on the power of documents to authorize fantasy and violence. Medievalist films' framing manuscript-scenes are revealing cinematic instances of 'documentary undecidability': they are, paradoxically, a portal into the film's premodern past but also a reminder of the impossibility of unmediated access to that past. That this premodernity is a creative back-projection of the modern is evident in the fact that so many of these 'medieval' manuscript pages are manifestly modern creations; in the case of *The Hunchback of Notre Dame* the opening text borrows from the aesthetic codes of silent film intertitles as well as loosely conceived ideas of manuscript aesthetics. Taking this into account, *Ten Canoes* can seem to have a type of unfamiliar familiarity for viewers with knowledge of cinematic medievalism: its sophisticated

inclusion of an undecidable documentary archive grounds and author-
izes its story-telling, which is fictitious yet 'true', comprised of history
and legend.

But, lest this instance of *Ten Canoes*'s framing use of the Thomson
photos seem like an easy parallel to the use of the manuscript trope, it is
important to register the more complex ethical and metaphysical status
accorded to the photographs. Understanding the double valency of the
Thomson photos for the Yolŋu is key to understanding their particular
complexity and representational force. On the one hand, Louise
Hamby has pointed out that they document a very specific historical
moment in April–May 1937 when Thomson visited Ramingining to
record the way of life there; this period of contact, according to Hamby,
is actually known among the locals as 'Thomson Times'.[58] Others,
conversely, such as de Heer himself, claim that the photographs do
not simply record a moment of contact, but rather, have a more
metaphysical status as documentation of vital surviving traditional
practices which reach far back into the pre-contact past. Tom Crosbie
points out that Thomson's photos have come to be regarded, by
Aboriginal people and *balanda* alike, as a 'cherished...evocation of
lost, rarely seen moments of non-settler-influenced culture'.[59] Lest this
seem contradictory to a Western perspective that would locate the
photographs firmly in the colonial contact era, Deger enjoins Westerners viewing Aboriginal texts to 'approach the dynamics of looking
relations...with an attentiveness to the ways that local modes of
perception and imaging practices can shape—and in turn be shaped
by—different modes of visual communication'.[60] For de Heer, the
decision to base the film's black-and-white section on reconstructions
of these photos reflects his collaborators' 'initial thinking' to portray
Yolŋu 'living life a thousand years ago,...showing the world how to
make canoes and how they catch [goose eggs]'.[61] Moreover, the photographic encounter between the Yolŋu and Thomson, he claims, has
been 'completely consumed into their culture as though it had always

[58] Louise Hamby, 'Thomson Times and Ten Canoes (de Heer and Djigirr, 2006)',
Studies in Australasian Cinema 1.2 (2007), 127–8.
[59] Tom Crosbie, 'Critical Historiography in "Atanarjuat the Fast Runner and Ten
Canoes"', *Journal of New Zealand Literature* 24.2 (2007), 140.
[60] Deger, 'Seeing the Invisible', 104.
[61] Quoted in Hamby, 'Thomson Times', 143.

been that way',[62] rather than being rejected as an intrusion of Western anthropology.

Yet while it is true that Yolŋu culture has a capacious and highly responsive way of incorporating meaningful outside influences into its storytelling and its ritual practices—the absorption of Makassan prayer is another case in point—this does not fully deflect the Thomson photographs' implication in ethnographic method, with its colonizing intent of rendering indigenous people 'knowable' to Western audiences. Anne Rutherford puts it well when she describes Thomson's process as 'a kind of double helix' in which 'the photos themselves reproduce something that was, in some ways, Thomson's imaginary— his reconstruction of the pre-contact past'.[63] Part of this construction involved Thomson requesting that his subjects remove their modern clothing for the photographs. Rutherford in turn describes the reproduction of Thomson's images in *Ten Canoes* as 'endlessly recursive';[64] by re-embodying the photographs the film further naturalizes their effect of premodernity, which is in turn reinforced by de Heer's statement that its 'middle' episode took place a millennium ago. De Heer's interchangeable use of 'a thousand years ago', 'ancestral' and 'always' introduces further strain into his commentary on the operations of time and history in the film. By creating an equivalence between these terms he not only re-locates the ancestral layer of the film's Yolŋu story in a deep and unchanging past ('it had always been that way'), but, in a gesture recognizable from the previous chapter, uses a time coeval with the Middle Ages as a hinge into that deep past.

None of what is raised here is intended to diminish the remarkable cross-cultural achievement of *Ten Canoes*. Rather, returning in a different way to the question of deep time posed in the previous chapter, I am chiefly interested here in the implications of de Heer inviting viewers to locate the film in a past that invokes the western calendar but also defamiliarizes it. His representation of this black-and-white Yolŋu 'Middle Age' offers, I suggest, an especially teasing instance of world medievalism, or (to again invoke Mead's term) 'medievalism on Country', because its 'middleness' parallels but radically differs from, and

---

[62] Quoted in Hamby, 'Thomson Times', 144.

[63] Rutherford, '*Ten Canoes* as "Inter-Cultural Membrane"', 139.

[64] Rutherford, '*Ten Canoes* as "Inter-Cultural Membrane"', 139.

relativizes, the middleness of the post-Roman cultures of Europe collectively referred to as medieval cultures. Kathleen Davis has argued, in an argument that accords with McClintock's in *Imperial Leather* but applies it specifically to the mobilization of the 'Middle Ages' as a category 'to legitimize, classify, and make sense of colonial policies, practices, and encounters', that:

> [I]t is salutary to remember that the Middle Ages was constituted as European (more specifically, western European) and that...non-European areas were excluded from fundamental histories (politics, sovereignty, law, philosophy) conceived as moving from ancient Greece and Rome, through the power centers of Europe's Christian Middle Ages, and to fruition in modern Europe.... This territorial history is part of the colonial logic of the Middle Ages.[65]

By this construction, de Heer's remark prompts Western audiences to view the film in a way that displaces Eurocentric accounts of what was taking place a thousand years ago, offering an alternative temporal imaginary. By another construction, however, as I will now go on to discuss, these remarks can be seen to operate as a post hoc domestication of the Aboriginal understanding of time that underpins the film. By considering this gesture in conjunction with the film's use of the Thomson photos, it is possible to see the simultaneously liberatory and colonizing impulses that underlie it, and thereby the complexities of medievalism's engagement with Aboriginal texts and culture.

A fundamental difficulty in de Heer's invocation of 'a thousand years ago' is that, in order to make the film more intelligible to his Western audience, he locates the action within a temporal ontology that is essentially linear, thereby downplaying his Yolŋu collaborators' entirely different conception of the dynamics of time. This compromise is again symptomatic of *Ten Canoes*'s status as a cross-cultural text. Billy Griffiths states that the title of his 2018 study of Australian archaeology, *Deep Time Dreaming*, signals a corresponding tension in that field's negotiation of Western and Aboriginal worldviews: 'the deep time history, bound to notions of linear time, and the active and continuous time of the Dreaming, which is a self-referencing and self-affirming

---

[65] Kathleen Davis, 'Theory in Time', *PMLA* 130.3 (2015), 765.

system of meaning.'[66] Ambelin and Blaze Kwaymullina, while noting the particular influence of their own Palyku culture, set out to describe a general Aboriginal understanding of time, which they place within a broader worldview predicated on the experience and ethos of connectedness:

> In an Aboriginal worldview, time—to the extent that it exists at all— is neither linear nor absolute. There are patterns and systems of energy that create and transform, from the ageing process of the human body to the growth and decay of the broader universe. But these processes are not 'measured' or even framed in a strictly temporal sense, and certainly not in a linear sense.... Time, like all things, is relative to the enduring physical and metaphysical context of country. Even the Dreaming—the myriad of universe-making events from which all Aboriginal knowledge is derived—is not fixed in time. Rather, it is a complex ongoing happening that Aboriginal peoples engage with through songs, dance, ceremony, art and story.[67]

This broader definition, in which time is responsive to the dynamism of Country, is reiterated in the specific context of Yolŋu Country by the Gay'wu group of women in *Song Spirals*, who emphasize that their songs, which are expressions of deep law as well as maps of Country, exist in 'many times' at once—past, present, and future—and encompass both the eternal and the everyday.[68]

This fluid perception of time is clearly evident in *Ten Canoes*, in the Storyteller's use of continuous present tense to narrate events across the film's three stages. The use of oral story-telling, which moves across the visual track in a continuous present-tense, creates a seamless continuum between the present, Thomson-time, and the Dreaming. One important moment when it is especially apparent is in the initial transition from the colour scenes of the prologue to the black-and-white 'Middle Age' goose egg hunting section. As the audience, positioned almost like eavesdroppers within the swamp, see the group of hunters come into view, the Storyteller appeals for silence, saying 'shhhh, I can hear them coming—my ancestors'. In addition to the

---

[66] Griffiths, *Deep Time Dreaming*, 292.

[67] Ambelin Kwaymullina and Blaze Kwaymullina, 'Learning to Read the Signs: Law in an Indigenous Reality', *Journal of Australian Studies* 34.2 (2010), 199.

[68] Gay'wu Group of Women, *Song Spirals*, 20.

fact that his storytelling continues unbroken across a visually marked shift in timeframe, his continued use of present tense ('I can hear them') and his conspiratorial direct address ('shhhh') deftly collapses time into a continuous present, gathering Storyteller, audience, and ancestors into the same moment across a large but indefinite swathe of time. This continues as the Storyteller introduces us to the ancestors Minygululu and Dayindi, and tells us of the dilemma of Dayindi's desire for his brother's wife. Layers of time and identity fold into each other as Minygululu commences his cautionary tale for Dayindi, which the audience hears in the voice of the Storyteller: 'it is Minygululu's story for Dayindi back then, and it is my story for you now. It's a good story, but you better listen.' In establishing a multi-temporal time-frame, the film does not present Yolŋu culture in a state of static adherence to past edicts, but shows, rather, the wisdom of the Dreamtime as both sustained by and responsive to happenings and change. This closely reflects Kwaymullina and Kwaymullina's argument that the law of Country is abidingly dynamic:

> Aboriginal creation stories tell that law was given by the same Ancestors who made the world and continue to live within it, and that the purpose of the gift of law was to show all life how to sustain country. In this context, Aboriginal statements that 'something is to be done because the Ancestors did so'—historically often misinter-preted as indicating that an individual is blindly copying the behav-iour of previous generations—in fact reveal a complex legal system premised on the interconnection of life in country and of the place of human beings in sustaining that life.[69]

This fluid temporality is further reinforced by the shift back into colour for the Dreamtime frame, where the story of Ridjimiraril and Yeeral-paril unfolds. This shift in colour scheme, which links the Dreamtime visually to the colour world of the present-tense narrative frame, is intended, de Heer claims, to signify the ongoing vibrancy and imme-diacy of this past into the present. The use of colour might well have been driven by de Heer's contractual undertaking to feature the vivid palette of Arnhem Land, but it still managed to convey the living presence of the deep past, to the point that it attracted criticism from

---

[69] Kwaymullina and Kwaymullina, 'Learning to Read the Signs', 198.

some who argue that it perpetuates Western Romantic tropes of 'Dreamtime vitality'.[70] Although, as discussed before, there is a visual rupture created by the use of ethnographic black and white in the Thomson time frame, this layer is nevertheless woven together with the Dreamtime story both by their parallel narrative of forbidden desire and by the fact that both frames self-consciously recreate, animate, and narrativize a large number of Thomson's still photos, in black-and-white and in colour respectively. The film also documents a cultural continuum by observing Yolŋu kinship structures. This is strongly evident in the protocols followed for casting, in which care was taken to ensure that the Yolŋu actors recreating and animating the Thomson photos are themselves descendants of the corresponding figures in the photos. Hamby detects changes between the photographs and their recreations, particularly in the clothing and adornments, but the issue of first significance was the ancestral line between actor and character. Frances Djulibing, for instance, whose performance as Ridjimiraril's wife Nowalingu involved making and wearing adornments based on those worn by her grandmother in Thomson's photographs, claimed that participating in the film brought her into contact with her ancestors and their way of living.[71]

Taking all of this into account, then, even 'Thompson time' might both allude to the period of contact between Thomson and the Yolŋu *and* also connect in a continuous time to the distant past, and to the present. The visual technique of bringing the photos to life, by recreating them as momentarily suspended tableaux whose figures then move and speak, is an effective way for the filmmakers to unlock the images' temporal depth and put them literally into motion as part of a much more expansive story of connection, consistent with the understanding captured by Kwaymullina and Kwaymullina:

> To be temporally fixed is...to be isolated; frozen. In an Indigenous worldview, it is, in fact, an impossibility—for that which cannot move, cannot interact, and that which cannot interact is inanimate. And there is nothing inanimate in country.[72]

[70] Davis, 'Remembering our Ancestors', 10.

[71] Hamby, 'Thomson Times', 132–4.

[72] Kwaymullina and Kwaymullina, 'Learning to Read the Signs', 200.

The fact that the ancestral people in the photos are embodied in their descendants brings a material immediacy to the interaction between times. It is possibly in recognition of this that de Heer later attempted to 'unfix' the film from his original thousand-year designation, realizing that it made little sense for him to nominate a specific and fixed timeframe for any part of *Ten Canoes*, let alone one that is intelligible in terms of its coevalness with the Anglo-European Middle Ages. As this book has shown at length, medievalism is itself a multi-temporal phenomenon, which exposes in its many iterations how the past continues to live on in the present, inflecting what for the sake of convenience is called the 'modern' or the postmedieval. Carolyn Dinshaw describes the 'asynchrony' of the medievalist encounter as comprising 'different time frames or temporal systems colliding in a single moment of *now*',[73] and apprehending 'the present power of past things, past bodies, past lives'.[74] To that end, scholars of medievalism are well-placed to grasp *Ten Canoes*'s refusal of linear temporality and its portrayal of a 'now' that is thick with layers of deep and recent time. Nevertheless, it is vital to be attentive to the differences between this and the deep multi-temporality registered in *Ten Canoes* as a Yolŋu collaborative text. Medievalism's registering of multi-temporality, and the disorientation that this brings with it, still relies implicitly on recognizing a linear model of temporal and historical unfolding that is disrupted by the reintroduction or retention of an earlier time into a later time, whether deliberately or inadvertently. Even though the notion of a 'Middle Age' is essentially relative rather than absolute, and as such can be set in motion, it still marks a place on a line. The continuous present of *Ten Canoes*, however, while temptingly similar to the asynchrony of medievalism, is just one component of the interconnective living web of Country. Again, Kwaymullina and Kwaymullina offer an evocative summation of this networked apprehension of time: '[l]ife does not move through time; rather, time moves through life.'[75]

[73] Carolyn Dinshaw, *How Soon is Now?: Medieval Texts, Amateur Readers and the Queerness of Time* (Durham: Duke University Press, 2012), 5.
[74] Dinshaw, *How Soon Is Now?*, 148.
[75] Kwaymullina and Kwaymullina, 'Learning to Read the Signs', 200.

As the film attempts to negotiate the differing perceptions and interests of Aboriginal and *balanda* audiences, the Storyteller, as mentioned before, kindly but definitively tells the viewer 'it's my story, not your story'. Access to Yolŋu knowledge is not denied *balanda* audiences in the cinematic release version, but there is a careful signification of the custodianship of this knowledge and its mythic representations. This statement of custodianship, along with the black-and-white visual language of Thomson time, clarifies not just the impossibility but, moreover, the *undesirability* of unmediated access to those viewers who do not have ownership of the continuous oral, material, and spiritual culture of the Yolŋu. This is of urgent importance in an ideologically charged environment of cultural recovery such as Aboriginal Australian culture. Through its complex, intercultural depiction of time, *Ten Canoes* also exposes and redirects the politics of the possession of the past.

This book began by discussing a sliver of coast at the tip of a Southern continent that had been excluded from an imagined medieval globe, as an entry point into asking what it means for medievalism to exclude the East and especially the South, while privileging the West and the North as the 'true' locations of the medieval. Later chapters have continued this inquiry, starting from the West and then following medievalism's trajectory eastward and then southward, exploring how it has fruitfully expanded the modern medievalist imaginary, but also how it has threatened to occlude the great depth of human history that lies beyond Europe. I have ended the book by reaching another coastal tip of a different Southern land—this time a non-imaginary one—asking what it means to contain the deep human and more-than-human past of this place within the framework of medievalism. I have sought to show that medievalism can offer the experience of trans-temporal world disclosure, and can expand the geopolitical ambit of 'the medieval', as well as offering a discourse for embracing or rejecting 'the global' in its numerous iterations. But I have also shown where medievalism's capacity to scale up, attaching the Middle Ages to deeper times and more distant places, becomes strained. Its potential for reduction and assimilation is exposed by its attempts to use the medieval to encompass deep human history and the planetary past; and it finally reaches its limits when it arrives on Aboriginal Country, whose stories are rightly told by others.

Eurocentric medievalism has had a long and complicit relationship with colonialism; if practitioners and scholars of world medievalism are to traverse new terrains, this cannot be a neocolonial venture. We must be attentive to how medievalism can open up the world beyond Europe; but we must also know when to refrain from using 'the medieval' to claim sovereignty over the past.

BIBLIOGRAPHY

Primary texts

Abu-Jaber, Diana, *Crescent* (W. W. Norton and Company, 2003).

Ali, Tariq, *Can Pakistan Survive? The Death of a State* (London: Penguin Books, 1983).

Ali, Tariq, *Shadows of the Pomegranate Tree* (London: Verso, 1992).

Ali, Tariq, *The Book of Saladin* (London: Verso, 1998).

Ali, Tariq, *A Sultan in Palermo* (London: Verso, 2005).

Ali, Tariq, *The Clash of Fundamentalisms: Crusades, Jihads and Modernity* (London: Verso, 2002).

Ali, Tariq, and Howard Brenton, *Iranian Nights* (London: Nick Hern Books, 1989).

Anon. (Frank Renar), 'Prolific Australia: The Continent of the British Race', *The Lone Hand* 1 (1907), 68.

Ashour, Radwa, *Granada: A Novel*, trans. William Granara, foreword by Maria Rosa Menocal (Syracuse, New York: Syracuse University Press, 2003).

Benioff, David, and D. B. Weiss, *Game of Thrones* (New York: HBO, 2011–19).

Boldrewood, Rolf, *A Sydney-Side Saxon* (London, Macmillan; Sydney, Cornstalk Publishing, 1894/1925).

Bordihn, Maria R., *The Falcon of Palermo* (New York: Atlantic Monthly Press, 2005).

Camus, Renaud, *Le Grand Remplacement*, 1st edn (Paris: David Reinharc, 2011).

Chahine, Youssef, *Al Nasser Salah Ad-Din* (*Saladin the Victorious*) (Assia, 1963).

Chahine, Youssef, *al-Masir* (*Destiny*) (Pyramide/MSR International Films, 1997).

Chesterton, G. K., *The Outline of Sanity* (London: Methuen, 1926).

Crichton, Michael, *Eaters of the Dead* (New York: Knopf, 1976).

Daley, Victor, 'An Australian Mummy', in *Creeve Roe: Poetry by Victor Daley*, ed. Muir Holburn and Marjorie Pizer, foreword by E. J. Brady, drawings by Roderick Shaw (Sydney: Pinchgut Press), 128–32.

De Heer, Rolf, and Peter Djigirr, *Ten Canoes* (Palace Films, 2006).

De Mille, Cecile B., *The Crusades* (Paramount Pictures, 1935).

Enard, Mathias, *La Boussole* (Arles: Actes Sud, 2015).

Enard, Mathias, *Compass*, trans. Charlotte Mandel (New York: New Directions, 2017).

Ferrari, Jérôme, *Où j'ai laissé mon âme* (Paris: Éditions Actes Sud, 2010).

Ferrari, Jérôme, *Sermon sur la chute de Rome* (Paris: Éditions Actes Sud, 2012).

Ferrari, Jérôme, *Sermon on the Fall of Rome*, trans. Geoffrey Strachan (London: Maclehose Press, 2016).

Finkielkraut, Alain, *L'Identité malheureuse* (Paris: Stock, 2013).

Gularri: That Brings Unity, dir. Bangana Wunungmurra (CAAMA Productions and WankwarrpuynguYolngu Media, Australia, 1997).

Heine, Heinrich, *Almansor*, in *Gesamtausgabe der Werke*, ed. Manfred Windfuhr, (Hamburg, 1973–97), Bild 5.

Holland, Cecelia, *Great Maria* (Naperville, IL: Sourcebooks Landmark, 1974/2010).

Houellebecq, Michel, *Soumission* (Paris: Groupe Flammarion, 2015).

Houellebecq, Michel, *Submission*, trans. Lorin Stein (London: William Heinemann, 2015).

James, Marlon, *Black Leopard, Red Wolf* (New York: Riverhead Books, 2019).

Lawson, Joseph J., *Clash of the Empires* (Asylum Pictures, 2012).

Ludlow, Jack, *Conquest Trilogy* (London: Allison & Busby, 2009–10).

McTiernan, John, *The 13th Warrior* (Touchstone Pictures, 1999).

Martin, George R. R., *A Song of Ice and Fire* Series (New York: Bantam Books; London: Voyager Books, 1996–).

Martin, George R. R., Elio M. Garcia, and Linda Antonsson, *The World of Ice & Fire: The Untold History of Esteros and The Game of Thrones* (London: Harper Voyager, 2014).

Martin, George R. R., and Jonathan Roberts, *The Lands of Ice and Fire: Maps from King's Landing to Across the Narrow Sea* (New York: Random House, 2012).

Overo-Tarimo, Ufuoma, *The Miller's Tale: Wahala Dey O!*, ed. Jessie Lockhart (self-published, 2018).

Rouart, Jean-Marie, *Adieu à la France qui s'en va* (Paris: Éditions Grasset, 2003).

Scott, Sir Ridley, *Kingdom of Heaven* (Twentieth Century Fox, 2005).

Scott, Sir Walter, *Ivanhoe* (Harmondsworth: Penguin, 1820/2000).

Scott, Sir Walter, *The Talisman*, 1825, Penn State Electronic Classics, file://D:/Users/mq20160735/Documents/crusades/talisman.pdf.

Ten Canoes Press Kit, 2006, https://www.metromagazine.com.au/tencanoes/pdf/background.pdf.

Tolkien, J. R. R., *Tree and Leaf, Including the Poem Mythopoeia* (Boston: Houghton Mifflin, 1989).

Unsworth, Barry, *The Ruby in her Navel* (London: Hamish Hamilton, 2006).

Warner Bros Entertainment Inc, New Line Cinema LLC, New Line Productions Inc., Metro-Goldwyn-Meyer Studios Inc., and the Paul Zaentz Company, Plaintiffs v The Global Asylum Inc., Defendant, 2012, Complaint, United States District Court, Central District of California.

Ye'or, Bat, *The Dhimmi: Jews and Christians under Islam*, trans. David Maisel, Paul Fenton, and David Littman (Rutherford, NJ: Fairleigh Dickinson University Press, 1985).

Ye'or, Bat, *Eurabia: The Euro-Arab Axis* (Cranbury, NJ: Fairleigh-Dickinson University Press, 2005).

Zaidan, Jurji, *The Conquest of Andalusia*, trans. with an Afterword and Study Guide by Roger Allen (Bethesda, MD: The Zaidan Foundation, 2010).

Zaidan, Jurji, *The Battle of Poitiers: Charles Martel and 'Abd al-Rahman*, trans., with a study guide, by William Granara (Bethesda, MD: The Zaidan Foundation, 2011).

Zaidan, Jurji, *Saladin and the Assassins*, trans. Paul Starkey (Bethesda, MD: The Zaidan Foundation, 2011a).

Zemmour, Éric. *Mélancolie Française: L'histoire de France racontée par Éric Zemmour* (Paris: Librarie Anthème Fayard et Éditions Denoël, 2010).

Zemmour, Éric, *Le Suicide français* (Paris: Éditions Albin Michel, 2014).

Secondary texts

Abu-Lughod, Janet, *Before European Hegemony: The World System AD 1250–1350* (Oxford: Oxford University Press, 1989).

Agbabi, Patience, 'Stories in Stanza'd English: A Cross-Cultural Canterbury Tales', *Literature Compass* 15.6 (2018), e12455.

Ahmed, Sara, *The Promise of Happiness* (Durham: Duke University Press, 2010).

Ahmed, Talat, 'Interview: Tariq Ali', *Socialist Review* 311, November 2006, 6–9. http://socialistreview.org.uk/311/interview-tariq-ali.

Akbari, Suzanne Conklin, 'Modeling Medieval World Literature', *Middle Eastern Studies* 20.1 (2017), 2–17.

Akbari, Suzanne Conklin, and Karla Mallette (eds), *A Sea of Languages: Rethinking the Arabic Role in Medieval Literary History* (Toronto: University of Toronto Press, 2013).

Ali, Daud, 'The Idea of the Medieval in the Writing of South Asian History: Contexts, Methods and Politics', *Social History* 39.3 (2014), 382–407.

Ali, Tariq, 'From the Ashes of Gaza', *The Guardian*, 30 December 2008, https://www.theguardian.com/commentisfree/2008/dec/30/gaza-hamas-palestinians-israel1.

Altschul, Nadia, *Geographies of Philological Knowledge: Postcoloniality and the Transatlantic National Epic* (Chicago: University of Chicago Press, 2012).

Alush-Levron, Merav, 'The Politics of Ethnic Melancholy in Israeli Cinema', *Social Identities* 21.2 (2015), 169–83.

Amalfi, Carmelo, and Leigh Dayton, 'Hobbits May Be Earliest Australians', *The Australian*, 8 December 2005, https://www.freerepublic.com/focus/news/1535978/posts.

Amari, Michele, *Storia dei Musulmani di Sicilia*, 3 vols, ed. Carlos Alfonso Nallino (Catania: Prampolini, 1933–9).

Amer, Sahar, and Laura Doyle, 'Introduction: Reframing Postcolonial and Global Studies in the Longue Durée', *PMLA* 130.2 (2015), 331–5.

Apter, Emily, 'Afterword: The "World" in World Literature', in *Transnational French Studies: Postcolonialism and Littérature-monde*, ed. Alec G. Hargreaves, Charles Fosdick, and David Murphy (Liverpool: Liverpool University Press, 2012), 287–95.

Apter, Emily, *Against World Literature: On the Politics of Untranslatability* (New York: Verso, 2013).

Arsan, Andrew, John Karam, and Akram Khater, 'On Forgotten Shores: Migration in Middle East Studies and the Middle East in Migration Studies', *Mahjar & Mashriq: Journal of Middle East Migration Studies* 1.1 (2013), 1–7, http://lebanesestudies.ojs.chass.ncsu.edu/index.php/mashriq/article/view/1/2.

Atelier Daynès, Reconstruction of *homo floresiensis*, https://www.elisabethdaynes.com/paleoart-reconstructions/.

Aveling, Harry, 'A Malay Knight Speaks the White Man's Tongue', *Indonesia and the Malay World* 44.130 (2016), 389–408.

Bawaka Country, Sarah Wright, Sandie Suchet-Pearson, Kate Lloyd, Laklak Burrarwanga, Ritjilili Ganambarr, Merrkiyawuy Ganambarr-Stubbs, Banbapuy Ganambarr, and Djawundil Maynuru, 'Working With and Learning From Country: Decentring Human Author-ity', *Cultural Geographies* 22.2 (2015), 269–83.

Barbero, Alessandro, *The Day of the Barbarians: The Battle That Led to the Fall of the Roman Empire*, trans. John Cullen (New York: Walker & Company, 2007).

Barrington, Candace, 'Global Medievalism and Translation', in *The Cambridge Companion to Medievalism*, ed. Louise D'Arcens (Cambridge: Cambridge University Press, 2016), 180–95.

Bashford, Alison, 'Terraqueous Histories', *The Historical Journal* 60.2 (2017), 253–72.

Bayeh, Jumana, 'Anglophone Arab or Diasporic? The Arab Novel in Australia, Britain, Canada, the United States of America', *Commonwealth Essays and Studies* 39.2 (2017), 13–26.

Beaujard, Philippe, 'The Indian Ocean in Eurasian and African World-Systems before the Sixteenth Century', *Journal of World History* 16.4 (2005), 411–65.

Belloni, Matthew, '"Hobbit" Lawyers Threaten "Age of the Hobbits" Movie', *The Hollywood Reporter*, 17 October 2012, https://www.hollywoodreporter.com/thr-esq/hobbit-lawyers-threaten-age-hobbits-377892, accessed 29 May 2019.

Bentley, Jerry H., 'The Task of World History', in *The Oxford Handbook of World History*, ed. Jerry H. Bentley (Oxford University Press, 2011), 1–18.

Bentley, Jerry H., 'Cross-Cultural Interaction and Periodization in World History', *American Historical Review* 101.3 (1996), 749–70.

Betz, Hans-Georg, 'Nativism across Time and Space', *Swiss Political Science Review* 23.4 (2017), 335–53.

Bildhauer, Bettina, *Filming the Middle Ages* (London: Reaktion Books, 2011).

Bloch, R. Howard, and Stephen G. Nichols, *Medievalism and the Modernist Temper* (Baltimore: Johns Hopkins University Press, 1996).

Bloembergen, Marieke, and Martijn Eickhoff, 'Decolonizing Borobudur: Moral Engagements and the Fear of Loss. The Netherlands, Japan, and (Post) Colonial Heritage Politics in Indonesia', in *Sites, Bodies and Stories: Imagining Indonesian History*, ed. Susan Legêne, Bambang Purwanto, and Henk Schulte Nordholt (Singapore: NUS Press, 2015), 33–66.

Bock, Pauline, 'How Right-Wing Thinker Eric Zemmour Is Fuelling France's Identity Wars', *New Statesman*, 30 October 2019, https://www.newstatesman.com/world/europe/2019/10/how-right-wing-thinker-eric-zemmour-fuelling-france-s-identity-wars.

Bon, François, '34,000 avant J.-C: Inventer le monde dans les entrailles de la Terre', in *Histoire mondiale de la France*, ed. Patrick Boucheron (Paris: Éditions de Seuil, 2017), 19–23.

Boucheron, Patrick, et al., *Histoire mondiale de la France* (Paris: Éditions de Seuil, 2017).

Boucheron, Patrick, et al., *France in the World: A New Global History*, ed. Stéphane Gerson (New York: Other, 2019).

Brann, Ross, 'Andalusi "Exceptionalism"', in *A Sea of Languages: Rethinking the Arabic Role in Medieval Literary History*, ed. Suzanne Conklin Akbari and Karla Mallette (Toronto: University of Toronto Press, 2013), 119–134.

Braudel, Fernand, *La Méditerranée et le Monde Méditerranéen a l'époque de Philippe II*, 3 vols, 9th edn (Paris: A. Colin, 1949/1990).

Brigg, Morgan, 'Old Cultures and New Possibilities: Marege'-Makassar Diplomacy in Southeast Asia', *The Pacific Review* 24.5 (2011), 601–23.

Britt, Karen C., 'Roger II of Sicily: Rex, Basileus, and Khalif? Identity, Politics, and Propaganda in the Cappella Palatina', *Mediterranean Studies* 16 (2007), 21–45.

Brown, P., T. Sutikna, et al., 'A Small-Bodied Hominin from the Late Pleistocene of Flores, Indonesia', *Nature* 431.28 (2004), 1055–61.

Bull, Hedley, *The Anarchical Society: A Study of Order in World Politics* (New York: Columbia University Press, 1977).

Callaway, Ewen, 'Tales of the Hobbit', *Nature* 514, 23 October 2014, 422–6.

Carroll, Shiloh, *The Medievalism of Game of Thrones* (Cambidge: Boydell and Brewer, 2018).

Caruth, Cathy, *Unclaimed Experience: Trauma, Narrative and History* (Baltimore: Johns Hopkins University Press, 1996).

Catlos, Brian A., *Muslims of Medieval Latin Christendom c.1050–1614* (Cambridge: Cambridge University Press, 2014).

Chahine, Youssef, and Joseph Massad, 'Art and Politics in the Cinema of Youssef Chahine', *Journal of Palestine Studies* 28.2 (1999), 77–93.

Chakrabarty, Dipesh, *Provincializing Europe: Postcolonial Thought and Historical Difference* (Princeton, NJ: Princeton University Press, 2000).

Chambers, Claire, 'Tariq Ali', in *British Muslim Fictions: Interviews with Contemporary Writers* (Basingstoke: Palgrave Macmillan, 2011), 33–55.

Chazan, Robert, *Reassessing Jewish Life in Medieval Europe* (Cambridge: Cambridge University Press, 2010).

Chaudhuri, K. N., *Trade and Civilization in the Indian Ocean: An Economic History from the Rise of Islam to 1750* (Cambridge: Cambridge University Press, 1985).

Cheah, Peng, 'World against Globe: Toward a Normative Conception of World Literature', *New Literary History* 45.3 (2014), 303–29.

Chism, Christine, 'Tawaddud/Teodor and the Stripping of Medieval Mastery', *Digital Philology* 8.1 (2019), 123–37.

Citron, Suzanne, 'A propos de Clovis', *Le Monde*, 28 February 1996, http://www.maphilosophie.fr/voir_un_texte.php?$cle=A%20propos%20de%20Clovis.

Clarke, Anne, 'Winds of Change: An Archaeology of Contact in the Groote Eylandt Archipelago, Northern Australia', 1994 PhD thesis, Australian National University.

Clarke, Anne, and Ursula Frederick, 'Making a Sea Change: Rock Art, Archaeology and the Enduring Legacy of Frederick McCarthy's Research on Groote Eylandt', in *Exploring the Legacy of the 1948 Arnhem Land Expedition*, ed. Martin Thomas and Margo Neale (Canberra: ANU E Press, 2011), 135–55.

Cohen, Jeffrey Jerome, and Linda Elkins-Tanton, *Earth* (New York, etc.: Bloomsbury, 2017).

Cohen, Mark, *Under Crescent and Cross: The Jews in the Middle Ages* (Princeton, NJ: Princeton University Press, 1994).

Cole, Douglas, ' "The Crimson Thread of Kinship": Ethnic Ideas in Australia, 1870–1914', *Historical Studies* 14 (1971), 511–25.

Collins-Gearing, Brooke, et al., 'Listenin' Up: ReImagining Ourselves through Stories of and from Country', *M/C Journal* 18.6, December 2015, 1, ezproxy. newcastle.edu.au/login? url=http://search.ebscohost.com/login.aspx?direct=true&db=ufh&AN=111814601&site=edslive.

Connell, Raewyn, *Southern Theory: The Global Dynamics of Knowledge in Social Science* (Sydney: Allen and Unwin, 2007/New York: Routledge, 2020).

Cooppan, Vilashini, 'World Literature and Global Theory: Comparative Literature for the New Millenium', *Symplokē* 9.1 (2001), 15–43.

Corn, Aaron, and Brian Djangirrawuy Garawirrtja, 'The Legacy of Yolŋu-Makassan Contact: Before the First Wave', in *The First Wave: Exploring Early Coastal Contact History in Australia*, ed. Gillian Dooley and Danielle Clode (Mile End, South Australia: Wakefield Press, 2019), 104–32.

Crosbie, Tom, 'Critical Historiography in "Atanarjuat the Fast Runner and Ten Canoes"', *Journal of New Zealand Literature* 24.2 (2007), 135–52.

Dalton, Heather, Jukka Salo, Pekka Niemelä, and Simo Örmä, 'Australasian Cockatoo: Symbol of Détente between East and West and Evidence of the Ayyubids' Global Reach', *Parergon* 35.1 (2018), 35–60.

Dalton, Rex, 'More Evidence for Hobbit Unearthed as Diggers Are Refused Access to Cave', *Nature* 437.13 (2005), 934–5.

Damrosch, David, *What Is World Literature?* (Princeton, NJ: Princeton University Press, 2003).

D'Arcens, Louise, 'Inverse Invasions: Medievalism and Colonialism in Rolf Boldrewood's *A Sydney-Side Saxon*', *Parergon* 22.2 (2005), 159–82.

D'Arcens, Louise, 'Response to Bruce Holsinger: In Praise of Feral Medievalism', *Postmedieval* 1.3 (2010), 344–6.

D'Arcens, Louise, *Old Songs in the Timeless Land* (Cawley/Turnhout: University of Western Australia Press/Brepols, 2011).

D'Arcens, Louise, *Comic Medievalism: Laughing at the Middle Ages* (Cambridge: Boydell and Brewer, 2014).

D'Arcens, Louise, 'Introduction: Medievalism: Scope and Complexity', in *The Cambridge Companion to Medievalism*, ed. Louise D'Arcens (Cambridge: Cambridge University Press, 2016), 1–13.

D'Arcens, Louise, 'Nostalgia, Melancholy, and the Emotional Economy of Replacement: Feeling for *la France profonde* in the Novels of Michel Houellebecq', *Exemplaria* 30.3 (2018), 257–73.

Davis, Kathleen, *Periodization and Sovereignty: How Ideas of Feudalism and Secularization Govern the Politics of Time* (Philadelphia: University of Pennsylvania Press, 2008).

Davis, Kathleen, 'Theory in Time', *PMLA* 130.3 (2015), 759–67.

Davis, Kathleen, and Michael Puett, 'Periodization and "The Medieval Globe": A Conversation', *The Medieval Globe* 2.1 (2015), 1–14.

Davis, Kathleen, and Nadia Altschul, *Medievalisms in the Postcolonial World: The Idea of 'The Middle Ages' outside Europe* (Baltimore: Johns Hopkins University Press, 2009).

Davis, Therese, 'Remembering our Ancestors: Cross-Cultural Collaboration and the Mediation of Aboriginal Culture and History in *Ten Canoes* (Rolf de Heer, 2006)', *Studies in Australasian Cinema* 1.1 (2007), 5–14.

De la Cadena, Marisol, and Mario Blaser (eds), *A World of Many Worlds* (Durham and London: Duke University Press, 2018).

Deger, Jennifer, 'Seeing the Invisible: Yolngu Video as Revelatory Ritual', *Visual Anthropology* 20.2–3 (2007), 103–21.

Dellheim, Charles, *The Face of the Past: The Preservation of the Medieval Inheritance in Victorian England* (New York: Cambridge University Press, 1982).

Democracy Now interview with Tariq Ali, 6 July 2016, https://www.democracynow.org/2016/7/6/tariq_ali_on_chilcot_iraq_report.

Détroit, F., A. S. Mijares, J. Corny, G. Daver, C. Zanolli, E. Dizon, E. Robles, R. Grün, and P. J. Piper, 'A New Species of *Homo* from the Late Pleistocene of the Philippines', *Nature* 568.7751 (2019), 181–6.

De Vos, John, 'Receiving an Ancestor in the Phylogenetic Tree: Neanderthal Man, Homo Erectus, and Homo Floresiensis: *L'histoire se Répète*', *Journal of the History of Biology* 42 (2009), 361–79.

Dimock, Wai Chee, 'Literature for the Planet', *PMLA* 116.1 (2001), 173–88.

Dimock, Wai Chee, 'Introduction: Planet as Duration and Extension', in *Through Other Continents: American Literature across Deep Time* (Princeton, NJ and Oxford: Princeton University Press, 2009), 1–6.

Dinshaw, Carolyn, *How Soon Is Now? Medieval Texts, Amateur Readers, and the Queerness of Time* (Durham: Duke University Press, 2012).

Doyle, Laura, *Inter-imperiality: Vying Empires, Gendered Labor, and the Literary Arts of Alliance* (Durham and London: Duke University Press, 2020).

Dreyfus, Hubert L., *Commentary on Being and Time* (Cambridge: MIT Press, 1999).

Dreyfus, Hubert L., and Mark A. Wrathall, 'Martin Heidegger: An Introduction to his Thought, Work, and Life', in *A Companion to Heidegger*, ed. Hubert L. Dreyfus and Mark A. Wrathall (Malden, MA: Blackwell, 2005), 1–15.

Emery, Elizabeth. 'J. K. Huysmans, Medievalist.' *Modern Language Studies* 30.2 (2000), 119–31.

Eng, David L., and Shinhee Han, 'A Dialogue on Racial Melancholia', in *Loss: The Politics of Mourning*, ed. David L. Eng and David Kazanjian (Berkeley: University of California Press, 2003), 343–71.

Evans, Nicholas, 'Macassan Loanwords in Top End Languages', *Australian Journal of Linguistics* 12.1 (1992), 45–91.

Fabian, Johannes, *Time and the Other: How Anthropology Makes its Object* (New York: Columbia University Press, 1983).

Farinelli, Marcel A., 'Island Societies and Mainland Nation-Building in the Mediterranean: Sardinia and Corsica in Italian, French, and Catalan Nationalism', *Island Studies Journal* 12.1 (2017), 21–34.

Fauvelle, François-Xavier, '719: L'Afrique frappe à la porte du pays des Francs', in Patrick Boucheron et al., *Histoire mondiale de la France* (Paris: Éditions de Seuil, 2017), 91–4.

Feichtinger, Johannes, 'Komplexer k.u.k. Orientalismus: Akteure, Institutionen, Diskurse im 19. und 20. Jahrhundert in Österreich', in *Orientalismen in Ostmitteleuropa: Diskurse, Akteure und Disziplinen vom 19. Jahrhundert bis zum Zweiten Weltkrieg*, ed. Robert Born and Sarah Lemmen (Bielefeld: Transcript Verlag, 2014), 31–64.

Flood, Josephine, *Archaeology of the Dreamtime*, rev. edn (Sydney: Collins, 2004).

Flores Tourism website, 'The Hobbit Liang Bua', http://florestourism.com/places/the-hobbit-liang-bua/.

Forth, Gregory, *Beneath the Volcano: Religion, Cosmology and Spirit Classification among the Nage of Eastern Indonesia* (Leiden: KITLV Press, 1998).

Forth, Gregory, 'Hominids, Hairy Hominoids, and the Science of Humanity', *Anthropology Today* 12.3 (2005), 13–17.

Forth, Gregory, 'Flores after Floresiensis: Implications of Local Reaction to Recent Palaeoanthropological Discoveries on an Eastern Indonesian Island', *Bijdragen tot de Taal-, Land- en Volkenkunde* 162.2/3 (2006), 336–49.

Frank, Andre Gunder, and Barry K. Gills (eds), *The World System: Five Hundred Years or Five Thousand?* (London, New York: Routledge, 1993).

Freud, Sigmund, 'Mourning and Melancholia', in *The Standard Edition of the Complete Psychological Works of Sigmund Freud*, trans. and ed. James Strachey, in collaboration with Anna Freud, Volume XIV (London: Hogarth Press, 1917/1957), 243–58.

Gana, Nouri, 'In Search of Andalusia: Reconfiguring Arabness in Diana Abu-Jaber's Crescent', *Comparative Literature Studies* 45.2 (2008), 228–46.

Ganguly, Debjani, 'Literary Globalism in the New Millenium', *Postcolonial Studies* 11.1 (2008), 119–33.

Ganim, John M., *Medievalism and Orientalism: Three Essays on Literature, Architecture and Cultural Identity* (Basingstoke, New York: Palgrave Macmillan, 2005).

Ganim, John M., 'Cosmopolitanism, Sovereignty and Medievalism', *Australian Literary Studies* 26.3–4 (2011), 6–20.

Gay'wu Group of Women, *Song Spirals: Sharing Women's Wisdom of Country through Songlines* (Sydney: Allen & Unwin, 2019).

Gee, Henry, *The Science of Middle Earth*, rev. 2nd edn (Golden, CO: Reanimu Press, 2014).

Ghosh, Bishnupriya, 'Once There Was Cosmopolitanism: Enchanted Pasts as Global History in the Contemporary Novel', *Ariel: A Review of International English Literature* 42.1 (2011), 11–33.

Gill, Richard, 'Oikos and Logos: Chesterton's Vision of Distributism', *Logos: A Journal of Catholic Thought and Culture* 10.3 (2007), 64–90.

Goh, Geok Yian, 'Beyond the World-System: A Buddhist Ecumene', *Journal of World History* 25.4 (2014), 493–513.

Gopnik, Adam, 'The First Frenchman', *The New Yorker*, 7 October 1996, 44–5.

Gould, Stephen Jay, 'Bushes and Ladders in Human Evolution', in *Ever Since Darwin: Reflections in Natural History* (New York, London: W. W. Norton, 1977), 56–62.

Graizbord, David, 'Pauline Christianity and Jewish "Race": The Case of João Baptista D'Este', in *Race and Blood in the Iberian World*, ed. Max S. Hering Torres, María Elena Martínez, and David Nirenberg (Münster, etc.: LIT Verlag, 2012), 61–79.

Granara, William, 'Ibn Ḥamdīs and the Poetry of Nostalgia', in *The Literature of Al-Andalus*, ed. María Rosa Menocal, Raymond P. Scheindlin, and Michael Sells (Cambridge: Cambridge University Press, 2000), 388–403.

Granara, William, 'Nostalgia, Arab Nationalism, and the Andalusian *Chronotope* in the Evolution of the Modern Arabic Novel', *Journal of Arabic Literature* 36.1 (2005), 57–73.

Griffiths, Billy, *Deep Time Dreaming: Uncovering Ancient Australia* (Melbourne: Black Inc., 2018).

Griffiths, Billy, and Lynette Russell, 'What We Were Told: Responses to 65,000 Years of Aboriginal History', *Aboriginal History* 42 (2018), 31–53.

Griffiths, Tom, *Hunters and Collectors: The Antiquarian Imagination in Australia* (Cambridge, etc.: Cambridge University Press, 1996).

Grossman, Avraham, *Pious and Rebellious: Jewish Women in Medieval History* (Hanover, NH: Brandeis University Press, 2004).

Gurche, John, Reconstruction of *Homo Floresiensis*, http://gurche.com/homo-floresiensis.

Guzmán, María Costanza, 'Reviewed Work: *Granada: A Novel* by Radwa 'Ashour, William Granara, María Rosa Menocal', *The Arab Studies Journal* 13/14 (2005/6), 129–32.

Hamby, Louise, 'Thomson Times and Ten Canoes (de Heer and Djigirr, 2006)', *Studies in Australasian Cinema* 1.2 (2007), 127–46.

Hamdani, Abbas, 'An Islamic Background to the Voyages of Discovery', in *The Legacy of Muslim Spain*, ed. Salma Khadra Jayyusi (Boston: Brill, 1994), 289–93.

Hanafi, Hassan, 'The Middle East, in Whose World?', in *The Middle East in a Globalized World: Papers from the Fourth Nordic Conference on Middle Eastern Studies, Oslo, 1998*, ed. Bjørn Olav Utvik and Knut S. Vikør (Bergen, London: Nordic Society for Middle Eastern Studies, 2000), 1–9.

Handel, James, '"Age of the Hobbits" Is Now "Clash of the Empires"', *The Hollywood Reporter*, 12 December 2012, https://www.hollywoodreporter.com/thr-esq/age-hobbits-is-clash-empires-401897.

Haydock, Nickolas, 'Introduction: "The Unseen Cross upon the Breast": Medievalism, Orientalism, and Discontent', in *Hollywood in the Holy Land: Essays on Film Depictions of the Crusades and Christian-Muslim Clashes*, ed. Nickolas Haydock and E. L. Risden (Jefferson, NC and London: McFarland & Company, Inc., 2009), 1–30.

Hayes, Susan, Thomas Sutikna, and Mike Morwood, 'Faces of *Homo floresiensis* (LB1)', *Journal of Archaeological Science* 40 (2013), 4400–10.

Heidegger, Martin, *Being and Time*, trans. J. Macquarrie and E. Robinson (Oxford: Blackwell, 1962).

Heinzelmann, Martin, 'Heresy in Books I and II of Gregory of Tours' *Historiae*', in *After Rome's Fall: Sources of Early Medieval History. Essays Presented to Walter Goffart*, ed. Alexander Callander Murray (Toronto, Buffalo, London: University of Toronto Press, 1998), 67–82.

Hegel, G. W. F., *Lectures on the Philosophy of World History*, trans. H. B. Nisbet (Cambridge: Cambridge University Press, 1975).

Heng, Geraldine, 'Reinventing Race, Colonization, and Globalisms across Deep Time: Lessons from the Longue Duree', *PMLA* 130.2 (2015), 358–66.

Heng, Geraldine, *The Invention of Race in the European Middle Ages* (Cambridge: Cambridge University Press, 2018).

Heng, Geraldine, and Lynn Ramey, 'Early Globalities, Global Literatures: Introducing a Special Issue on the Global Middle Ages', *Literature Compass* 11.7 (2014), 389–94.

Heyns, Michael, 'An Epistemology of Engagement', *Koers* 71.1 (2006), 73–99.

Hiatt, Alfred, *Terra Incognita: Mapping the Antipodes before 1600* (Chicago: University of Chicago Press, 2008).

Hillebrand, Carole, *The Crusades: Islamic Perspectives* (Edinbugh: Edinburgh University Press, 1999).

Hillebrand, Carole, 'The Evolution of the Saladin Legend in the West', in *Crusades: Medieval Worlds in Conflict*, ed. T. Madden (Aldershot: Ashgate, 2011), 9–23.

Hodgson, Marshall G. S., 'The Role of Islam in World History', *International Journal of Middle East Studies* 1.2 (1970), 99–123.

Holmes, Catherine, and Naomi Standen, 'Introduction: Towards a Global Middle Ages', *Past and Present* 238, Supplement 13 (2018), 1–44.

Holsinger, Bruce, *Neomedievalism, Neoconservatism, and the War on Terror* (Chicago: Prickly Paradigm Press 2007).

Holsinger, Bruce, 'Neomedievalism and International Relations', *The Cambridge Companion to Medievalism*, ed. Louise D'Arcens (Cambridge: Cambridge University Press, 2016), 165–79.

Horsman, Reginald, *Race and Manifest Destiny: The Origins of American Racial Anglo-Saxonism* (Harvard: Harvard University Press, 1981).

Hsy, Jonathan, *Antiracist Medievalisms: From 'Yellow Peril' to Black Lives Matter* (Amsterdam: Amsterdam University Press, 2021).

Hynes, Gerard, '"Beneath the Earth's Deep Keel"', *Tolkien Studies* 9 (2012), 21–36.

Janke, Terri, *Pathways and Protocols: A Filmmaker's Guide to Working with Indigenous People, Culture, and Concepts* (Australian Government: Screen Australia, 2009).

Johnson, Rebecca C., 'Importing the Novel: The Arabic Novel in and as Translation', *Novel: A Forum on Fiction* 48.2 (2015), 243–60.

Jungers, William, and Karen Baab, 'The Geometry of Hobbits: *Homo Floresiensis* and Human Evolution', *Significance*, December 2009, 159–64.

Kahf, Mohja, *Western Representations of the Muslim Woman: From Termagant to Odalisque* (Austin: University of Texas Press, 1999).

Karras, Alan, and Laura J. Mitchell, 'Writing World Histories for our Times', in *Encounters Old and New in World History: Essays Inspired by Jerry H. Bentley*, ed. Alan Karras and Laura J. Mitchell (Honolulu: University of Hawai'i Press, 2017), 1–12.

Kaufman, Amy S., and Paul B. Sturtevant, *The Devil's Historians: How Modern Extremists Abuse the Medieval Past* (Toronto: University of Toronto Press, 2020).

Keene, Bryan C., 'Introduction: Manuscripts and their Outlook on the World', in *Toward a Global Middle Ages: Encountering the World through Illuminated Manuscripts*, ed. Bryan C. Keene (Los Angeles: The J. Paul Getty Museum, 2019), 5–31.

Kim, Dorothy, 'Introduction to Literature Compass Special Cluster: Critical Race and the Middle Ages', *Literature Compass* 16.e12549 (2019), https://doi.org/10.1111/lic3.12549.

Kinoshita, Sharon, 'Deprovincializing the Middle Ages', in *The Worlding Project: Doing Cultural Studies in the Era of Globalization*, ed. Rob Wilson and Christopher Leigh Connoly (Santa Cruz: New Pacific Press, 2007), 61–75.

Kinoshita, Sharon, 'Translatio/n, Empire, and the Worlding of Medieval Literature: The Travels of *Kalila wa Dimna*', *Postcolonial Studies* 11.4 (2008), 371–85.

Korzybski, Alfred, 'A Non-Aristotelian System and its Necessity for Rigour in Mathematics and Physics', a paper presented before the American Mathematical

Society at the New Orleans, Louisiana, meeting of the American Association for the Advancement of Science, 28 December 1931.

Kwaymullina, Ambelin, and Blaze Kwaymullina, 'Learning to Read the Signs: Law in an Indigenous Reality', *Journal of Australian Studies* 34.2 (2010), 195–208.

Laffan, Michael, 'Crossroads Region: Southeast Asia', in *The Cambridge World History*, vol. 6, ed. Jerry H. Bentley, Sanjay Subrahmanyam, and Merry E. Wiesner-Hanks (Cambridge: Cambridge University Press, 2017), 372–92.

Lafont, Cristina, 'Hermeneutics', in *A Companion to Heidegger*, ed. Hubert L. Dreyfus and Mark A. Wrathall (Malden, MA: Blackwell, 2005), 265–84.

Larrington, Carolyne, *Winter Is Coming: The Medieval World of Game of Thrones* (London: I. B. Taurus, 2015).

Laurentin, Emmanuel, '2015: Le retour du drapeau', in *Histoire mondiale de la France*, ed. Patrick Boucheron (Paris: Éditions du Seuil, 2017), 763–6.

Lee, Justin, 'Hobbit Makers Ban Uni from Using "Hobbit"', *Newshub*, 24 October 2012, https://www.newshub.co.nz/nznews/hobbit-makers-ban-uni-from-using-hobbit-2012102417.

Leibniz, G. W., *La Monadologie*, ed. E. Boutroux (Paris: Librairie Générale Française, 1892/1991).

Leys, Ruth, and Marlene Goldman, 'Navigating the Genealogies of Truma, Guilt, and Affect: An Interview with Ruth Leys', *University of Toronto Quarterly* 79.2 (2010), 656–79.

Lipton, Sara, *Dark Mirror: The Medieval Origins of Anti-Jewish Iconography* (New York: Metropolitan Books, 2014).

McClintock, Anne, *Imperial Leather: Race, Gender, and Sexuality in the Colonial Context* (New York, London: Routledge, 1995).

McClure, Julia, 'A New Politics of the Middle Ages: A Global Middle Ages for a Global Modernity', *History Compass* 13.11 (2015), 610–19.

McIntosh, Ian, 'Islam and Australia's Aborigines? A Perspective from North-East Arnhem Land', *Journal of Religious History* 20.1 (1996), 53–77.

McIntosh, Ian, 'Life and Death on the Wessel Islands: The Case of Australia's Mysterious African Coin Cache', *Australian Folklore* 27 (2012), 9–26.

McIntosh, Ian, 'The Ancient African Coins of Arnhem Land', *Australasian Science*, May 2014, 19–21.

Maalouf, Amin, *Les Croisades vues par les Arabes* (Paris: J. T. Lattès, 1983).

Magennis, Hugh, 'Michael Crichton, Ibn Fadlan, Fantasy Cinema: *Beowulf* at the Movies', *OEN* 35.1 (2001), 34–8.

Mallette, Karla, 'Poetries of the Norman Courts', in *The Literature of Al-Andalus*, ed. María Rosa Menocal, Raymond P. Scheindlin, and Michael Sells (Cambridge: Cambridge University Press, 2000), 377–87.

Mallette, Karla, 'Orientalism and the Nineteenth-Century Nationalist: Michele Amari, Ernest Renan, and 1848', *The Romanic Review* 96.2 (2005), 233–52.

Mallette, Karla, '*I nostri saracini*: Writing the History of the Arabs of Sicily', *California Italian Studies* 1.1 (2010), 1027.

Mead, Jenna, 'Medievalism on Country', in *The Global South and Literature*, ed. Russell West-Pavlov (Cambridge: Cambridge University Press, 2018), 264–306.

Meijer, Hanneke J. M., Lars van den Hock Ostende, Gert van den Bergh, and John de Vos, 'The Fellowship of the Hobbit: The Fauna Surrounding *Homo Floresiensis*', *Journal of Biogeography* 37 (2010), 995–1006.

Menocal, María Rosa, *The Arabic Role in Medieval Literary History: A Forgotten Heritage* (Philadelphia: University of Pennsylvania Press, 1987).

Menocal, María Rosa, *The Ornament of the World: How Muslims, Jews, and Christians Created a Culture of Tolerance in Medieval Spain* (Boston, New York: Little, Brown and Company, 2002).

Metcalfe, Alex, *The Muslims of Medieval Italy* (Edinburgh: Edinburgh University Press, 2009).

Mignolo, Walter, 'The Global South and World Dis/order', *Journal of Anthropological Research* 67.2 (2011), 165–88.

Mitchell, Philip Irving, '"Legend and History Have Met and Fused": The Interlocution of Anthropology, Historiography, and Incarnation in J. J. R Tolkien's "On Fairy Stories"', *Tolkien Studies* 8 (2011), 1–21.

Miyashiro, Adam, 'Our Deeper Past: Race, Settler Colonialism, and Medieval Heritage Politics', *Literature Compass* 16.e12550 (2019), https://doi.org/10.1111/lic3.12550.

Moore, Robert I., 'The Global Middle Ages', in *The Prospect of World History*, ed. James Belich, John Darwin, Margret Frenz, and Chris Wickham (Oxford: Oxford University Press, 2016), 80–92.

Morag, Raya, 'Perpetrator Trauma and Contemporary Israeli Documentary Cinema', *Camera Obscura* 80 (2012), 93–133.

Moreton-Robinson, Aileen, *The White Possessive: Property, Power and Indigenous Sovereignty* (Minneapolis: University of Minnesota Press, 2015).

Morwood, M. J., R. P. Soejono, et al., 'Archaeology and Age of a New Hominin from Flores in Eastern Indonesia', *Nature* 431, 28 October 2004, 1087–91.

Morwood, Mike, and Penny van Oosterzee, *A New Human: The Startling Discovery and Strange Story of the 'Hobbits' of Flores, Indonesia* (Walnut Creek, CA: Left Coast Press, 2007).

Nagib, Lúcia, 'Towards a Positive Definition of World Cinema', in *Remapping World Cinema: Identity, Culture and Politics in Film*, ed. Stephanie Dennison and Song Hwee Lim (London: Wallflower Press, 2006), 30–7.

Nakata, Martin, *Disciplining the Savages, Savaging the Disciplines* (Canberra: Aboriginal Studies Press, 2007).

Nancy, Jean-Luc, *The Creation of the World or Globalization*, trans. and intro. François Raffoul and David Pettigrew (Albany, NY: SUNY Press, 2007).

Ng, Su Fang, 'Global Souvenirs: Bridging East and West in the Malay Alexander Romance', *Literature Compass* 11.7 (2014), 395–408.

Nirenberg, David, *Communities of Violence: Persecution of Minorities in the Middle Ages* (Princeton, NJ: Princeton University Press, 1996).

Nirenberg, David, 'Was There Race before Modernity? The Example of "Jewish" Blood in Late Medieval Spain', in *The Origins of Racism in the West*, ed. Miriam Eliav-Feldon, Benjamin Isaac, and Joseph Ziegler (Cambridge: Cambridge University Press, 2009), 232–64.

Norwich, John Julius, *The Kingdom in the Sun, 1130–1194* (London: Longman, 1970).

Norwich, John Julius, *Sicily: An Island at the Crossroads of History* (New York: Random House, 2015).

Pappalardo, Salvatore, 'From Ibn Ḥamdīs to Giufà: Leonardo Sciascia and the Writing of a Siculo-Arab Literary History', *Italian Culture* 36.1 (2018), 32–47.

PASTTIME podcast, 'Episode 10 Field Guide: The Hobbit—An Unexpected Discovery', http://www.pasttime.org/2014/01/episode-10-field-guide-the-hobbit-an-unexpected-discovery/.

Paterson, Alistair, *A Millenium of Cultural Contact* (Walnut Creek, CA: Left Coast Press, 2011).

Pearson, Noel, 'A Rightful Place: Race, Recognition, and a More Complete Commonwealth', *Quarterly Essay* 55 (Melbourne: Black Inc., 2014).

Peled, M., 'Creative Translation: Towards the Study of Arabic Translations of Western Literature since the 19th Century', *Journal of Arabic Literature* 10 (1979), 129–50.

Pennock, Caroline Dodds, and Amanda Power, 'Globalizing Cosmologies', *Past and Present* 238, Supplement 13 (2018), 88–115.

Phillips, Jonathan, ' "Unity! Unity between All the Inhabitants of our Lands!" The Memory and Legacy of the Crusades and Saladin in the Near East, c.1880 to c.1925', in *Perceptions of the Crusades from the Nineteenth to the Twenty-First Century*, ed. Mike Horswell and Jonathan Phillips (New York: Routledge, 2018), 79–106.

Phillips, Richard, 'Remembering Islamic Empires: Speaking of Imperialism and Islamophobia', *New Formations* 70 (2010), 94–112.

Powell, Anna, *Deleuze, Altered States, and Film* (Edinburgh: Edinburgh University Press, 2007).

Rastegar, Kamran, 'Literary Modernity between Arabic and Person Prose: Jurji Zaydan's *Riwayat* in Persian Translation', *Comparative Critical Studies* 4.3 (2007), 359–78.

Rateliff, John D., '"And All the Days of her Life Are Forgotten": *The Lord of the Rings* as Mythic Prehistory', in *The Lord of the Rings 1954–2004: Scholarship in Honor of Richard E. Blackwelder*, ed. Wayne G. Hammond and Christina Scull (Milwaukee: Marquette University Press, 2006), 67–100.

Roberts, Richard 'Bert', and Thomas Sutikna, 'A Decade On and the Hobbit Still Holds Secrets', *The Conversation*, 30 October 2014, https://theconversation.com/a-decade-on-and-the-hobbit-still-holds-secrets-33454.

Rouse, Robert, 'Indigenising the Medieval; or How Did Maori and Awabakal Become Inscribed in Medieval Manuscripts?' *Parergon* 32.2 (2015), 233–50.

Runciman, Steven, *A History of the Crusades*, 3 vols (Cambridge: Cambridge University Press, 1951–4).

Rutherford, Anne, '*Ten Canoes* as "Inter-Cultural Membrane"', *Studies in Australasian Cinema* 7.2–3 (2013), 137–51.

Sabo, Deborah, 'Archaeology and the Sense of History in J. R. R. Tolkien's Middle-Earth', *Mythlore* 99/100 (2007), 91–112.

Safran, Janina M., 'The Politics of Book Burning in Al-Andalus', *Journal of Medieval Iberian Studies* 6.2 (2014), 148–68.

Said, Edward, *Orientalism* (New York: Vintage Books, 1979).

Said, Edward, *Culture and Imperialism* (New York: Knopf, 1994).

Salleh, Muhammad Haji, 'A Malay Knight Speaks the White Man's Tongue: Notes on Translating the *Hikayat Hang Tuah*', *Indonesia and the Malay World* 34.10 (2006), 395–405.

Salmon, Wesley, *Logic* (Englewood Cliffs, NJ: Prentice-Hall, 1984).

Salter, Jessica, 'Peter Frankopan: "This Idea of Globalisation as Something Facebook Taught Us Is Rubbish"', Interview, *The Telegraph*, 28 August 2015, https://www.telegraph.co.uk/books/authors/peter-frankopan-interview/.

Sassen, Saskia, *Territory, Authority, Rights: From Medieval to Global Assemblages* (Princeton, NJ: Princeton University Press, 2006).

Sciascia, Leonardo, *La Sicilia come metafore: Intervista di Marcelle Padovani* (Milan: Arnoldo Mondadori, 1979).

Shih, Shu-Mei, 'World Studies and Relational Comparison', *PMLA* 130.2 (2015), 430–8.

Simmons, Clare, *Reversing the Conquest: History and Myth in Nineteenth-Century British Literature* (New Brunswick: Rutgers University Press, 1990).

Smail, Daniel Lord, *On Deep History and the Brain* (Berkeley, Los Angeles: University of California Press, 2008).

Smail, Daniel Lord, 'The Original Subaltern', *Postmedieval* 1–2 (2010), 180–6.

Smail, Daniel Lord, and Andrew Shryock, 'History and the "Pre"', *American Historical Review* 118.3 (2013), 709–37.

Spire, Alexis, '1974: Reflux migratoires', in *Histoire mondiale de la France*, ed. Patrick Boucheron (Paris: Éditions du Seuil, 2017), 712–15.

Stephenson, Peta, 'Andrish St-Clare and the Trepang Project: The "Creative Intermediary" in an Indigenous-Asian Theatrical Production', *Journal of Australian Studies* 32.2 (2008), 163–78.

Stevenson, Kylie, '"It Could Change Everything": Coin Found Off Northern Australia May Be from Pre-1400 Africa', *The Guardian*, 12 May 2019, https://www.theguardian.com/australia-news/2019/may/12/it-could-change-everything-coin-found-off-northern-australia-may-be-from-pre-1400-africa.

Sturtevant, Paul, 'TPM Special Series: Race, Racism, and the Middle Ages', *The Public Medievalist*, 2017, https://www.publicmedievalist.com/race-racism-middle-ages-toc/.

Sutikna, Thomas, et al., 'Revised Stratigraphy and Chronology for *Homo Floresiensis* at Liang Bua in Indonesia', *Nature* 532, 21 April 2016, 366–9, plus appendix.

Symes, Carol, 'Introducing the Medieval Globe', *The Medieval Globe* 1.1 (2014), 1–8.

Szpiech, Ryan, 'The Convivencia Wars: Decoding Historiography's Polemic with Philology', in *A Sea of Languages: Rethinking the Arabic Role in Medieval Literary History*, ed. Suzanne Akbari and Karla Mallette (Toronto: University of Toronto Press, 2013), 135–61.

Taçon, Paul S. C., and Sally K. May, 'Rock Art Evidence for Macassan-Aboriginal Contact in Northwestern Arnhem Land', in *Macassan History and Heritage: Journeys, Encounters and Influences*, ed. Marshall Clark and Sally K. May (Canberra: ANU E-Press, 2013), 127–40.

Terrio, Susan J., 'Crucible of the Millennium? The Clovis Affair in Contemporary France', *Society for the Comparative Study of Society and History* 41.3 (1999), 438–57.

Tickner, Arlene B., and Ole Waever, eds, *International Relations Scholarship around the World* (New York: Routledge, 2009).

Trigg, Stephanie (ed.), *Medievalism and the Gothic in Australian Culture* (Turnhout: Brepols, 2005).

Tudball, Libby, and Robert Lewis, *Ten Canoes: A Film by Rolf de Heer and the People of Ramingining* (Film Finance Corporation/Australian Teachers of Media, Inc., 2006), www.tencanoes.com.au 10.

Vernon, Matthew X., *The Black Middle Ages: Race and the Construction of the Middle Ages* (Basingstoke, New York: Palgrave Macmillan, 2018).

Vidal, Stéphanie. 'Interview de Mathias Enard—Fragments d'un discourse amoureux entre l'Orient et l'Occident', *ONORIENT*, 28 September 2015, http://onorient.com/interview-de-mathias-enard-fragments-dun-discours-amoureux-entre-lorient-locident-9056-20150928.

Vineyard, Jennifer, 'George R. R. Martin on What Not to Believe in *Game of Thrones*', *Vulture*, 6 November 2014, https://www.vulture.com/2014/11/george-rr-martin-new-book.html.

Wade, Geoff, 'Early Muslim Expansion in South East Asia, Eighth to Fifteenth Centuries', in *The New Cambridge History of Islam*, vol. 3, ed. David O. Morgan and Anthony Reid (Cambridge: Cambridge University Press, 2010), 366–408.

Wallace, David, *Premodern Places: Calais to Surinam, Chaucer to Aphra Behn* (Malden, MA, Oxford, Carlton: Blackwell, 2004).

Warren, Michelle, *Creole Medievalism: Colonial France and Joseph Bédier's Middle Ages* (Minneapolis: University of Minnesota Press, 2010).

Waters, Sarah, 'French Intellectuals and Globalisation: A War of Worlds', *French Cultural Studies* 22.4 (2011), 303–20.

Waters, Sarah, 'The 2008 Economic Crisis and the French Narrative of Decline: Une causalité diabolique.' *Modern and Contemporary France* 21.3 (2013), 335–54.

West, Alex J., 'Manuscripts and the Medieval Tropics', in *Toward a Global Middle Ages: Encountering the World through Illuminated Manuscripts*, ed. Bryan C. Keene (Los Angeles: The J. Paul Getty Museum, 2019), 94–8.

York, Richard, '*Homo Floresiensis* and Human Equality: Enduring Lessons from Stephen Jay Gould', *Monthly Review* 56.10 (2005), 14–19.

Young, Helen, *Race and Popular Fantasy Literature: Habits of Whiteness* (New York: Routledge, 2015).

Yousef, Nisreen T., 'Historiographic Metafiction and Renarrating History', in *Routledge Companion to Pakistani Anglophone Writing*, ed. Aroosa Kanwal and Saiyma Aslam (New York: Routledge, 2018), 116–24.

Zúquete, José Pedro, *Missionary Politics in Contemporary Europe* (Syracuse: Syracuse University Press, 2007).

Zutter, Natalie, 'Marlon James to Write Fantasy Trilogy Inspired by *Lord of the Rings* and African Mythology', *Tor.Com*, Tuesday 10 January 2017, https://www.tor.com/2017/01/10/marlon-james-dark-star-trilogy-fantasy-african-mythology/.

INDEX

For the benefit of digital users, indexed terms that span two pages (e.g., 52–53) may, on occasion, appear on only one of those pages.